"The Devil hath been raised"

uch mischief hath follow

Devil hath been raised am

nible, & when he shall

ly knows. But now that th

to such distress, is a great gri

& Reverend neighbours, wh

nevertheless, I do truly hope, & bel

r the Lord, & am well satisfy

did it ignorantly, from

from other ignorant, or

bound, to protest against

to the Devil, for keys agan

irections from Nature, or Go

ecounted by godly Protestant

Diabolical, & therefore

"The Devil hath been raised"

A Documentary History
of the Salem Village
Witchcraft Outbreak
of March 1692

Richard B. Trask

Published for the
DANVERS HISTORICAL SOCIETY
DANVERS, MASSACHUSETTS

By
PHOENIX PUBLISHING
West Kennebunk, Maine
1992

Witch Hysteria of Salem Village
Danvers, Massachusetts
1 6 9 2 • 1 9 9 2

The Salem Village Witchcraft Tercentennial
Committee of Danvers deems this publica-
tion to be educationally useful and accurate.

Library of Congress C.I.P. Data

Trask, Richard B.
  The devil hath been raised : a documentary history of
of the Salem Village witchcraft outbreak / Richard B.
Trask.
  p. cm.
  Includes index.
  ISBN 0-914659-58-8
  1. Witchcraft—Massachusetts—Salem—History—
Sources. I. Danvers Historical Society. II. Title.
BF1576.T73   1992
133.4'3'097445—dc20   92-16196
                                                          CIP

Printed in the United States of America

Contents

Acknowledgments

MOST BOOKS, no matter their size or style, take much painstaking effort on the part of many people to bring forth a final product. This book is no exception. I am both pleased and grateful that the Danvers Historical Society believed it important and was willing to invest significant funds to sponsor the publication of a scholarly volume on the subject of Salem Village witchcraft as part of its participation in the 300th anniversary commemoration of that event. Dr. Anthony Patton, President of the Danvers Historical Society, and the Publications Committee chaired by Esther Usher, as well as the Society's Executive Board have been very encouraging and supportive of this project.

My thanks also go to Mary Jane Wormstead, Sally Symmes, Ann McNamara and Madeline Crane who assisted in typing and proofreading the text and primary source material.

For their kind and generous permission to publish these witchcraft-related papers, I wish to express my gratitude to the following institutions and individuals: The Board of County Commissioners of the County of Essex, Massachusetts; The Clerk of Courts for Essex County, James Dennis Leary, Esq.; The Essex Institute, Salem, Massachusetts, and its Director of the Library William T. La Moy and Curator of Manuscripts Jane E. Ward; The Massachusetts Historical Society, Boston, Massachusetts, and its Director Louis L. Tucker and Librarian Peter Drummey; The New York Public Library, New York City, and Wayne Furman of the Office of Special Collections and Valerie Winfield of the Rare Books and Manuscripts Division; The Connecticut Historical Society, Hartford, Connecticut, and Head Librarian Everett Wilkie; my good friends at the First Church of Danvers, Congregational; and my own institution, The Danvers Archival Center, Peabody Institute Library of Danvers, where I am Town Archivist and Douglas Rendell is Librarian.

My greatest appreciation is reserved for the two people who have so greatly and consistently assisted me in every facet of this project—my wife Ethel B. Trask, whose skills and knowledge in so many fields continue to astonish me, and my friend Dr. Richard P. Zollo whom I regard as a trusted mentor and meticulous researcher and writer.

Finally, I want to dedicate this volume to the four women in my life who continually "bewitch" me with their love and support—Ethel Trask, Elizabeth Trask, Mildred Trask, and Polly Boghosian.

Samuel Parris

Introduction

"THE DEVIL hath been raised amongst us, & his Rage is vehement & terrible, & when he shall be silenc'd the Lord only knows." So wrote Samuel Parris, the pastor of Salem Village, in his church record book in late March 1692 when confronted with what was discovered to be a diabolical occurrence taking place in this small Massachusetts hamlet.

What at first seemed only a localized witchcraft outbreak soon would spread rapidly and by the end of May 1692 people from communities as distant and diverse as Salem, Billerica, Andover, Charlestown, Marblehead, Lynn, Reading, Topsfield, Gloucester, Malden, and Beverly would be accused by various "afflicted persons" of using witchcraft upon them. By the fall of 1692 over 150 people had been examined and sent to prison. Men and women, both rich and influential as well as poor and hapless, were enmeshed in frightening legal confrontation. Some 50 falsely confessed to being witches who, in exchange for special powers and favors, had made a covenant with the Devil to assist in his assault upon the people of the colony. Nineteen persons who staunchly maintained their innocence were tried, found guilty and hanged, while one old man was tortured to death, and at least five others died in prison succumbing to harsh conditions and treatment.

This portrait was found in 1982 among uncatalogued Endicott papers in the Massachusetts Historical Society. On the enclosing envelope William C. Endicott, Jr., had written, "Miniature of Rev. Mr. [Samuel] Parris." Parris in his 1720 will had made reference to bequeathing "my own picture" to his son Noyes, and in 1790 another son, Deacon Samuel Parris, bequeathed to his son Samuel, "my Grandfather's and father's pictures." An 1839 letter by Rev. G. W. Porter of Boston offered the loan "of the miniature Portrait of the Revd Mr. Paris of Salem" to artist Washington Allston for copying, an offer the artist declined. Although it is unknown how and where Endicott acquired this miniature, it is well known that he was an avid late 19th and early 20th century collector of local history memorabilia.

The original brass-framed, color portrait measures 2 ¼ " high by 1 ¾ " wide and is of the style typical of late 17th century English artists. It portrays a fair-complected man with aquiline nose, dark brown eyes and light brown, shoulder-length hair. He appears to be in his 20s or 30s, is wearing a knotted cravat and may very well be Samuel Parris prior to his religious calling. If so, this is the only known portrait of any inhabitant of 1692 Salem Village.

Courtesy, Massachusetts Historical Society.

The story of the Salem Village witch hysteria is a minor, though well-known footnote in American colonial history. Its popular fascination has continued to make it the subject of innumerable scholarly as well as superficial books and articles. In our own time the expression "A Salem Witch Hunt" is often used as a universal phrase which points to a scapegoating position taken by people or groups emphasizing hysterical, blindly illogical and intolerant actions or expressions.

What was the cause of the historical 1692 Salem witch hunt, the largest witch outbreak in America, that occurred at a time when the earlier, massive witch hunts of Europe were on the wane? Writers and researchers since the last decade of the 17th century down to the present time have been trying to find a theory or an explanation to this question. Colonial clerics, including John Hale and Cotton Mather, saw these events as the direct intervention of the Devil attacking the Puritan Commonwealth and being partially successful as the result of a religious backsliding of New Englanders and the use by civil authorities of ill-conceived traditions and non-biblical principles to discover who was a witch. Later authors would come up with a wealth of hypotheses to describe the causes, postulating among other explanations that it resulted from the pranks of bored adolescents, the influence of oligarchical and power-hungry clergy, local petty jealousies and land grabs, mental aberrations, spiritualist goings-on, political instability, a conspiratorial holding action against the disintegration of Puritanism, mass clinical hysteria, a clash between agrarian and emerging commercial interests, a continuation of the suppression of certain types of women, and even physical reactions to ingested fungus. Besides the mysterious quality of the subject matter, the Salem cases have always afforded the researcher a fairly extensive accumulation of primary source documents representing a diversity of people, yet combined with a body of knowledge that is manageable enough to be examined in microcosm.

The ordinary English Puritan settler in 17th century New England believed, as did his European counterpart, in the existence of a literal Devil and the possibility of witchcraft affecting his everyday life. Witches were thought to be humans, typically women, who had agreed to serve the Devil. In return for favors and certain amazing powers from the Devil, they attempted to help "The Old Deluder" bring ruin upon the Christian community.

On continental Europe beginning in the 15th century, literally tens of thousands of "witches" had been discovered and put to death. There, witchcraft was considered a heresy against the church, and heretics were burned at the stake. Because of geography and certain cultural and religious differences, England had escaped the brunt of the continental-style witch hunts for many years. It was not until the mid-sixteenth century in England that witchcraft became a crime punishable by death. From then through the end of the 17th century an estimated one thousand English witches would be found out and hanged. In England witchcraft was considered a felony against the state, and felons were hanged. Major English witch outbreaks typically occurred during those periods of social or political strife as, for example, during the Civil War when in less than two years in the mid 1640s about 200 witches were executed following their discovery by a merciless and deceitful man named Matthew Hopkins, who was dubbed the "Witch Finder General."

The English settlers of 17th century New England did on occasion find witchcraft at work within their various communities, and although a large-scale witch outbreak did not occur prior to 1692, over 90 individual complaints and accusations took place before that date.

One of the larger Massachusetts Bay towns was Salem, first occupied by Englishmen in 1626. Soon a large migration of people followed from the mother country. By the mid 1630s with the available land of this coastal community quickly diminishing and the desire for larger and better farmland, a group of settlers established homesteads to the west of Salem some five to ten miles from the town center. This area soon became known as Salem Village, and by the 1660s included a substantial collection of widely scattered farms.

Once established, the farmers or "villagers," as they began to refer to themselves, saw that they had less and less in common with Salem and began to look towards their own self-interests. Many resented their subservient position to the more mercantile and distant townspeople, and beginning in 1667 with a group of villagers petitioning to be exempt from the Salem military watch, "considering how remote our dwellings are from the Town," the farmers pressed towards becoming independent from their mother community. Salem, having previously lost significant territory to other developing settlements, was not eager to grant any such new request. For the major part of a century through delaying counter-proposals, political clout and obstinacy the town staved-off losing the valuable and taxable village territory.

Turning to the General Court for possible relief, the villagers petitioned for permission at least to build their own meeting house and hire a minister to preach among them. In 1672 Salem relented to the religious argument, and the village was allowed to establish a parish.

A parish was not an independent church, however, and although the villagers could choose from among themselves a five-man committee to assess support for a minister and a building, the chosen minister was not an ordained pastor and theirs was not an independent, covenant church. Villagers who desired full church membership and participation in communion at the Lord's Table would continue to be required to travel the many miles to the Salem church. Though the villagers were free from paying Salem church rates, for all other purposes, taxing and political, they were legally part of Salem Town. Many but not all of the approximately 550 villagers still desired full independence, both ecclesiastical and political, from the town, and they pressed the issue on numerous occasions. It would not be until the 1750s, however, that Salem Village would be finally granted its full independence with the establishment of the Town of Danvers.

Even while they possessed a semblance of ecclesiastical independence, a divisive inter-village religious factionalism emerged resulting in much controversy during the three, short term, successive ministries which served the village from 1672 to 1688. Ministers James Bayley, George Burroughs, and Deodat Lawson seemed never to gain the endorsement and support of more than a simple majority of the villagers, and typically found themselves entangled in heated, uncharitable controversy with a vocal minority. Upon finding the situation not worth the fight, each would unhappily depart the village.

In a 1682 letter villager Jeremiah Watts complained concerning the local factionalism, "Brother is against brother and neighbors against neighbors, all quarreling and smiting one another." Still later in the 1680s during a dispute involving Rev. Lawson, a committee of arbitrators from Salem commented in their written advice to the village that "uncharitable expressions and uncomly reflections tost [sic] to and fro . . . have a tendency to make such a gap as we fear, if not timely prevented, will lett out peace and order and let in confusion and every evil work." Among the arbiters in this February 1687 communication were future witchcraft judges John Hathorne and Bartholomew Gedney.

Although much of the contentiousness and quarreling over village ministers was indeed homegrown, Salem Town shared part of the blame in its heavy-handed dealings with the village. Salem Village was in an unenviable position. It sorely lacked those traditional institutions meant to assist in the governing and the stability of New England communities. The village church could congregate, tax itself, and worship, but was denied performing its own sacraments or holding its own covenant. The Village Committee could be elected and meet, but it was a governing body in name only, not able to act on its own or the inhabitants' self-interest and forced to appeal to the town selectmen on any substantive issues. Though by no means the only explanation for the village's problems with factionalism, this vacuum of power greatly exacerbated its difficulties. A not inconsequential number of villagers also had a vision and an empathy more in keeping with the mercantile interests of Salem Town rather than with the agrarian outlook of Salem Village. With these significant political, religious, social, and economic differences existing from without and from within the village society, it is not difficult to understand why the area had acquired a regional reputation for provincialism and ill-feeling.

By 1689 the villagers in a seemingly unusual spirit of cooperation pushed hard for a completely independent church, while at the same time hiring their fourth successive minister, Samuel Parris. By a chance of circumstances, the request was granted from the Salem mother church and on November 19, 1689, the Rev. Mr. Samuel Parris was ordained pastor of the newly created and independent Church of Christ at Salem Village, with twenty-seven adults joining together in full covenant.

What at first seemed a fresh and positive beginning, soon took on the same old attitudes and style of former controversies. Thirty-five-year-old Rev. Parris was a novice to the ministerial calling, having engaged for much of his adult life in the mercantile field. After over a decade of attempting to make a successful living in the Barbados, West Indies, and then in Boston, Parris gradually changed his life's course to become a minister for Christ. Through truncated negotiations in 1688 and 1689 with various small committees purporting to fully represent the will of the village inhabitants, Parris eventually acquired for himself what he felt to be adequate terms for his calling among the farmers. Though his salary was smaller and included less hard currency than he had initially desired, he concluded that it was sufficient for him and his family. He had also wrangled the major concession of full ownership of the village-built 1681 parsonage and its two-acre lot.

Unfortunately everyone had not been privy to the full terms of the agreement, or at least later claimed this to be the case. A vociferous minority, primarily of non-church member inhabitants, saw the settlement agreement as unwarrantable and an illegal give-away of their village-owned parsonage. As a contemporary chronicler of the witchcraft events, Robert Calef, would write of the parsonage dispute, "This occasioned great Divisions both between the Inhabitants themselves, and between a considerable part of them and their said Minister, which Divisions were but the beginning or Praeludium to what immediately followed." Slowly festering, the controversy continued to build until by October 1691 the opposition faction made its move. In the annual election of the Village Committee, the old committee made up of the minister's church supporters was ousted and a new committee composed of Joseph Porter, Francis Nurse, Joseph Putnam, Daniel Andrews, and Joseph Hutchinson, most if not all strong opponents of Parris, was installed. When called upon by the church in November 1691 to begin the gathering of taxes to support the ministry, the committee, whose primary duty this was, chose instead inaction. Thereupon, the church voted to sue the committee in court. The two village institutions had set their course of confrontation, and villagers were placed in the unenviable position of choosing sides. Meanwhile, his firewood supply virtually depleted, the minister entreated his congregation to provide him with wood for heating and cooking. Even this request was tinged with controversy. Parris expected the wood to be brought forth and stacked upon his wood pile by his respectful congregation. Most villagers, however, believed Parris's salary included a wood allotment payment and that he should not presume to be above making arrangements for his own wood.

From the scant written sources which survive, Parris appears to have been a man of strong will who expected the deference from his people which was customarily given to respected community ministers. A good portion of the inhabitants were unwilling to give Parris, both as to his personal comfort among them and in their acknowledgment of him as their spiritual guide, either their generosity of spirit or of purse. An examination of Parris's surviving sermon outlines, particularly those written during the last quarter of 1691, seem to include thinly veiled references to his dissatisfaction with his lot among them. He often preached on the theme of conflict between good and evil, Christ and Satan, and enemies who are both within and without the church.

Besides these ever-present conflicts within the village and between the village and the town, the inhabitants of Salem Village were part of the larger community of the Massachusetts Bay and New England. The times were full of uncertainty and apprehension. Many clergy spoke of the backsliding of the current generation of New Englanders into a less God-fearing and righteous-living society, and suggested that in answer to these sins God might allow tribulation to befall His wayward people. Indians and the French to the north were a constant threat. In early 1692 Abenaki Indians had resumed bloody warfare by viciously attacking settlements in Maine, killing or carrying off inhabitants at York and Wells and burning many houses. These attacks led Essex County people to fear that this was the beginning of another war on the scale of the King Philip's War of the mid 1670s when many Salem Village soldiers had died and when the village had erected a watch house and fortified the meeting house. Indeed not too long before 1692 several young village men on duty elsewhere had died in Indian attacks.

The political scene in Massachusetts was also a matter of concern. In 1684 the colony had lost its self-governing charter and the Crown's newly appointed governor, Sir Edmund Andros, arrived in 1686. It was unclear during this period if the land granted under the old charter would be considered valid by the new power. With the excuse of the "Glorious Revolution" in England, Massachusetts in 1689 revolted against Andros and set up its own commonwealth based on the old charter. Rev. Increase Mather had been sent to England as advocate for Massachusetts concerning a new charter. The success or failure of his venture was unknown and the cause of much apprehension. Thus the bleak midwinter of 1691-1692 was a period of uneasiness in the colony. Little Salem Village with its divisive social structure and scattered population faced not only consternation from without, but also a continuation of the institutional difficulties with Salem and significant internal stress over its own religious community.

Just when a strange malady first struck several children in the minister's house and that of several of his neighbors' homesteads is unclear. By late January and early February of 1692, a number of locals knew that something was amiss, however. Two of the youngsters in the Parris household, daughter Betty, age 9, and niece Abigail Williams, age 11, together with Ann Putnam, Jr., the daughter of staunch Parris supporter Thomas Putnam, who lived less than a mile from the parsonage, were affected. Putnam's wife's niece, Mary Walcott, the 17-year-old daughter of Jonathan Walcott who lived within a stone's throw of the parsonage, was also " . . . afflicted by they knew not what distempers." While it would later be speculated that these adolescent girls and perhaps others were dabbling in unhealthy and sinful games of divination, attempting to find out by means of white witchcraft their future fate, what caused their fits is not clearly known. Though presumed by later writers, it is unclear if Tituba, Rev. Parris's Indian slave, had any hand in letting the impressionable girls have their forbidden sport and encouraged or at least did not prevent their irreligious games.

An undoubtedly chagrined Parris must have seen these young girls' actions as extremely dangerous signs. The fits they exhibited were not simply playful; and instead of diminishing over time, they seemed to intensify and infect others. Rev. John Hale of Beverly, an observer of many of these early happenings, would in later years, describe the symptoms:

> These children were bitten and pinched by
> invisible agents; their armes, necks, and backs turned
> this way and that way . . . . Sometimes they were
> taken dumb, their mouths stopped, their throats
> choked, their limbs wracked and tormented so as

might move an heart of stone, to sympathize with them, with bowels of compassion for them.

As these torments continued, they became the talk of the village, and many saw a clear comparison of what was presently occurring in Salem Village with the reported afflictions of the Goodwin children who had been tormented by a witch in Boston in 1689. Other classic English bewitchment cases were also brought to mind.

Rather than separating the affected children as had been done with successful results in the Boston case by Rev. Cotton Mather, the village parents seem to have allowed the children to keep together. This did not quiet the situation, but rather encouraged its festering. The anxious elders, undoubtedly guided by Rev. Parris, held prayer meetings with the children present. They also held private fasts and called upon the neighborhood ministers to visit and pray over the girls at the parsonage and elsewhere.

A local physician, most probably William Griggs, was also called to offer his assistance and advice. Finding no physical malady he could identify as to the cause, he suggested that their afflictions were likely to be the result of bewitchment, an explanation that others quickly embraced as logical considering the evidence. The teenage maid living with the Griggs family also became an early sufferer of this same strange affliction.

Once it was recognized that these were no epileptic-like seizures or anything of that type and that the problem was spreading to others, many felt that firm action had to be taken. The various private and public fasts and the patient, continual praying and the waiting upon Providence was too ineffectual for some. Concerned adults began pressing the young ones to discover who or what agent was hurting them.

Some sincere but meddling neighbors dabbled in white witchcraft in an attempt to discover the cause of the afflictions. Mary Sibley directed Parris's slaves to concoct a witch cake utilizing the children's urine, and when the minister later learned of this abomination occurring under his roof, he severely and publicly chastised the woman, and identified this occurrence as what he perceived to be the new and dangerous plateau of allowing the Devil entry into this sad and now horrific calamity.

Finally the girls, under now unknown pressures and from unclear sources, named three tormentors. The accused were the safe kind of victims to cry out upon. One, the minister's slave, another a destitute woman of ill repute possessing a sharp tongue, and the third a sickly woman who had avoided church attendance for over a year and whose unsavory marital past had been the occasion for much gossip, were safe choices. With the swearing out of warrants for their arrest issued on February 29, 1692, Tituba, Sarah

Good and Sarah Osburn would become the first to be examined in relation to the girls' afflictions. The events, the words and the actions that would transpire at their examination, and the testimony and evidence that would result would significantly transform this seemingly typical and local witch incident. And it would be during the critical first thirty-one days of the witch-craft outbreak that the course would be set, the confrontation joined and the community hysteria stoked, leading into the most dramatic, far reaching and deadly witch hunt in all of American history.

Richard B. Trask

Danvers, Massachusetts
March 1, 1992

March 1692

Sunday	Monday	Tuesday	Wednesday	Thursday	Friday	Saturday
		1	2	3	4	5
6	7	8	9	10	11	12
13	14	15	16	17	18	19
20	21	22	23	24	25	26
27	28	29	30	31		

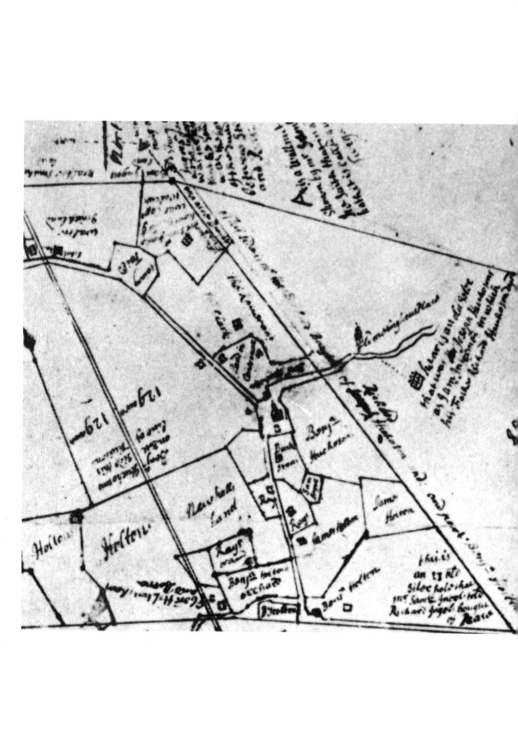

Notes

U NLIKE MOST previous witchcraft proceedings in New and old
England, a significant number of
the legal papers of the 1692 Salem cases have survived. Today there exist in
judicial archives and various manuscript repositories over 850 of these court
papers including complaints, warrants, examinations, indictments, sum-
monses, depositions, recognizances, petitions and confessions. Following the
establishment in May 1692 of the Court of Oyer and Terminer, which had
the authority to try the witch cases, Stephen Sewall of Salem was appointed
Clerk of the Court. It was he who took custody of most of the previous and
the newly generated legal papers. Yet even a cursory examination of the
surviving records will show that significant gaps appear in them today.

Cotton Mather in late 1692 requested Sewall to lend him a number of
the case records. Although most of those original documents which appear
in Mather's resulting book *Wonders of the Invisible World* are extant in their
original form, this borrowing of unique legal records placed their survival
in jeopardy. In the 1760s Lieutenant Governor Thomas Hutchinson, preparing a two volume history of Massachusetts, was also given access to original witchcraft documents. Several of those loaned to him survive only as

*This earliest extant map of the center of Salem Village was drawn in 1730 by surveyor
Joseph Burnap. It was created to assist in the settlement of the Nathaniel Ingersoll estate. The
road running up from the bottom and veering toward the left is present-day Centre Street. Among
the buildings located at the right of this road which were present in 1692 are from the bottom:
"Benj. Holton" (widow Sarah Holten in 1692), "James Holton" (Joseph Holten), "Rays"
(John Holten), and "Buckstons" (Thomas Haines). The 1701 Meeting House is located just
north of Buckstons; in 1692 this was the site of the Watch House. Down the road to the right,
represented by a wavy double line, is the location of the "old meeting house Place." This street
is now Hobart Street. It was at this first Meeting House that the witchcraft proceedings were
held. Back on Centre Street and just above the 1701 Meeting House is the Ingersoll house and
ordinary at the lot marked "Land in Controversy." Just above Ingersoll's lot is a house set back
from the road marked, "The Reverent Mr. Clark" being the village parsonage occupied in 1692
by Rev. Parris. Above this house is a lot reading "Taining Feild" where the local militia drilled.
The house to the right of the field is the "Capt. Walcutt" house occupied in 1692 by the Jonathan
Walcott family, including the "afflicted girl" Mary Walcott.
Courtesy, Danvers Archival Center.*

xix

reprinted in his second volume, the originals lost perhaps as a result of a 1765 anti-government riot when Boston radicals vandalized Hutchinson's house and threw valuable papers into the street or carried them off. Others besides Mather and Hutchinson were given access to the files, and over time many other papers disappeared including various transcripts of examinations and and the majority of the death warrants for the nineteen who were executed.

While summary records of witchcraft trials before the Superior Court of Judication held from January to May 1693 survive, virtually nothing in the way of documentation of the examinations and deliberations before the 1692 Court of Oyer and Terminer, if in fact set down, have been preserved.

Though a good part of the extant witchcraft records are made up of the repetitive, formulaic warrants and indictments, the richest body of surviving witchcraft documentation includes the transcripts of the preliminary hearings held to determine probable cause for jailing and eventually trying an accused person. Also rich in detail and giving us a sample of the speech patterns, vital concerns, and life of the 17th century common man are the depositions used in these preliminary examinations or in the trials themselves. These records are particularly interesting and worthy of cautious deliberation when two or more versions of the same event are recorded, as is the case in the early March examinations of Tituba, Sarah Good, and Sarah Osburn.

A researcher utilizing any of this 17th century material must understand that in reading it we see those events through the eyes, writing style and prejudice of the original recorder, whose perception of the reality of that time is not reality itself. Typically the men who wrote these examinations were not neutral court officers, but rather persons deeply concerned with and involved in the village community. They jotted down what they believed to be significant, and given the slowness of writing with pen and ink could not capture all the words and actions transpiring around them. Rev. Samuel Parris, a fervent believer in the reality of the witch attack on Salem Village, often was requested to take down examinations. Even with his built-in biases, he felt his obligation and undoubtedly attempted to do this duty well. At the the end of a May 2 transcript during the examination of one accused witch Parris notes, "The afflicted were much distressed during her examination. This is a true account of the Examination of Dorcas Hoar without wrong to any party according to my original, from characters at the moments thereof."

Thus it is that our approach to these existing witchcraft papers must be with the knowledge that they do include meaningful gaps of information and that they give us only a part of the reality of the events. Their significance and veracity must be judged on an item-by-item basis. Yet with such cautions in mind, these records are for us a valuable means of better understanding the 1692 witchcraft outbreak as seen and perceived by the participants themselves. This is the "best evidence" we possess in that it survives in its original form. Though it can at times be difficult to appreciate the antiquated language and lack of consistent punctuation and spelling of the originals, they can speak to the careful reader with more authority and power than through the interpretation and narrative of later writers and historians.

This present volume is in the tradition of several earlier, useful books which gathered together the witchcraft transcripts. In 1864 and 1865 W. Elliot Woodward printed at his own expense a two volume set titled *Records of Salem Witchcraft, Compiled From the Original Documents* which transcribed the 1692 witchcraft records preserved at the Essex County Court House in Salem. Though used by numerous writers ever since and reprinted several times in the 20th century, his work did not attempt to gather the significant number of documents housed elsewhere. The transcriptions made for Woodward by Ira J. Patch, though impressive in that the typesetting kept true to the originals, contained nonetheless a large number of errors. Woodward arranged the book according to individual cases with the names ordered generally by the date of the first mention of the accused appearing in the document group. The Woodward volume was a significant, though flawed publication.

In 1938 a Depression era Works Progress Administration (WPA) project resulted in a three volume, typescipt transcription of the Salem witchcraft papers. Supervised by Essex County Clerk of Courts Archie N. Frost, the group of researchers and typists meticulously gathered from the Suffolk County Court Archives, the New York and Boston Public Library, the Essex Institute and Massachusetts Historical Society and other sources all the known legal papers. These were combined in alphabetical order by case with the Essex County documents. Unfortunately this fine resource was underutilized, typescript copies of the volumes being available only at the court house itself, at the Essex Institute, and later at the Danvers Archival Center.

Unaware of the WPA work, David Levin in 1950 compiled a casebook on Salem witchcraft as part of a Harvard University course. Finding it of potential popularity to a larger market, Levin in 1952 and again in 1960 reissued the material in expanded form under the title *What Happened in Salem?* Among other source material in his volume, he included five of the witch cases with transcriptions based on the Woodward text. Then in 1977 Da Capo Press published a three volume set of books titled *The Salem Witchcraft Papers* based on the WPA transcripts. This collection generally remained true to the layout and transcription of the WPA work and was edited by Paul Boyer and Stephen Nissenbaum, who wrote a highly readable and useful introduction for it. Included in the work were additional documents that had come to light since 1938, as well as some other papers not presently extant in original form, but which had been reprinted in several pre-20th century publications.

The work currently before you acknowledges a debt to these earlier transcribed volumes and is in the tradition of other history casebooks. Though there are several similarities with those that have gone before it, there are also several important differences in both form and style. It is the intention of the editor of this current volume to allow the documents themselves to reveal the beginnings and growth of the Salem Village witchcraft from a small, fairly typical incident of this kind into an ever-expanding witch hunt.

We shall concentrate on only the first critical month of the almost full year's witchcraft occurrance. By concentrating on March 1692 through the surviving records, we shall see how the first examinations were conducted, and how the question of "spectral evidence" was approached. In following the sources to the end of the month, we will recognize that there was no safety valve and no powerful person or persons who understood what was occurring and attempted to slow down the expanding events. Ours will be a chronological approach allowing the documents themselves to unravel the story day by day and incident by incident. Included will be not only the legal records, but also the village church and civil records, a sermon by Rev. Deodat Lawson, (here reprinted in its entirety for the first time since a 1704 reprint), the extensive notes to an important sermon preached by Rev. Parris, and excerpts of several narrative accounts by persons who witnessed many of the events. During this month of March 1692, all of the accused and all of the accusers lived in the Salem Village area, and the incidents portrayed are all local. With the exception of the witchcraft warrant for the arrest of Rachel Clinton of Ipswich issued on March 29 not included within this Salem Village chronology, no persons outside the immediate village area had up until then been arrested. All this would change, however, during the ensuing months when over 150 persons from a number of Essex County towns and beyond were accused.

This volume attempts to be faithful to the original documents, whether they are the easy narrative writings of educated ministers or the close to illiterate, jumbled words and convoluted syntax of observations made by common yeomen. As previously noted, it is the editor's intention not to interpret the documents or comment on their significance, nor to offer new theories, but rather to let these surviving documents speak in their own words, and for themselves.

Now a few specifics about the form of the transcripts themselves. Though what follows is not a typographical facsimile, the general shape of the body of the original text is retained, as are paragraph layouts, punctuation, capitalization and spelling. Either the original documents themselves or photocopies of them were utilized throughout in the new transcription of the material. Capitalization in the originals is inconsistent and in this edition many initial letters of words were capitalized if it appeared from the original that the letters were considerably larger than the others around them. The letter "P" is most usually written in the 17th century text as a small case "p", while the initial letter "e" is conversely almost always written as a capital "E". The "y" representation for the "th" sound, so prevalent in 17th century text, has been retained. Thus "ye" was expressed as "the"; "ym" as "them"; "yr" as "their" and "yt" as "that".

The transcription in this edition is closer to what is known as "diplomatic transcription" wherein certain symbols or abbreviations are used rather than reproducing the document's exact physical appearance. As the old style "s" used as the initial letter or in the body of words and looking in print like an "f" without the full cross staff, cannot be easily produced in modern print, they have been exchanged for the familiar "s". Contractions in written text usually include the elevation of end letters above the line such as "wth" repesenting "with". As such superscript is again difficult for modern typesetting, the letters have been simply included on the same line of text such as "wth" for "with". Though the retention of these antiquated styles, the lack of consistent capitalization and punctuation may at first prove a bit difficult to follow, a little practice will soon allow the reader not only to understand the text, but to have a closer appreciation of its 17th century variety, spontaneity and richness than if it were thoroughly sanitized into modern usage. The nuggets of understanding and nearness to the people involved are well worth the effort of reading these originals in their original form.

In this edition the following symbols will be used in the transcripts: ★ denotes an original signature; X represents a mark made on a document representing a signature by someone who cannot write; # [ ] indicates a line through a readable crossed out word or passage in the original text.

The year used in the text of most of these documents will appear as "1691/2" or "1691-2." Until 1752 the English continued to follow the Julian rather than the "Catholic" Gregorian calendar. In the ancient Julian calendar the new year began on March 25 rather than January 1. From the last quarter of the 17th century, however, it became common usage for the English to acknowledge the more precise and accurate Gregorian calendar by writing the year of a date occurring between January 1 and March 24 with a double digit date. In all cases the year as written "1691/2" should read in actuality "1692". It is also of note that 1692 was a leap year.

As to the physical layout of the edited transcripts, each batch of documents of a specific date will be preceded by a heading stating that date in March 1692. In a number of cases, depositions written and/or sworn to after the fact will be included under the date about which they speak. A brief title description of the document, including the principal deposer or the name of the person's case involved, will be placed above the transcript. Spelling of names is not consistent in the original documents, and the editor has chosen to use from the evidence available, a spelling of the name which will be standard for the title descriptions and for the index. In some cases, just below the descriptive title heading will be found in italics explanatory notes about the document or its contents in those cases that the editor believes such information useful for the reader's understanding. If the full transcript of the document is not included either due to that information's being located elsewhere under a different date or excluded if it refers to post-March events, it will be so indicated with the words, "Document continues" in brackets [ ] printed just below and to the right side of the transcript. Following the document transcription, in small italics between parentheses, will be found the current location of the original documents.

The bulk of the witchcraft legal papers are in the possession of the Essex County court archives. In 1980 an agreement was made between the Essex County Clerk of Courts, and the Essex Institute of Salem for the long-term deposit of these documents at the Institute. Previously, this material was stored in three scrapbooks and included a number system replicated in various publications including the Boyer and Nissenbaum edition. When the papers were deposited at the Institute, the documents were dismounted from the scrapbooks, conserved and re-assigned numbers. These new numbers are used throughout this edition.

"The Devil hath been raised"

March 1692

Sunday	Monday	Tuesday	Wednesday	Thursday	Friday	Saturday
		1	2	3	4	5
6	7	8	9	10	11	12
13	14	15	16	17	18	19
20	21	22	23	24	25	26
27	28	29	30	31		

The Documentary Evidence

Warrant for the Apprehension of Sarah Good

Salem feby the 29th 1691/92

Whereas Mrs Joseph Hutcheson Thomas putnam Edward putnam and Thomas preston Yeomen of Salem Village in ye County of Essex personally appeared before us, and made Complaint on Behalfe of theire Majests against Sarah Good the Wife of William Good of Salem Village above sd, for suspition of Witchcraft by her Committed, and thereby much Injury donne to Eliz parris Abigail Williams Anna putnam and Elizabeth Hubert all of Salem Village aforesd Sundry times within this two moneths and Lately also don, at Salem Village Contrary to ye peace of our Sovern Ld and Lady Wm & mary King & Queen of Engld &c —You are therefore in theire Majesties names hereby required to apprehed & bring before us the said Sarah Good, to morrow aboute ten of ye clock in ye forenoon at ye house of Lt Nathaniell Ingersalls in Salem Village.or as soon as may be then & there to be Examined Relateing to ye abovesd premises and hereof you are not to faile at your perile Dated Salem feby 29th 1691/2—

To Constable George Locker.—   *John Hathorne
                                                             Assists.
                                           *Jonathan Corwin

(Essex County Court Archives, Salem Witchcraft Papers, I,4)

1

Warrant for the Apprehension of Sarah Osburn and Tituba

Salem febr. the 29th. day. 1691/2

Whereas mrs Joseph Hutcheson Thomas putnam Edward putnam and Thomas preston Yeomen of Salem Village, in ye County of Essex. personally appeared before us, And made Complaint on behalfe of theire Majesties against Sarah Osburne the wife of Alexa Osburne of Salem Village aforesd, and titibe an Indian Woman servant, of mr. Saml parris of sd place also; for Suspition of Witchcraft, by them Committed and thereby much injury don to Elizabeth Parris Abigail Williams Anna putnam and Elizabeth Hubert all of Salem Village aforesd Sundry times with in this two moneths and Lately also don; at sd Salem Village Contrary to ye peace and Laws of our Sovr Lord & Lady Wm & Mary of England &c King & Queene
You are there fore in theire Majts names hereby required to apprehend and forthwith or as soon as may be bring before us ye abovsd Sarah Osburne, and titibe Indian, at ye house of Lt Nathl Ingersalls in sd place and if it May be by to Morrow aboute ten of ye Clock in ye morning then and there to be Examined Relateing to ye abovesd premises--. You are likewise required to bring at ye same tyme Eliz. parris Abigl Williams Anna putnam and Eliz Hubert. or any other person or persons yt can give Evedence in ye abovesd Case. and here of you are not to faile
Dated Salem feby 29 1691/2
To Constable Joseph Herrick Const in Salem   *John Hathorne

Assists.

*Jonathan.Corwin

(Essex County Court Archives, Salem Witchcraft Papers, I,33)

TUESDAY, MARCH 1, 1692

Meeting of the Salem Village Inhabitants

Since the 1660s many in Salem Village had been seeking complete independence from the town of Salem. On the same day as the witch examinations, the villagers gathered to discuss the most recent in the string of proposals and counterproposals. Besides petitioning the General Court for assistance in this endeavor, in early January the village had sought greater autonomy from the town itself. The town presented a counter proposition which was being considered by the village on March 1. This vote, recorded by Joseph Putnam, would be the last item of business written into the official Village Record Book until December when the witchcraft accusations had generally abated. It

"the Devil hath been raised"

would not be until 1752 that a full political separation between the village and the town would occur with the establishment of the District of Danvers.

At a general meeting of the Inhabitants of Salem Village the first day of March 1691/92 it was agreed and voted by a generall concurrance that wee doe not exsept of what the Towne of Salem hath profered us that is to bee freed from the maintainance of there highways provided wee will maintaine all our one poor
2ly Voted that wee make choice of Capt John Putnam and his son Jonathan Putnam to manage our Petetione now depending in general Cort
3ly Voted that wee make choice of Mr. Daniell Andrew to informe the Towne of Salem that wee doe not except of what the Towne of Salem hath profered us

(Salem Village Book of Record, p. 57, from the First Church of Danvers, Congregationl, deposit collection of the Danvers Archival Center)

Constable Locker's Return of Sarah Good's Apprehension Warrant

I brought the person of Sarah Good the wife of william Good according to the tenor of the within warrant as is Attest by me
    1. March. 1691/2   ★George Locker Constable

(Essex County Court Archives, Salem Witchcraft Papers, I,4 reverse)

Constable Herrick's Return of Sarah Osburn and Tituba's Apprehension Warrant

according to this warrant I have apprehended the parsons with in mentioned and have brought them accordingly and have mad diligent sarch for Images and such like but can find non
    Salem village this 1th march 1691/92

                        p me ★Joseph Herrick Constable

(Essex County Court Archives, Salem Witchcraft Papers, I,33 reverse)

The Documentary Evidence

Examination of Sarah Good

During the examination of the three accused women several people recorded the proceedings. The first version, the magistrates' summary record, included all three examinations on the same document. For the sake of chronological clarity, this and the other versions will be divided into the three separate examinations.

Salem Village

March the 1t. 1691/2

Sarah Good the wife of Wm Good of Salem Village Labourer Brought before us by George Locker Constable in Salem. to Answer Mrs Joseph Hutcheson Thomas putnam &c of Salem Village yeomen (Complainants on behalfe of theire Majesties) against sd Sarah Good for suspition of Witchcraft by her Committed and thereby much Injury don to the Bodys of Elizabeth parris Abigaile Williams Anna putnam & Elizabeth Hubert all of Salem Village aforesd according to theire Complaints as pr warrants Dated Salem March 29th 1691/2

Sarah Good upon Examination denyed the matter of fact (viz) that she ever used any witchcraft. or hurt the abovesaid Children or any of them, The above named Children being all present positively accused her of hurting of them Sundry times within this two moneths and also that morneing

Sarah Good denyed yt she had benn: at theire houses in sd tyme, or neere them, or had don them any hurt

all the abovesaid children then presente accused her face to face, upon which they ware all dredfully tortred & tormented for a short space of tyme, and ye affliction and torters being over they charged sd Sarah Good againe. yt she had then soe tortered them, and came to them and. did itt. althow she was personally then keept at a Considerable distance from them

Sarah Good being Asked if yt she did not then hurt them; who did it, And the children being againe tortered, she looked upon them, And said yt it was one of them Wee brought into ye house with us, Wee Asked her who it was, shee then Answered and sayd it was Sarah Osburne, and Sarah Osburne was then under Custody & not in the house; — And the children being quickly after recovered out of there fitt sayd. yt itt was Sarah Good and also Sarah Osburne yt then did hurt & torment or aflict them althow both of them at ye same time at adistance or Remote from them personally: --their ware also sun dry other Questions put to her & Answers given thereunto by her.

"the Devil hath been raised"

according as is also given in.

[Document continues]

(Essex County Court Archives, Salem Witchcraft Papers, I,14)

Second Version of Sarah Good's Examination

A more detailed record of the March 1 examinations was written down by Ezekiel Cheever. This is the section of Cheever's account of the examination of Sarah Good.

The examination of Sarah Good before the worshipfull Assts John Harthorn Jonathan Curren
(H) Sarah Good what evil spirit have you familiarity with (S G) none (H) have you made no contract with the devil, (g) good answered no (H) why doe you hurt these children (g) I doe not hurt them. I scorn it. (H) who doe you imploy then to doe it (g) I imploy no body, (H) what creature doe you imploy then, (g) no creature but I am falsely accused (H) why did you go away muttering from mr Parris his house (g) I did not mutter but I thanked him for what he gave my child (H) have you made no contract with the devil (g) no (H) desired the children all of them to look upon her, and see, if this were the person that hurt them and so they all did looke upon her and said this was one of the persons that did torment them. presently they were all tormented. (H) Sarah good doe you not See now what you have done why doe you not tell us the truth. why doe you thus torment these poor children (g) I doe not torment them, (H) who do you imploy then (g) I imploy nobody I scorn it (H) how came they thus tormented, (g) what doe I know you bring others here and now you charge me with it (H) why who was it (g) I doe not know but it was some you brought into the meeting house with you (H) wee brought you into the meeting house (g) but you brought in two more (H) who was it then that tormented the children (g) it was osburn (H) what is it that you say when you goe muttering away from persons houses (g) if I must tell I will tell (H) doe tell us then (g) if I must tell I will tell it is the commandments I may say my commandments I hope (H) what commandment is it (g) if I must tell you I will tell, it is a psalm (H) what psalm (g) after a long time shee muttered over some part of a psalm (H) who doe you serve (g) I serve god (H) what god doe you serve (g) the god that made heaven and earth though shee was not willing mention the word God her answers were in a very wicked, spitfull manner reflecting and retorting aganst the authority with base and abusive words and many lies shee was taken in.it was here said that her husband had said that he was afraid that shee either was a witch or would be one very quickly the worsh mr Harthon asked him his reason why he said

The Documentary Evidence

so of her whether he had ever seen any thing by her he answered no not in this nature but it was her bad carriage to him and indeed said he I may say with tears that shee is an enimy to all good ――――――――――

[Document continues]

6

(Essex County Court Archives, Salem Witchcraft Papers, I, 11)

Third Version of Sarah Good's Examination

Still another version of the examinations was written by Joseph Putnam, though in very brief fashion. He begins his record with the examination of Good.

What Sarah Good saith

1 with non 2 shee saith that shee did doe them noe harme 3 shee implyd noe budey to doe the children 4 shee saith that shee hath made no contract nor covenant 5 shee saith that shee never did hurt the children 6 shee saith that she never had familyarity att the Devell 7 shee saith that shee never saw the children in such a condition shee saith that shee came nott to meting for want of cloase who is itt shee usially discorceseth with nobodey: but itt is a psalme or a comandement: hur God is the god that made heaven and earth she hops: she saith that shee never did noe harme to mr parr she saith itt was nott she itt is gamer osborne that doth pinch and aflicht the children
william good saith thatt she #[saith that she] is anenemy to all good shee saith shee is cleare of being a wich

[Document continues]

(Essex County Court Archives, Salem Witchcraft Papers, I,9)

Examination of Sarah Osburn

A continuation of the magistrates' summary record.

Salem Village March the 1 st 1691/2

Sarah Osburne the wife of Alexander Osburne of Salem Village. brought before us by Joseph Herrick Constable in Salem; to Answer Joseph Hutcheson & Thomas putnam &c yeomen in sd Salem Village Complainants on behalfe of theire Majests against sd Sarah Osburne, for Suspition of Witchcraft by her Committed, and thereby much Injury don to the bodys of Elizabeth parris Abigail Williams Anna putnam and Elizabeth Hubert

"the Devil hath been raised"

This ca. 1890 photograph is of the Prince-Osburn house on its original Spring Street location in Danvers. A First Period structure, the left side of the main building exhibits the remnant of a front overhang. Here lived in 1692 Sarah Osburn, one of the first three persons accused of practicing witchcraft. This house is now located at 273 Maple Street. Courtesy, Danvers Archival Center.

all of Salem Village aforesaid, according to theire Complaint, according to a Warrant Dated Salem febuy 29 th 1691/2

Sarah Osburne upon Examination denyed ye matter of fact (viz) that she ever understood or used any Witchcraft or used any Witchcraft, or hurt any of ye aboves children

The children abovenamed being all personally present accused her face to face which being don, they ware all hurt afflicted and tortured very much: which being over and they out of theire fitts they said yt said Sarah Osburne did then Come to them and hurt them, Sarah Osburn being then keept at a distance personally from them.   S. Osburne was asked why she then hurt them she denyed it: it being Asked of her how she could soe pinch & hurt them and yet she be at that distance personally from ym she Answered she did not then hurt them.nor never did.she was Asked who

The Documentary Evidence

then did it, or who she Imployed to doe it, she Answered she did not know that the divell goes aboute in her likeness to doe any hurt. Sarah Osburn being told that Sarah Good one of her Companions had upon Examination accused her. she nottwithstanding denyed ye same, according to her Examination, wch is more at Large given in as therein will appeare

[Document continues]

(Essex County Court Archives, Salem Witchcraft Papers, I,14)

Second Version of Sarah Osburn's Examination

A continuation of Ezekiel Cheever's account of the three examinations.

Sarah Osburn her examination

(H) what evil spirit have you familiarity with (O) none. (H) have you made no contact with the devill (O) no I never saw the devill in my life (H) why doe you hurt these children (O) I doe not hurt them (H) who do you imploy then to hurt them (O) I imploy no body (H) what familiarity have you with Sarah Good (O) none I have not seen her these 2 years. (H) where did you see her then (O) one day agoing to Town (H) what communications had you with her (O) I had none, only how doe you doe or so, I did not know her by name (H) what did you call her then Osburn made a stand at that at last said, shee called her Sarah (H) Sarah good saith that it was you that hurt the children (O) I doe not know that the devil goes about in my likeness to doe any hurt. Mr Harthorn desired all the children to stand up and look upon her and see if they did know her which they all did and every one of them said that this was one of the woman that did afflict them and that they had constantly seen her in the very habit that shee was now in throe evidence do stand that shee said this morning that shee was more like to be bewitched than that she was a witch Mr Harthorn asked her what made her say so shee answered that she was frighted one time in her sleep and either saw or dreamed that shee saw a thing like an indian all black which did pinch her in her neck and pulled her by the back part of her head to the dore of the house (H) did you never see anything else (O) no. it was said by some in the meeting house that shee had said that shee would never be teid to that lying spirit any more. (H) what lying spirit is this hath the devil ever deceived you and been false to you. (O) I doe not know the devil I never did see him (H) what lying spirit was it then. (O) it was a voice that I thought I heard (H) what did it porpound to you. (O) that I should goe no more to meeting but I said I would and did goe the next Sabbath day (H) wee you never tempted

"the Devil hath been raised"

furder (O) no (H) why did you yeild thus far to the devil as never to goe to meeting since. (O) alas I have been sike and not able to goe her housband and others said that shee had not been at meeting this yeare and two months.

[Document continues]   9

(Essex County Court Archives, Salem Witchcraft Papers, I,11)

Third Version of Sarah Osburn's Examination

A continuation of Joseph Putnam's account of the three examinations.

What gamer osborn saith—
1 shee saith she had noe hand in hurting the children nether by hur self by instrements
she saith that shee saith that #[shee] was more lickley bee wicht then a wich shee said shee would never beeleave the devell, the devell did propound to hur that shee should never goe to meting noe more and att that time nothing was sugested to hur elce
Why did she pinch the young woaman shee never did nor dont know who did

[Document continues]

(Essex County Court Archives, Salem Witchcraft Papers, I, 9)

Examination of Tituba

A continuation of the magistrates' summary record. Tituba is examined and the magistrates order the holding of all three suspects.

Salem Village
March 1 st 1691

Titiba an Indian Woman brought before us by Const Jos Herrick of Salem upon Suspition of Witchcraft by her Commited according to ye Complt of Jos. Hutcheson & Thomas putnam &c of Salem Village as appeares p Warrant granted Salem 29 febry 1691/2

Titiba upon Examination, and after some denyall acknowledged ye matter of fact according to her Examination given in more fully will appeare and who also charged Sarah Good and Sarah Osburne with the same

The Documentary Evidence

Salem Village
March ye 1th 1691/2

10   Sarah Good Sarah Osborne and Titiba an Indian Woman all of Salem Village
Being this day brought before us upon Suspition of Witchcraft &c by them
and Every one of them Committed. titiba an Indian Woman acknowledging ye matter of fact. and Sarah Osburne and Sarah Good denying the same
before us: but there appeareing in all theire Examinations sufficient Ground
to secure them all. And in order to further Examination they Ware all p mittimus sent to ye Goales in ye County of Essex.

[Document continues]

(Essex County Court Archives. Salem Witchcraft Papers, I,14)

Second Version of Tituba's Examination

The concluding section of Ezekiel Cheever's account of the three examinations.

The examination of Titibe

(H) Titibe what evil spirit have you familiarity with (T) none (H) why do
you hurt these children (T) I do not hurt them (H) who is it then (T) the devil
for ought I know (H) did you never see the devil. (T) the devil came to me
and bid me serve him (H) who have you seen (T) 4 women sometimes hurt
the children (H) who were they? (T) goode Osburn and Sarah good and I
doe not know who the other were Sarah good and Osburn would have me
hurt the children but I would not shee furder saith there was a tale man of
Boston that shee did see (H) when did you see them (T) Last night at Boston
(H) what did they say to you they said hurt the children (H) and did you hurt
them (T) no there is 4 women and one man they hurt the children and then
lay all upon me and they tell me if I will not hurt the children they will hurt
me (H) but did you not hurt them (T) yes but I will hurt them no more (H)
are you not sorry you did hurt them. (T) yes. (H) and why then doe you hurt
them (T) they say hurt children or we will doe worse to you (H) what have
you seen   a man come to me and say serve me (H) what service (T) hurt the
children and last night there was an appearance that said Kill the children and
if I would no go on hurting the children they would do worse to me (H) what
is this appearance you see (T) sometimes it is like a hog and some times like
a great dog this appearance shee saith shee did see 4 times (H) what did it
say to you (T) the black dog said serve me but I said I am a fraid he said if
I did not he would doe worse to me (H) what did you say to it (T) I will serve

"the Devil hath been raised"

you no longer then he said he would hurt me and then he lookes like a man and threatens to hurt me shee said that this man had a yellow bird that keept with him and he told me he had more pretty things that he would give me if I would serve him (H) what were these pretty things (T) he did not show me them (H) what else have you seen (T) two rats, a red rat and a black rat (H) what did they say to you (T) they said serve me (H) when did you see them (T) Last night and they said serve me but shee said I would not (H) what service (T) shee said hurt the children (H) did you not pinch Elizabeth Hubbard this morning (T) the man brought her to me and made me pinch her (H) why did you goe to thomas putnams Last night and hurt his child (T) they pull and hall me and make goe (H) and what would have you doe Kill her with a knif   Left. fuller and others said at this time when the child saw these persons and was tormented by them that she did complain of a knif that they would have her cut her head off with a knife (H) how did you go (T) we ride upon stickes and are there presently (H) doe you goe through the trees or over them (T) we see no thing but are there presently (H) why did you not tell your master (T) I was a fraid they said they would cut off my head if I told (H) would not you have hurt others if you could (T) they said they would hurt others but they could not (H) what attendants hath Sarah good (T) a yellow bird and shee would have given me one (H) what meate did she give it (T) it did suck her between her fingers (H) Did not you hurt mr Currins child (T) goode good and goode Osburn told that they did hurt mr Currens child and would have had me hurt him two but I did not (H) what hath Sarah Osburn (T) yesterday shee had a thing with a head like a woman with 2 leggs and wings Abigail williams that lives with her uncle mr Parris said that shee did see this same creature and it turned into the shape of goode osburn (H) what else have you seen with g osburn (T) an other thing hairy it goes upright like a man it hath only 2 leggs (H) did you not see Sarah good upon elisebeth Hubbard last Saturday (T) I did see her set a wolfe upon her to afflict her the persons with this maid did say that shee did complain of a wolf T shee furder said that shee saw a cat with good at another time (H) what cloathes doth the man go in (T) he goes in black clouthes a tal man with white hair I thinke (H) how doth the woman go (T) in a white whood and a black whood with a top knot (H) doe you see who it is that torments these children now (T) yes it is goode good she hurts them in her own shape (H) & who is it that hurts them now (T) I am blind now I cannot see

Salem Village
March the 1 t 1691/2

(Document continued on next page)

The Documentary Evidence

12   *(Essex County Court Archives, Salem Witchcraft*
Papers, I,11 & 12)

Third Version of Tituba's Examination

The concluding section of Joseph Putnam's account of the three examinations.

What the Indyen woman saith

they have don noe harme to hur shee saith she doth nott know how the dveill works — Who it it that hurts them the devell frot I know there is fowre that hurts the children 2 of the women are gamer Osburn and gamer Good and they say itt is shee one of the women is atall and short women and they would have hur goe with them to Boston and shee oned that shee did itt att first butt butt she was sorry for itt: itt was the apearance of a man that came to hur and told hur that she must hurt the Children and she said that 4 times shaps of a hodg or adodge and bid her sarve him she said that shee could nott then she said he would hurt hur shee all soe said that shee seed a yalow # [catt] burd that said unto hur sarve me and shee seed 2 catts and they said sarve me she murst more pinch the children she saith she sends the catt to bid hur pinch them: and the man brings the maid and bids hur pinch hur: and they doe pull hur and make hur goe with them to mr putman to perplex them: and they make hur ride upone apoall and they hould the poll and osband and good all soe rids upon poalls and they the 2 women would have hur cill thomas putmans child The 2 women and the man told hur that if she told to hur master they would cutt of hur heed and yester day tetaby abigall sayd that she say athing with wings and 2 leedgs and vanished into the chape of osborn and the indgon oneth the same: and all soe atends osborn a short and hary thing with 2 ledgs and to Whings all soe tetaby oneth that sary good sent a wolfe to scare the dr maid

Written by Jos putnam
Salem Village
March the 1t 1691/2

(Essex County Court Archives, Salem Witchcraft Papers, I,9)

"the Devil hath been raised"

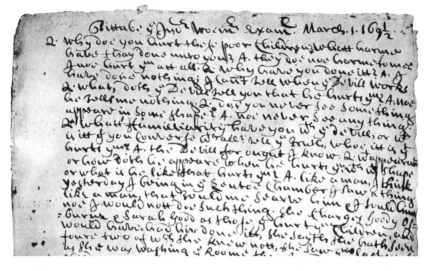

The first portion of the March 1, 1692, examination of the Parris slave Tituba, this testimony was recorded by Salem magistrate Jonathan Corwin.   *Courtesy, Danvers Archival Center.*

Fourth Version of Tituba's Examination

Tittube ye Indn Woemns Examd March. 1. 1691/2

Q. Why doe you hurt these poor Children? whatt harme have thay done unto you? A. they doe noe harme to me I noe hurt ym att all. Q. why have you done itt? A. I have done nothing; I Can't tell when ye Devill works Q. what, doth ye Devill tell you that he hurts ym? A. noe he tells me nothing. Q. doe you never see Something appeare in Some shape? A. noe never See any thing. Q. whatt familliarity have you wth ye devill, or wt is itt yt you Converse wth all? tell ye truth, whoe itt is yt hurts ym? A. the Devill for ought I know. Q. wt appearanc or how doth he appeare when he hurts ym, wth wt shape or what is he like that hurts ym? A. like a man I think yesterday I being in ye Lentoe Chamber I saw a thing like a man, that tould me Searve him & I tould him noe I would nott doe Such thing. she charges Goody Osburne & Sarah Good as those yt hurt ye Children, and would have had hir done itt, she sayth she hath Seen foure two of wch she knew nott,she Saw ym last night as she was washing ye Roome, thay tould me hurt the Children & would have had me gone to Boston, ther was.5. of ym with ye man, they tould me if I would nott goe & hurt ym thay would doe soe to mee att first I did agree wth ym

The Documentary Evidence

butt afterward I tould ym I doe soe noe more Q. would ya have had you hurt ye Children ye Last Night A. yes, butt I was Sorry & I sayd, I would doe Soe noe more, but tould I would feare God. Q. butt why did nott you doe Soe before? A. why thay tell mee I had done Soe before & therefore I must goe on, these were the.4.woemen & ye man, butt she knew none butt Osburne & Good only, ye others were of Boston. Q. att first begining wth ym, wt then appeared to you wt was itt like yt Got you to doe itt A. one like a man Just as I was goeing to sleep Came to me this was when ye Children was first hurt he sayd he would kill ye Children & she would never be well, and he Sayd if I would nott Serve him he would do soe to mee Q. is yt ye Same man yt appeared before to you yt appeared ye last night & tould you this? A. yes. Q. wt other likenesses besides a man hath appeared to you? A. Sometimes like a hogge Sometimes like a great black dogge, foure tymes. Q. but wt did thay Say unto you? A. thay tould me Serve him & yt was a good way; yt was ye black dogge I tould him I was afrayd, he tould me he would be worse then to me. Q. wt did you say to him then after that? A. I answer I will Serve you noe Longer he tould me he would doe me hurt then. Q. wt other Creatures have you seene A. a bird.Q. wt bird? A. a little yellow Bird. Q. where doth itt keep? A. wth ye man whoe hath pretty things there besides. Q. what other pretty things? A. he hath nott showed ym unto me, but he sd he would show ym me tomorrow, and tould me if I would Serve him, I should have ye Bird. Q. wt other Creatures did you see? A. I saw 2 Catts, one Red, another black as bigge as a little dogge. Q. wt did these Catts doe? A. I dont know, I have seen ym two tymes. Q. wt did they say? A. thay Say serve them. Q. when did you see ym? A. I saw them last night. Q. did thay doe any hurt to you or threaten you? A. thay did scratch me. Q. when? A. after prayer; and scratched mee, because I would not serve them and when ya went away I could nott see but thay stood before ye fire. Q. what Service doe thay expect fro you? A. thay Say more hurt to ye Children. Q. how did you pinch ym when you hurt ym? A. the other pull mee & hall me to ye pinch ye Childr, & I am very sorry for itt, what made you hould yor arme when you were Searched? wt had you there? A. I had nothing Q. doe nott those Catts suck you? A. noe never yett I would nott lett ym but ya had almost thrust me into ye fire. Q. how doe you hurt those yt you pinch? doe you gett those Catts? or other thing to doe it for you? tell us, how is it done? A. ye man sends ye Catts to me & bids me pinch ym, & I think I went over to mr Grigg's & have pinched hir this day in ye morning. the man brought mr Grigg's mayd to me & made me pinch hir. Q. did you ever goe wth these woe-

men? A. they are very strong & pull me & make me goe wth them. Q.
where did you goe? A. up to mr putnams & make me hurt the Child. Q.
whoe did make you goe? A. man yt is very strong & these two woeman,
Good & Osburne but I am Sorry. Q. how did you goe? Whatt doe you
Ride upon? A. I Rid upon a stick or poale & Good & Osburne behind
me, we Ride takeing hold of one another don't know how we goe for
I Saw noe trees, nor path, but was presently there. when wee were up.
Q. how long Since you began to pinch mr parriss Children? A. I did nott
pinch ym att ye first, butt he make me afterward. Q. have you Seen Good
and Osburne Ride upon a poule? A. yes & have held fast by mee: I was
nott att mr Griggs's but once, butt it may be Send Something like mee,
with or would I have gone, butt yt ya tell me, they will hurt me; last night
thay Tell me I must kill Some body with ye knife. Q. who were thay yt
told you Soe? A. Sarah Good & Osburne & ya would have had me killed
Thomas putnam's Child last night. the Child alsoe affirmed yt att ye Same
tyme thay would have had hir Cutt #[hir own throat] of hir own head
for if she would nott yn tould hir Tittubee would Cutt itt off & yn she
Complayned att ye Same Time of a knife Cutting of hir when hir master
hath asked hir about these things she sayth thay will nott lett hir tell, butt
Tell hir if she Tells hir head shall be Cutt off. Q. whoe Tells you Soe?
A. ye man, Good & Osburnes Wife. Goody Goody Came to hir last night
wn hir master was att prayr & would not lett hir hear & she Could nott
hear a good whyle. Good hath one of these birds ye yellow bird & would
have given mee itt, but I would not have itt & in prayer tyme she stoped
my eares & would nott lett me hear. Q. wt should you have done with
itt. A. give itt to ye Children. wch yellow bird hath bin severall tymes
Seen by ye Children I saw Sarah Good have itt on hir hand when she
Came to hir when mr parris was att prayr: I saw ye bird suck Good
betwene ye fore finger & Long finger upon the Right hand. Q. did you
never practise witchcraft in your owne Country? A. Noe Never before
now. Q. did you See ym doe itt now? A. yes. to day, butt yt was in ye
morneing. Q. butt did you see them doe itt now while you are Examin-
ing. A. noe I did nott See ym butt I Saw ym hurt att other tymes. I saw
Good have a Catt beside ye yellow bird wch was with hir Q. what hath
Osburne gott to goe wth hir? Some thing I dont know what itt is. I can't
name itt, I don't know how itt looks she hath two of ym one of ym hath
wings & two Leggs & a head like a woeman. the Children Saw ye Same
butt yesterday w'ch afterward turned into a woeman. Q. What is ye other
thing yt Goody Osburne hath? A. a thing all over hairy, all ye face hayry
& a long nose & I don't know how to tell how ye face looks, wth two

15

Leggs, itt goeth upright & is about two or three foot high & goeth upright like a man & last night itt stood before ye fire In mr parris's hall. Q. Whoe was yt appeared like a Wolfe to Hubbard as she was goeing fro proctures? A. itt was Sarah Good & I saw hir Send ye Wolfe to hir. Q. what Cloathes doth ye man appeare unto you in? A. black Cloaths Some times, Some times Searge Coat of other Couler, a Tall man wth White hayr, I think. Q. What apparrell doe ye woeman ware? A. I don't know wt couller. O. What Kind of Cloathes hath she? A. a black Silk hood wth a White Silk hood under itt, wth top knotts, wch woeman I know not butt have Seen hir in boston when I lived there. Q. what Cloathes ye little woeman? A. a Searge Coat wth a White Cap as I think. the Children having fits att this Very time she was asked whoe hurt ym, she Ansr Goody Good & ye Children affirmed ye same, butt Hubbard being taken in an extreame fit after she was asked whoe hurt hir & she Sayd she Could nott tell, but sayd they blinded hir, & would nott lett hir see & after yt was once or twice taken dumb hirself

[Document continues]

(Witchcraft – Tituba, Rare Books and Manuscripts Division, The New York Public Library, Astor, Lenox and Tilden Foundations)

Expenses at Ingersoll's Ordinary

Sometime after July 1692, Nathaniel Ingersoll submitted an itemized bill of expenses incurred at his ordinary by the magistrates and court officers while on county business.

March ye 1st 1691/2

Uppon a meeteing of ye Majestrates Mr Jno:Hathorne and Jonathan Corwin Esqrs: in an Inquirere after Witchcraft Expences upon ye Countrys Accot for Majestrates Marshalls Constables & Asistance at my Howse Vizt

		£	s.	d.
Impr	To ye Majestrate Dinner & Drink		8	
	To ye Marshalls 2 Constables			
	& Assistance Victeills		3	
	To 43d Cakes 6 qts Sider		2	
	To 2 Constables att 2 qts of 3d Sider on Cake .			9
	To Rum			6
	To Majestrates Horses			6
	To ye Marshall & Constable Herricks Horses .			6

"the Devil hath been raised"

Ye 3d Instant the Marshall Expences   6
Ye Marshall & his Horse 1 pott Sider   6

[Reverse]
Nath Ingersolls acco. expenses in some of the witch cases.

(Essex County Court Archives, Salem Witchcraft Papers, II,131)

Depositions by the Afflicted Girls

These seven depositions were written and filed after March 1, 1692, in the names of the afflicted children. The depositions of Elizabeth Hubbard, Ann Putnam, Jr., and Abigail Williams refer back to incidents in late February and particularly on March 1 during the examination of the three accused women.

The Deposistion of Elizabeth Hubbard agged about 17 years who testifieth and saith that on the 26 february 1691/92 I saw the Apperishtion of Sarah good who did most greviously afflect me by pinching and pricking me and so she continewed hurting of me tell the first day of march being the day of her examination and then she did also most greviously afflect and tortor me also dureing the time of her examynation and also severall times sence she hath afflected me and urged me to writ in hir book: also on the day of hir examination I saw the Apperishtion of Sarah good goe and hurt and afflect the bodyes of Elizabeth parish Abigail williams and Ann putnam junr and also I have seen the the Apperishtion
of Sarah Good afflecting:the body of   mark
Sarah vibber
                                            Eliz: X   Hubbard

[Reverse]

also in the Night after Sarah goods Examination: Sarah Good came to me barefoot and bareledged and did most grevously torment me by pricking and pinching me and I veryly beleve that Sarah good hath bewicked me also that night Samuell Sibly that was then attending me strock Sarah good on hir Arme

Elizabeth Hubbard
agt Sarah Good.

(Essex County Court Archives, Salem Witchcraft Papers I,20)

The Documentary Evidence

The Deposistion of Elizabeth Hubburd aged about 17 years who testifieth and saith that on the 27th of february 1691/92 I saw the Apperishtion of sarah osborn the wife of Alexander osborn who did most greviously tortor me by pricking and pinching me most dreadfully and so she continewed hurting me most greviously tell the first of march 1691/92:being the day of hir examination #[being first of march] and then also sarah osborn did tortor me most greviously by pinching and pricking me most dreadfully and also severell times sence sarah osborn has afflected me and urged me to write in hir book

(Essex County Court Archives, Salem Witchcraft Papers I, 28)

The Deposistion of Elizabeth Hubbard agged about 17 years who testifieth that on the 25th february 1691/92 I saw the Apperishtion of Tituba Indian which did Immediatly most greviously torment me by pricking pinching and almost choaking me. and so continewed hurting me most greviously by times #[hurting] tell the day of hir examination being the first of march and then also at the beginning of hir examination but as soon as she began to confess she left ofe hurting me and has hurt me but litle sence

[Reverse]

Eliz: Hubbard contra Titaba

(Essex County Court Archives, Salem Witchcraft Papers I,32)

The Deposition of Ann putnam Jur who testifieth and saith, that on the 25th of february 1691/92 I saw the apperishtion of Sarah good which did tortor me most greviously but I did not know hir name tell the 27th of february and then she tould me hir name was Sarah good and then she did prick me and pinch me most greviously: and also sense severall times urging me vehemently to writ in hir book and also on the first day of march being the day of hir Examination Sarah good did most greviously tortor me and also severall times sence: and also on the first day of march 1692 I saw the Aperishtion of sarah good goe and afflect and tortor the bodys of Elizabeth parish Abigail williams and Elizabeth Hubburd also I have seen the Apperishtion of Sarah good afflecting the body of Sarah vibber.

mark

Ann   X   putnams

ann putnam owned this har testimony to be the truth one har oath. before the Juriars of Inqwest this 28: of June 1692

"the Devil hath been raised"

And further says that shee verily believes that Sarah Good doth bewitch & afflicte her

Sworn before the Court

[Reverse]

Ann puttnam agt. Sarah Good

(Essex County Archives, Salem Witchcraft Papers, I,19)

The Deposistion of Ann putnam who testifieth and saith that on the 25 th of february 1691/92 I saw the Apperishtion of sarah osborn the wife of Allexandar osborn who did immediatly tortor me most greviously by pinching and pricking me dreadfully and so she continewed most dreadfully to afflect me tell the first day of march being the day of hir examination and then also she did tortor me most dreadfully in the time of hir examination: and also severall times sence sarah osborn has afflected me and urged me to writ in hir book

[Reverse]

Ann putnam agt Sarah Osborne

(Essex County Court Archives, Salem Witchcraft Papers, I,27)

The deposition of Ann putnam who testifieth and saith that on the 25 th of february 1691/92 I saw the Apperishtion of Tituba Mr. parishes Indian woman which did tortor me most greviously by pricking and pinching me most dreadfully tell the first day of march being the day of hir examination and then also most greviously allso at the beginning of hir examination: but senc she confessed she has hurt me but little

[Reverse]

Ann putnam agst Tittuba I[ndian]

(Essex County Court Archives, Salem Witchcraft Papers, I,35)

The testimony of Abigail Williams testifyh & saith that severall times last February she hath been much afflicted with pains in her head & other parts & often pinched by the apparition

The Documentary Evidence

of Sarah Good, Sarah Osburne & Tituba Indian all of Salem Village & also excessively afflicted by the said apparition of said Good, Osburne, & Tituba at their examination before authority the. 1 st March last past 1691/2

Farther the said Abigail Williams testifyeth that she saw the apparition of said Sarah Good at her examination pinch Eliz: Hubbard & set her into fits & also Eliz: Parris, & Ann Putnam

The mark of

Abigail X Williams.

Testified before us by Abigail Williams Salem May: the.23d, 1692

*John Hathorne
*Jonathan Corwin
P ordr of ye General Councill

[Reverse]

[illegible]   Contra Titiba

(Essex County Court Archives, Salem Witchcraft Papers, I,31)

Deposition of Samuel Parris, Thomas Putnam & Ezekiel Cheever

The body of this deposition is in the handwriting of Rev. Samuel Parris. It refers to events of March 1st, though possibly not written until May 23, at the time of its being "Jurat in Curia" or sworn in court. An additional notation on this document, written in another hand, shows that Parris also swore to this deposition again in late June.

The Deposition of Sam: Parris aged about thirty & nine years testifyeth & saith that Eliz: Parris junr & Abigail Williams & Ann Putnam junr & Eliz: Hubbard were most greivously & severall times tortured during the examination of Sarah Good, Sarah Osburne & Tituba Indian before the Magistrates at Salem village 1. March. 1691/2 And the said Tituba being the last of the abovesaid that was examined they the abovesd afflicted persons were greivously distressed until the said Indian began to confess & then they were immediately all quiet the rest of the said Indian womans examination. Also Tho: Putnam aged about fourty years & Ezek: Cheevers aged about thirty & six years testify to the whole of the abovesd & all the three deponents afore-

"the Devil hath been raised"

said farther testify that after the said Indian began to confess she was her self very much afflicted & in the face of authority at the same time & openly charged the abovesaid Good & Osburne as the persons that afflicted her the aforesaid Indian

Sworne Salem May the 23d 1692 Before us *John Hathorne
*Jonathan. Corwin

P ordr of ye Governr & Councill
Jurat in Curia

mr paris on his oath owned this to be the truth before the Juryars for inquest this 28 of Jun: 1692

[Reverse]
The depion of S. Parris Tho: putnam & Ezek: Cheevers

	Sarah Good
agst.	Sarah Osburne
	Tituba Indian

(Essex County Court Archives, Salem Witchcraft Papers, I,34)

Samuel Sibley Vs. Sarah Good

This testimony relates to the continued affliction of Elizabeth Hubbard during the evening following the examination of Sarah Good.

Samuell Sibly aged about :34: years Testefieth and saith that I being at the house of doctter grides that night after: that Sary good was examened and Elizebeth Hubbard said that ther sands Sary good #[stands] apon the tabel by you with all hear naked brast and bar footed bar lagded and said.o.nast slout if .I. had sum thing.I. wood kill hear then.I. struk with my staf wher she said Sary good stud and Elizabeth hubbard cried out you have heet har right acors the back you have a most killd hear if any body was there they may see it

Jurat in Curia

(Essex Institute, Salem, Mass., Salem Witchcraft Papers, Fowler Collection)

The Documentary Evidence

Joseph Herrick, Sr. & Mary Herrick Vs. Sarah Good

The Deposistion of Joseph Herrick senr. who testifieth and saith that on the first day of March 1691/2: I being then Constable for Salem: there was delivered to me by warrant from the worshipfull Jno. Hathorne and Jonathan Corwine Esqrs. Sarah good for me to cary to their majesties Gaol at Ipswich and that night I sett a gard to watch her at my own house namely Samul: Braybrook michaell dunell Jonathan Baker . . and the affore named parsons Informed me in the morning that that night Sarah good was gon for some time from them both bare foot and bare legde: and I was also Informed that: that night Elizabeth Hubburd one of the Afflected parsons Complaned that Sarah Good came and aflected hir:being bare foot and bare ledged and Samuell Sibley that was one that was attending of Eliza Hubburd strock Sarah good on the Arme as Elizabeth Hubburd said and Mary Herrick and wife of the above said Joseph Herick testifieth that on the 2th: March 1691/2 in the morning I took notis of Sarah Good in the morning and one of her Armes was Blooddy from a little below the Elbow to the wrist: and I also took notis of her armes on the night before and then there was no signe of blood on them

Joseph harrik senr and mary harrik appearid before us the Jary for Inquest: and did on the oath which the had taken owne this their evidense to the truth;the 28:of June 1692

Sworne in Court

[Reverse]
Joseph Herrick and his wife against Sarah Good

Memento. Sam Sibley to br served Michll. Dunwill
Jona. Bacar ver. Sa Good

(Essex County Court Archives, Salem Witchcraft Papers, I,16)

William Allen & John Hughes Vs. Sarah Good, Sarah Osburn & Tituba

This first section of a statement concerns strange sights and sounds observed by two men the night of March 1.

March 5th 1691/2

Wm Allin saith yt on ye 1 st:of March att night he heard a strange noyse not useually heard and so continued for many times so yt hee was afrighted and coming nearer on to it he there saw a strange and unuseall beast lyeing on

"the Devil hath been raised"

the Grownd so yt goeing up to it ye sd Beast vanished away and in ye sd
place starte up 2 or 3 weemen and flew from mee not after ye manner of other
weemen but swiftly vanished away out of our sight which weemen wee took
to bee Sarah Good Sarah Osborne and Tittabe ye time was a bout an hour
within night and I John Hughes saith ye same beeing in Company then wth
sd allin as wittness our hands

*william Allen
*john hughes

[Document continues]

(Essex County Court Archives, Salem Witchcraft Papers, I,29)

WEDNESDAY, MARCH 2, 1692

Examination of Osburn & Tituba

*Brief notation from the magistrates' summary record of the further examination of
two of the accused women.*

Salem March 2d Sarah Osburne againe Examined and also titiba as will appear
in their Examinations given in

[In margin]

titiba again acknowledged ye for & also accused ye other two.

[Document continues]

(Essex County Court Archives, Salem Witchcraft Papers, I,14)

Examination of Tituba

*This detailed transcript of Tituba's March 2 examination was recorded by magis-
trate Jonathan Corwin. It continues on the same document as he had used to record her
March 1 examination.*

Second Examination. March. 2.1691/2

Q. What Covenant did you make wth yt man yt came to you? What did he
tell you. A. he Tell me he god, & I must believe him & Serve him Six

The Documentary Evidence

yeares & he would give me many fine things. Q. how long a gone was this? A. about Six weeks & a little more, fryday night before Abigall was Ill. Q. wt did he Say you must doe more? did he Say you must write anything? did he offer you any paper? A. yes, the Next time he Come to me & showed me some fine things, Some thing like Creatures, a little bird something like green & white. Q. did you promiss him then when he spake to you then what did you answer him. A. I then sayd this I tould him I could nott believe him God, I tould him I ask my maister & would have gone up but he stopt mee & would nott lett me. Q. whatt did you promiss him? A. the first tyme I believe him God & then he was Glad. Q. what did he Say to you then? what did he Say you must doe? A. then he tell me they must meet together: Q. wn did he Say you must meet together? A. he tell me wednesday next att my m'rs house, & then they all meet together & thatt night I saw ym all stand in ye Corner, all four of ym & ye man stand behind mee & take hold of mee to make mee stand still in ye hall. Q. where was your master then? A. in ye other Roome. Q. What time of night? A. a little before prayr time. Q. What did this man Say to you when he took hold of you? A. he Say goe & doe hurt to them. and pinch ym & then I went in, & would nott hurt ym a good while, I would nott hurt Betty, I loved Betty, but ye hall me & make me pinch Betty & ye next Abigall & then quickly went away altogether & I had pinch ym Q. did they pinch A. Noe, but they all lookt on & See mee pinch ym Q. did you goe into yt Room in your own person & all ye rest? A. yes, and my master did nott See us, for ya would nott lett my Master See. Q. did you goe wth ye Company? A. Noe I stayd & ye Man stayd wth mee. Q. whatt did he then to you? A. he tell me my master goe to prayer & he read in book & he ask me what I remember, but don't you remember anything. Q. did he ask you noe more but ye first time to Serve him or ye secon time? A. yes, he ask me againe, yt I Serve him, Six yeares & he Come ye Next time & show me a book. A. and when would he come then? A. ye next fryday & showed me a book in ye day time betimes in ye morneing. Q. and what Booke did he Bring a great or little booke? A. he did nott show it me, nor would nott, but had itt in his pockett. Q. did nott he make you write yor Name? A. noe nott yett for my mistris Called me into ye other roome. Q. whatt did he say you must doe in that book? A. he Sayd write & sett my name to itt. Q. did you write? A. yes once I made a marke in ye Booke & made itt wh red like Bloud. Q. did he gett itt out of your body? A. he Said he must gett itt out ye Next time he Come againe, he give me a pin tyed in a stick to doe itt wth, butt he noe Lett me bloud wth itt as yett butt Intended another time when he

"the Devil hath been raised"

Come againe. Q. did you See any other marks in his book? A. yes a great many Some marks red, Some yellow, he opened his booke a great many marks in itt. Q. did he tell you ye Names of ym? A. yes of two noe more Good & Osburne & he Say thay make ym marks in that book & he showed them mee. Q. how many marks doe you think there was? A. Nine. Q. did they write there Names? A. thay made marks, Goody Good Sayd she made hir mark, butt Goody Osburne would nott tell she was Cross to mee. Q. when did Good tell you, She Sett hir hand to ye Book? A. the same day I Came hither to prison. Q. did you See ye man thatt morneing? A. yes a litle in ye morneing & he tell me ye Magistrates Come up to Examine mee. Q. wt did he Say you must Say? A. he tell me, tell nothing, if I did he would Cutt my head off. Q. tell us tru how many woemen doe use to Come when you Rid abroad? A. foure of ym these two Osburne & Good & those two strangers. Q. you Say yt there was Nine did he tell you whoe ya were? A. noe he noe lett me See but he tell me I should See ym ye next tyme Q. what sights did you see? A. I see a man, a dogge, a hogge, & two Catts a black and Red & ye strange monster was Osburne yt I mentioned before this was ye hayry Imp ye man would give itt to mee, but I would nott have itt. Q. did he show you in ye Book wch was Osburne & wch was Goods mark? A. yes I see there marks. Q. butt did he tell ye Names of ye other? A. noe sr. Q. & what did he say to you when you made your Mark? A. he sayd Serve mee & always Serve mee the man wth ye two women Came fro Boston. Q. how many times did you goe to Boston? A. I was goeing & then came back againe I was never att Boston. Q. whoe came back wth you againe? A. ye man came back wth mee & ye woemen goe away, I was nott willing to goe? Q. how farr did you goe, to what Towne? A. I never went to any Towne I see noe trees, noe Towne. Q. did he tell you where ye Nine Lived? A. yes, Some in Boston & Some here in this Towne, but he would nott tell mee wher thay were, X

(Witchcraft-Tituba, Rare Books and Manuscripts Division, The New York Public Library, Astor, Lenox and Tilden Foundations)

William Allen, William Good, John Hughes & Samuel Braybrook Vs. Sarah Good

This is a continuation of the March 5 statement made by William Allen and others relating to strange occurrences witnessed by them on March 2.

William Allen further saith yt on ye 2d day of march ye sd Sarah Good vissabley appeared to him in his chamber sd allen beeing in bed and brought an unuseuall light in wth her ye sd Sarah came and sate upon his foot ye sd allen went to kick att her upon which shee vanished and ye light with her

———

william Good saith yt ye night before his sd wife was Examined he saw a wort or tett a little belowe her Right shoulder which he never saw before and asked Goodwife Engersol whether she did not see it when shee searched her.

———

John Hughes further saith yt on ye 2d day of march yt comeing from Good-man Sibleys a boute Eight of ye clock in ye night hee saw a Great white dogg whome he came up to but he would not stire but when He was past hee ye sd dogg followed him about 4 or 5 pole and so disapeared ye same night ye sd John Hughes beeing in Bed in a clossd Roome and ye dore being fast so yt no catt nor dogg could come in ye sd. John saw a Great light appeare in ye sd Chamber and Risseing up in his bed he saw a large Grey Catt att his beds foot

———

March ye 2d Saml Brabrook saith yt Carrieng Sarah Good to ippswhich ye sd Sarah leapt of her horse 3 times which was Between 12 and 3 of ye clock of ye same day wch ye daughter of Thomas Puttman declared ye same att her fathers house ye sd Brabrook further saith yt sd Sarah Good tould him that shee would not owne her selfe to bee a wicth unless she is provd one shee saith yt there is but one Evidence and yts and Indian and therefore she fears not and so Continued Rayling against ye Majestrates and she Endevered to kill herselfe.

(Essex County Court Archives, Salem Witchcraft Papers, I, 29)

THURSDAY, MARCH 3, 1692

Further Examination of Osburn & Tituba

An additional notation taken from the magistrates' summary record shows that two of the women were again examined. The record of this examination is not extant.

Salem March 3d Sarah Osburn and titiba Indian againe Examined ye Examination now Given in

"the Devil hath been raised"

[Document continues]

SATURDAY, MARCH 5, 1692

An Additional Examination of Sarah Good & Tituba

This notation is also taken from the magistrates' summary record and concludes with acknowledging signatures.

Salem March 5th Sarah Good and titiba againe Examined. & in theire Examination titiba acknowledg ye same she did formerly and accused ye other two abovesd -

P us *John Hathorne
*Jonathan Corwin Assists.

[In margin]
titiba againe sd ye same

[Document continues]

(Essex County Court Archives, Salem Witchcraft Papers, I, 14)

SUNDAY, MARCH 6, 1692

Ann Putnam, Jr. Vs. Elizabeth Procter

In a sworn deposition presented to court on June 30, 1692, Ann Putnam, Jr., spoke to events of March 3 and 6 at which times she claimed Elizabeth Procter first began afflicting her. It would not be until early April 1692 that Elizabeth Procter, the wife of John Procter of Salem Farmes, would be arrested, examined, and jailed.

The Deposition of Ann putnam Jur who testifieth and saith that on the 3th of march 1691/92 I saw the Apperishtion of gooddy procktor amongst the wicthes & she did almost choake me Immediatly and bite and pinch me but I did not know who she was tell the 6'th of march that I saw hir att meeting and then I tould them that held me that yt woman was one that did afflect me: and severall times sence she hath greviously afflected me by biting pinch-

(Document continued on next page)

The Documentary Evidence

ing and almost choaking me urging me vehemently to writ in hir book:
[Document continues]
[Reverse]
Ann puttnam agt Eliza. procter

(Essex County Court Archives, Salem Witchcraft Papers, I, 101)

MONDAY, MARCH 7, 1692

Sarah Good, Sarah Osburn & Tituba Sent To Prison

A postscript notation made at the conclusion of the magistrates' summary record.

Salem
March 7th:1691/2
Sarah Good Sarah Osburne and Titiba an Indian Woman all sent to the Goale in Boston according to theire Mittimes then sent to theire Majests Goale Keeper

(Essex County Court Archives, Salem Witchcraft Papers, I, 14)

WEDNESDAY, MARCH 9, 1692

John Arnold's Expenses

In mid-1692 Boston jailer John Arnold submitted an account of his expenses for keeping prisoners. Heading the list of expenses were items obtained in March 1692 to be used on witch suspects.

Boston   Ye Countrey is . . . . Dr.
1691/2

March 9.   To Chaines for Sarah Good & Sarah Osbourn   £ – 14 –

[Document continues]

(Massachusetts Archives,vol. 135,#24)

"the Devil hath been raised"

At the rear of 67 Centre Street in present day Danvers is the archaeological site of the 1681 Salem Village parsonage. Here lived the Rev. Samuel Parris family including his slave Tituba, and here began the Salem Village witchcraft outbreak of 1692. This site is today owned by the Town of Danvers and includes original foundations and interpretive signs. Under the direction of Richard Trask, the site was excavated beginning in 1970.   Photo by the author.

FRIDAY, MARCH 11, 1692

Day of Prayer

This is an account of a prayer meeting held in the village parsonage. The account is taken from a book written by Robert Calef and printed in 1700.

March the 11th.   Mr. Parris invited several Neighboring Ministers to join with him in keeping a Solemn day of prayer at his own House; the time of the exercise those Persons were for them most part silent, but after any one Prayer was ended, they would Act and Speak strangely and Ridiculously, yet were such as had been well Educated and of good Behaviour, the one a girl of 11 or 12 years old, would sometimes seem to be in a Convulsion Fit, her Limbs being twisted several ways, and very stiff, but presently her Fit would be over.

(Robert Calef, More Wonders of the Invisible World *[London, 1700] p. 91)*

The Documentary Evidence

SATURDAY, MARCH 12, 1692

Edward Putnam & Ezekiel Cheever Vs. Martha Cory

This deposition, sworn in court on September 8, 1692, recounts a visit by Putnam and Cheever to the houses of Thomas Putnam and Giles Cory. The visitors were attempting to discover if a new spectre, that of village covenant church member Martha Cory, was in fact afflicting Ann Putnam, Jr., as it had been accused. Edward Putnam was a deacon of the village church as well as an uncle of Ann Putnam, Jr. Much of the discussion in the deposition centers around whether or not the spectre's clothes were the same as that which Martha wore.

The deposition of Edward Putnam aged about 36 years and Ezekiel Cheever aged about 37 years testifieth and sayeth that wee being often complained unto by An Putnam that goode Corie did often appear to her and torter her by pinching and other wayes thought it our duty to goe to her and see what shee would say to this complaint shee being in church covenant with us. and accordingly upon the 12'th day of march about ten of the clock we appointed to goe about the midle afternoon, and wee desired An Putnam to take good notice of what cloathes goode Corie came in that so we might see whither shee was not mistaken in the person, and accordingly wee went to the house of Thomas Putnam before we went to goode Corie to see what An could say about her cloathes. and shee told us that presently after we had #[spoken] told her that we would goe and talke with goode Corie she came and blinded her but told her that her name was Corie and that shee should see her no more before it was night because she should not tell us what cloathes shee had on and then shee would come again and pay her off. then wee went both of us away from the house of Thomas Putnum to the house of Giles Corie where we found go the abovesaid Corie all alone in her house.and as soone as we came in. in a smiling manner shee sayeth I know what you are come for you are come to talke with me about being a witch but I am none I cannot helpe peoples talking of me Edward Putnam answered her that it was the afflicted person that did complain of her that was the occasion of our coming to her. she presently replied but does shee tell you what cloathes I have on we made her no answer to this at her first asking where upon shee asked us again with very great eagernes but does she tell you what cloathes I have on. at which questions with that eagernes of mind. with which shee did aske made us to thinke of what An Putnam had told us before wee went to her. #[to which] and wee told her no shee did not for shee told us that you came and blinded her and told her that shee should see you no more before it was night

"the Devil hath been raised"

that so shee might not tell us what cloathes you had on. shee made but litle answer to this but seemed to smile at it as if shee had showed us a pretty trick. we had a great deal of talke with her about the complaint that was of her and how greatly the name of God and religion and thee church was dishonured by this meanes but shee seemed to be no way conserned for any thing about it but only to stop the mouthes of people that they might not say thus of her shee told us that shee did not thinke that there were any witches we told her wee were fully satisfied about the first knoe that they were such persons as they were arrested for. shee said if they were wee could not blame the devill for making witches of them for they were idle sloathfull persons and minded nothing that was good. but we had no reason to thinke so of her for shee had made a profession of christ and rejoyced to go and hear the word of god and the like. but we told her it was not her making an out ward profession that would clear her from being a witch for it had often been so in the would that witches had crept into the churches : much more discourse we had with her but shee made her profession a cloake to cover all she furder told us that the devill was come down amongst us in great rage and that God had for-saken the earth . and after much discourse with her being to much here to be related we returned to the house of the above said Thomas Putnam and we found that shee had done as shee said shee would for shee came not to hurt the above said Putnam as #[shee] An Putnam told us all this time but after we were gone we understand that shee came again as shee did use to doe before greatly afflicting of her

[Document continues]

[Reverse]
Edwd. Putnam & Eliza. Cheevir Deposition

(Essex County Court Archives, Salem Witchcraft Papers, I, 39)

MONDAY, MARCH 14, 1692

Edward Putnam Vs. Martha Cory

In this undated testimony, most likely presented in September 1692, during Cory's trial, Edward Putnam recounts the terrifying afflictions which took place when Martha Cory visited the Thomas Putnam house on March 14 to confront Ann Putnam, Jr., about her accusations.

The disposistion of Edward Putnam aged about 38 yeares ho testifieth and saith one the 14 day of march 1692 martha Cory the wife of giles Cory Came to the house of Thomas Putnam: she being desired to Come and see his dauter

The Documentary Evidence

ann Putnam: ho had Charged martha Cory to her face that she had hurt her by witchcraft but no sonner did martha Cory Come in to the hous of thomas putnam but ann putnam fell in to grevious feets of Choking blinding feat and hands twisted in a most grevious manner and told martha Cory to her face that she did it, and emediately hur tonge was dran out of her: mouth and her teeth fasned upon it in a most grevious maner after ann putnam had libberty to speeke she said to martha Cory ther is a yellow burd a sucking betwen your fore finger and midel finger I see it said ann putnam I will Come and see it said she: so you may said martha Cory: but before an Came to her I saw martha Cory put one of her fingers in the place whear ann had said she saw the burd and semed to give a hard rub ann putnam Came and said she see nothing but emediately she was blinded after this ann putnam tryed to go to her and when she Came allmost to her shee fell down blindad and Cold not Come at her any more: ann putnam allso told her she put her hands upon the face of Joseph poops wife one the Sabath day at meeting and shu- ing. her how she did it emediately her hands ware.fasned to her eyes that they Cold not be pulled from them except they should have ben broaken. off, after this ann putnam said hear is a speet at the fier with a man apon it and Goo- dey Cory you be a turnning of it then marcy lues toock a stick and struck at it and then it went away but emediately it apered again and marcy lues ofred to strike it again but ann putnam said do not if you love your self but presently marcy lues Cryed out with a grevious pane in her arme as if one had struck her with a stick upon her arme and ann putnam told goodey Corey she see her strike marcy lues with a Iron rood apon her arme: and marcy lues and ann putnam gru so bad with panes we desired goodey Cory to be gone and marcy lues said she saw shadows like women but Cold not disarn ho they were but presently Cryed out in a very loud maner I onte I onte and being asked what they wold have her do she said they wold have me to right and emediately she was Choked and blinded her neck twicted her teeth and mouth #[shet] shut and gru to such feets as wold put two or three men to it to hold her and was this evening drawn toward the fier by unseen hands as she sat in a Chare and two men hold of it yet she and Chare mooved toward the fier tho they labored to the Contrary her feat going formost and I seeing it steped to her feat and lifted with my stringht together with the other two and all littel enuf to prevent her from going in to the fier with her feat for- most and this destres held tell about a leven of the Cloack in the night—I have allso seen maney bitees before and sence apon ouer aflicted parsons that

"the Devil hath been raised"

have told me martha Cory did it the prisner now at the bar--
*Edward Putnam
Jurat in Curia
S Sewall Cle

(Massachusetts Historical Society, Salem Witchcraft Papers)

FRIDAY & SATURDAY, MARCH 18 & 19, 1692

Ann Putnam, Sr. Vs. Martha Cory & Rebecca Nurse

This is the first part of a deposition written in the handwriting of Thomas Putnam concerning his wife, Ann, the mother of Ann Putnam, Jr. In her testimony Mrs. Putnam tells of being afflicted not only by the spectre of Goody Cory, but also by a new spectral tormentor, Rebecca Nurse. Nurse was a Salem Village inhabitant and wife of Francis Nurse. She was also a covenant member of the Salem Church. This deposition was sworn to on May 31, 1692.

The Deposition of Ann putnam the wife of Thomas putnam agged about 30 years who testifieth and saith that on the 18th march 1691/92 I being wearied out in helping to tend my poor afflected Child and Maid: about the middle of the affternoon I layd me down on the bed to take a little Rest: and Immediatly I was allmost prest and Choaked to death: that had it not been for the mircy of a gratious God and the help of those that ware with me: I could not have lived many moments: and presently I saw the Apperishtion of Martha Cory who did torter me so as I cannot Express Redy to tare me all to peaces: and yn departed from me alitle while: but before I could recover strenth or well take breath the Apperishtion of Martha Cory fell upon me again with dreadfull tortors and hellish temtations to goe along with hir and she also brought to me a little Red book in hir hand and a black pen urging me vehemently to writ in hir book: and severall times that day she did most greviously tortor me allmost redy to kill me and on the 19 th march: Martha Cory againe appeared to me and also Rebekah nurs the wife of frances nurs sen r:and they both did tortor: me agrate many times this day with such tortors as no toungu can express because I would not yeald to their Hellish temtations that had I not been upheild by an Allmighty Arme I could not have lived while night ye 20 th march being sabboth day I had agrat deal of Respitt. between my fitts:

[Document continues]

(Essex Institute, Salem, Mass., Salem Witchcraft Papers, #22)

The Documentary Evidence

SATURDAY, MARCH 19, 1692

Warrant for the Apprehension of Martha Cory

Salem March the 19 th.1691/2

There being Complaint this day made before us. By Edward putnam and Henery Keney Yeoman both of Salem Village, Against Martha Cory the wife of Giles Cory of Salem farmes for Suspition of haveing Comitted sundry acts of Witchcraft and thereby donne much hurt and injury unto the Bodys of Ann Putnam the wife of Thomas putnam of Salem Village Yeoman And Anna Putnam the daughter of sd Thomas putnam and Marcy Lewis Single woman Liveing in sd putnams famyly; also abigail Williams one of mr parris his family and Elizabeth Hubert Doctor Grigs his maid---

You are therefore in theire Majests names hereby required to apprehend and bring; before us. Martha Cory the wife of Giles Cory abovesaid on Munday next being the. 21t day of this Instant month, at the house: of Lt Nathaniell Ingersalls of Salem Village aboute twelve of the Clock in ye day in order to her Examination Relateing to the premises and hereof you are not to faile Dated Salem March. the 19th 1691/2

P vs   *John:Hathorne
           *Jonathan. Corwin   Assists

To Geo Herrick Marshall
of the County of Essex—
or any Constable in Salem

(Essex County Court Archives, Salem Witchcraft Papers, I, 38)

Deodat Lawson's Narrative

Rev. Deodat Lawson had served as minister at Salem Village from 1684 to 1688. Upon hearing about the witchcraft outbreak in the village and that several members of his family may have previously died there under "the malicious operations of the infernal powers," Lawson decided to visit his former abode to learn what was happening. Lawson's observations during the latter part of March and the first of April were subsequently written into a 10-page pamphlet titled A Brief and True Narrative *and printed by Benjamin Harris of Boston. These short though tantalizing descriptions give a broader perspective than many of the surviving court records.*

On the Nineteenth day of March last I went to Salem Village, and lodged at Nathaniel Ingersols near to the Minister Mr. P[arris]'s house, and presently

"the Devil hath been raised"

Among the thousands of artifacts excavated at the village parsonage archaeological site were these items. The ca. 1690 Rhenish stoneware jug combines uncolored incised decoration and elaborate cobalt ornamental tulips, while the dark green bottle neck with a string rim is typical of squat wine bottles of the late 17th century. The metal plate fragment contains the punched initials S^{P}E indicating that the original was a monogrammed personal plate belonging to Samuel and Elizabeth Parris.   *Photo by the author.*

The Documentary Evidence

after, I came into my Lodging Capt. Walcuts Daughter Mary came to Lieut. Ingersols and spake to me, but, suddenly after as she stood by the door, was bitten, so that she cried out of her Wrist, and looking on it with a Candle, we saw apparently the marks of Teeth both upper and lower set, on each side of her wrist.

In the beginning of the Evening, I went to give Mr. P. a visit. When I was there, his Kins-woman, Abigail Williams, (about 12 years of age,) had a grievous fit; she was at first hurryed with Violence to and fro in the room; (though Mrs. Ingersol endeavoured to hold her,) sometimes makeing as if she would fly, stretching up her arms as high as she could, and crying "Whish, Whish, Whish!" several times; Presently after she said there was Goodw N[urse]. and said, "Do you not see her? Why there she stands!" And the said Goodw. N. offered her The Book, but she was resolved she would not take it, saying Often, "I wont, I wont, I wont, take it, I do not know what Book it is: I am sure it is none of Gods Book, it is the Divels Book, for ought I know." After that, she run to the Fire, and begun to throw Fire Brands, about the house; and run against the Back, as if she would run up Chimney, and, as they said, she had attempted to go into the Fire in other Fits.

(Deodat Lawson, A Brief and True Narrative
[Boston, 1692] p. 3)

SUNDAY, MARCH 20, 1692

Meeting House Disruptions

Rev. Lawson notes several unusual interruptions which occurred during his participation as a visiting clergyman at the Sunday Salem Village Meeting House service.

On Lords Day, the Twentieth of March, there were sundry of the afflicted Persons at Meeting, as, Mrs. Pope, and Goodwife Bibber, Abigail Williams, Mary Walcut, Mary Lewes, and Doctor Grigg's Maid. There was also at Meeting, Goodwife C[ory]. (who was afterward Examined on suspicion of being a Witch:) They had several Sore Fits, in the time of Publick Worship, which did something interrupt me in my First Prayer; being so unusual. After Psalm was Sung, Abigail Williams said to me, "Now stand up, and Name your Text!" And after it was read, she said "It is a long Text." In the beginning of Sermon, Mrs. Pope, a Woman afflicted, said to me, "Now there is enough of that." And in the Afternoon, Abigail Williams, upon my referring to my Doctrine said to me, "I know no Doctrine you had, If you did name one, I have forgot it."

"the Devil hath been raised"

In Sermon time when Goodw C was present in the Meetinghouse Ab. W. called out, "Look where Goodw. C sits on the Beam suckling her Yellow bird betwixt her fingers!" Anne Putnam another Girle afflicted said there was a Yellow-bird sat on my hat as it hung on the Pin in the Pulpit: but those that were by, restrained her from speaking loud about it.

(Deodat Lawson, A Brief and True Narrative
[Boston, 1692] p. 3-4)

MONDAY, MARCH 21, 1692

Constable Herrick's Return of Martha Cory's Apprehension Warrant

March 21.st I have taken Martha Cory and brought to ye house of Leut Nath: Engersoll where she is in ye Costody of some persons by mee Required and is forth Comeing att demand

   per : mee   *Joseph Herrick Constable for Salem

(Essex County Court Archives, Salem Witchcraft Papers, I, 38)

Rev. Lawson's Narrative of the Examination of Martha Cory

Lawson captures much of the emotion of the examination in his description of the scene and of the many physical happenings between the afflicted persons and the accused. Taken with the record as transcribed by Rev. Samuel Parris, a less than impartial though seemingly careful observer, the March 21 examination of Cory is one of the best recorded of any of the witchcraft proceedings.

On Monday the 21st. of March, The Magistrates of Salem appointed to come to Examination of Goodw C[ory]. And about twelve of the Clock, they went into the Meeting-House, which was Thronged with Spectators: Mr. Noyes began with a very pertinent and pathetic Prayer; and Goodwife C. being called to answer to what was Alledged against her, she desired to go to Prayer, which was much wondred at, in the presence of so many hundred people: The Magistrates told her, they would not admit it; they came not there to hear her Pray, but to Examine her, in what was Alledged against her. The Worshipful Mr. Hathorne asked her, Why she Afflicted those Children? she said, she did not Afflict them. He asked her, who did then? she said, "I do not know; How should I know?" The Number of the Afflicted Persons were about that time Ten, *viz.* Four Married Women, Mrs. Pope, Mrs. Putman, Goodw. Bibber, and an Ancient Woman, named Goodall, three

The Documentary Evidence

Maids, Mary Walcut, Mercy Lewes, at Thomas Putman's, and a Maid at Dr. Griggs's, there were three Girls from 9 to 12 Years of Age, each of them, or thereabouts, *viz.* Elizabeth Parris, Abigail Williams and Ann Putman; these were most of them at G. C's Examination, and did vehemently accuse her in the Assembly of afflicting them, by Biting, Pinching, Strangling, etc. And that they did in their Fit,see her Likeness coming to them, and bringing a Book to them, she said, she had no Book; they affirmed, she had a Yellow-Bird, that used to suck betwixt her Fingers, and being asked about it, if she had any Familiar Spirit, that attended her, she said, She had no Familiarity with any such thing. She was a Gospel Woman: which Title she called her self by; and the Afflicted Persons told her, "ah! She was, A Gospel Witch." Ann Putman did there affirm, that one day when Lieutenant Fuller was at Prayer at her Fathers House, she saw the shape of Goodw. C. and she thought Goodw. N[urse]. Praying at the same time to the Devil, she was not sure it was Goodw. N. she thought it was; but very sure she saw the Shape of G. C. The said C. said, they were poor, distracted, Children, and no heed to be given to what they said. Mr. Hathorne and Mr. Noyes replyed, it was the judgment of all that were present, they were Bewitched, and only she, the Accused Person said, they were Distracted. It was observed several times, that if she did but bite her Under lip in time of Examination the persons afflicted were bitten on their armes and wrists and produced the Marks before the Magistrates, Ministers and others. And being watched for that, if she did but Pinch her Fingers, or Graspe one hand hard in another, they were Pinched and produced the Marks before the Magistrates, and Spectators. After that, it was observed, that if she did but lean her Breast, against the Seat, in the Meeting House, (being the Barr at which she stood,) they were afflicted. Particularly Mrs. Pope complained of grievous torment in her Bowels as if they were torn out. She vehemently accused said C. as the instrument, and first threw her Muff at her; but that flying not home, she got off her Shoe, and hit Goodwife C. on the head with it. After these postures were watched, if said C. did but stir her feet, they were afflicted in their Feet, and stamped fearfully. The afflicted persons asked her why she did not go to the company of Witches which were before the Meeting house mustering? Did she not hear the Drum beat. They accused her of having Familiarity with the Devil, in the time of Examination, in the shape of a Black man whispering in her ear; they affirmed, that her Yellow-Bird sucked betwixt her Fingers in the Assembly; and order being given to see if there were any sign, the Girl that saw it, said, it was too late now; she had removed a Pin, and put it on her head; which was found there sticking upright.

They told her, she had Covenanted with the Devil for ten years, six of

"the Devil hath been raised"

them were gone, and four more to come. She was required by the Magistrates to answer that Question in the Catechism, "How many persons be there in the God-Head?" she answered it but oddly, yet was there no great thing to be gathered from it; she denied all that was charged upon her, and said, "They could not prove a Witch"; she was that Afternoon Committed to Salem-Prison; and after she was in Custody, she did not so appear to them, and afflict them as before.

(Deodat Lawson, A Brief and True Narrative *[Boston, 1692] p. 4-5)*

Examination of Martha Cory

21·March 1691/2

Mr Hathorne. You are now in the hands of Authority tell me now why you hurt these persons

Martha Kory. I do not.

who doth?

Pray give me leave to goe to prayer

This request was made sundry times

We do not send for you to go to prayer But tell me why you hurt these?

I am an innocent person: I never had to do with Witchcraft since I was born. I am a Gospel woman

Do not you see these complain of you

The Lord open the eyes of the Magistrates & Ministers: the Lord show his power to discover the guilty.

Tell us who hurts these children.

I do not know.

If you be guilty of this fact do you think you can hide it.

The Lord knows—

Well tell us wt you know of this matter

Why I am a Gosple-woman, & do you think I can have to do with witchcraft too

How could you tell then that the Child was bid to observe what cloths you wore when some came to speak wth you.

Cheevers. Interrupted her & bid her not begin with a lye & so Edwd Putman declared the matter

Mr Hath: Who told you that

K. He said the child said

The Documentary Evidence

Cheev:	you speak falsly
	Then Edw: Putman read again
Mr H.	Why did you ask if the child told wt cloths you wore
	My husband told me the others told
	Who told you about the cloaths? Why did you ask that question.
	Because I heard the children told wt cloaths the other wore
	Goodm: Kory did you tell her
	The old man denyed that he told her so.
	Did you not say your husband told you so
K.	—
H.	Who hurtes these children now look upon them.
K.	I cannot help it
H	Did you not say you would tell the truth why you askt yt question: how come you to the knowledge—
	I did but ask
	You dare thus to lye in all this assembly You are now before Authority, I expect the truth, you promised it, Speak now & tell#[what cloths] who told you what cloths
K	No body
H	How come you to know yt ye children would be examined what cloth yu wore
	Because I thought ye child was wiser than any body if she knew
	Give an answer you said your husband told you
	He told me the children said I afflicted them
	How do you know wt they came for, answer me this truly, will you say how you came to know what they came for
	I had heard speech that the children said I #[afflicted them] troubled them & I thought that they might come to examine
	But how did you know it
	I thought they did.
	Did not you say you would tell the truth, who told you wt they came for
	No body
	How did you know
	I did think so
	But you said you knew so
Childr:	There is a man whispering in her ear.
HQ	What did he say to you.

"the Devil hath been raised"

We must not beleive all that these distracted children say
Cannot #[he tell] you tell what that man whispered
I saw no body
But did not you hear
No, here was Extream agony of all the afflicted

41

If you expect mercy of God, you must look for it in Gods
way by confession
Do you think to find mercy by aggravating your sins—
A true thing
Look for it then in Gods way
So I do
Give glory to God & confess then
But I cannot confess
Do not you see how these afflicted do charge you
We must not beleive distracted persons
Who do you improve to hurt them
I improved none
Did not you say our eyes were blinded you would open them
Yes to accuse the innocent
Then Crossly gave in evidence
Why cannot the girl stand before you
I do not know.
What did you mean by that
I saw them fall down
It seems to be an insulting speech as if they could not stand
before you.
They cannot stand before others.
But you said they cannot stand before you
Tell me what was that turning upon the Spit by yu
You beleive the Children that are distracted I saw no spit
Here are more than two that accuse you for witchcraft What
do yu say
I am innocent
Then mr Hathorn read farther of Croslys evidence
What did you mean by that the Devil could not stand before
you
She denyed it
3. or 4. Sober witnesses confirm'd it.
What can I do many rise up against me
Why confess.

The Documentary Evidence

		So I would if I were guilty

So I would if I were guilty
Here are sober persons what do you say to them
You are a Gosple woman, will you lye:

42   **Abigail**   cryed out next Sab: is sacrament day, but she shall not come there

Kory   I do not care

You charge these children with distraction: it is a note of distraction when persons vary in a minute, but these fix upon you, this is not the manner of distraction—
When all are against me wt can I help it
Now tell me ye truth will you, why did you say that the Magistrates & Ministers eyes were blinded you would open them
She laught & denyed it.
Now tell us how we shall know

———

Who doth hurt these if you do not
Can an innocent person be guilty
Do you deny these words
Yes
Tell us who hurts these: We came to be a Terror to evil doers
You say you would open our eyes we are blind
If you say I am a Witch
You said you would show us
She denyed it.
Why do you not now show us
I cannot tell: I do not know
What did you strike the maid at Mr. Tho: Putmans with.
I never struck her in my life
Here are two that see you strike her with an iron rod.
I had no hand in it
Who had
Do you beleive these children are bewitcht
They may for ought I know I have no hand in it.
You say you are no Witch, may be you mean you never Covenanted with the Devil. Did you never deal wth any familiar
No never
What bird was that the children spoke of
Then Witnesses, spoke

"the Devil hath been raised"

What bird was it.

I know no bird.

It may be: you have engaged you will not confess. but God knows.

So he doth

Do you beleive you shall go unpunished

I have nothing to do wth withcraft

Why was you not willing your husband should come to the former Session here

But he came for all

Did not you take the Saddle off

I did not know what it was for

Did you not know wt it was for

I did not know that it would be to any benefit

Some body said that she would not have them help to find out witches.

Did you not say you would open our eyes why do you not

I never thought of a Witch

Is it a laughing matter to see these afflicted persons

She denyed it

Severall prove it

Ye are all against me & I cannot help it

Do not you beleive there are Witches in the Countrey

I do not know that there is any

Do not you know that Tituba Confessed it

I did not hear her speak

I find you will own nothing without severall witnesses & yet you will deny for all

It was noted wn she bit her lip severall of the afflicted were bitten

When she was urged upon it that she bit her lip saith she what harm is there in it:

Mr. Noyes.   I beleive it is apparent she practiseth Witchcraft in the congregation there is no need of images

What do you say to all these thing that are apparent

If you will all go hang me how can I help it.

Were you to serve the Devil ten years tell how many

She laught

The Children cryed there was a yellow bird with her

The Documentary Evidence

When Mr Hathorn askt her about it she laught
When her hands were at liberty the afflicted persons were pincht
Why do not you tell how the Devil comes in your shape & hurts these; you said you would
How can I know how
Why did you say you would show us
She laught again
What book is that you would have these children write in
What book: were should I have a book I showed them none, nor have none nor brought none.
The afflicted cryed out there was a man whispering in her ears
What book did you carry to Mary Walcott
I carryed none; if the Devil appears in my shape
Then Needham said that Parker some time agoe thought this woman was a Witch
Who is your God
The God that made me
Who is that God
The God that made me
What is his name
Jehovah
Do you know any other name
God Almighty
Doth he tell you that you pray to that he is God Almighty
Who do I worship but ye God yt made
How many Gods are there
One
How many persons
Theree
Cannot you say so there is one God in three blessed persons
[illegible]
Do not you see these children & women are rational & sober as their neighbours when your hands are fastened
Immediately they were seized with fitts & the standers by said she was squeezing her fingers her hands being eased by them that held them on purpose for triall
Quickly after the Marshall said she hath bit her lip & immediately the afflicted were in an uproar
[torn] you hurt these, or who doth

"the Devil hath been raised"

She denyeth any hand in it
Why did you say if you were a Witch you should have no pardon.
Because I am a [   ] Woman

Salem Village March the 21t. 1691/2

The Revert mr Samll parris being desired to take in wrighting the Examination of Martha Cory, hath returned it as aforesd Upon hearing the aforesd and seing what wee did then see, togather with ye charges of the persons then present Wee Committed Martha Cory the wife of Giles Cory of Salem farmes, unto the Goale in Salem as p mittimus then Given out ---

*John Hathorne   } Assists
*Jonathan Corwin

[Reverse]
Martha Kory Exam

(Essex Institute, Salem, Mass., Salem Witchcraft Papers, #1)

Expenses at Ingersoll's Ordinary

Upon Examination of Goodwife Corry
To ye Marshall for Horses & Drink . . . .   ”   ”   6
To ye Majestrates Horses; Drink
and Entertainment . . . .   ”   4   ”

[Document continues]

(Essex County Court Archives, Salem Witchcraft Papers, II,131)

Edward Putnam, Ezekiel Cheever & Thomas Putnam Vs. Martha Cory

This is the final portion of a deposition (see March 12) sworn to in court on September 8, 1692, concerning observations of the three men. This section deals with the afflictions caused by Cory at her March 21 examination.

we doe furder testifie that upon her examination shee accordeng to what was said of her that shee would open thee eyes of the magistrates and ministers. so shee did for shee made a most clear discovery witchcraft for by biting her lip it was observed that the afflicted #[children] persons were bit when that was discovered then we observed that shee would #[pinch] pinch them by

The Documentary Evidence

niping her foyers togeather and when that was discovered and her hands held then shee afflict them by working with her foot and when that was discovered then shee pressed upon the seate with her breast and mistress Pope was greatly afflicted by great pressure upon her stomack

Jurat in Curia Sept. 8. 92

[Reverse]

Mr Ezekell Cheevers : affimd : to ye Jury of inquest : that he saw Martha wife of Giles Cory examined before ye majestrates: at which time he observed that ye sd Cory some times did bite her lip : and when she bit her lip : mercy Lewis and Elizath Hubbard and others of ye afflicted persons : were bitten also when sd Cory : pinched her fingers to gether : then mercy lewis & elizabeth Hubbard and others were pinched : and #[when] according to : ye motions of sd martha Coryes body; so was ye afflicted persons : afflicted : this he affirmd to be true according to ye best of his observation : Mr. Edward Putnam affirmed ye same : to the Jury of inquest that : Mr. Cheevers doth. Mr. Thomas Putnam affirmed the same : all upon oathe all of them

[In margin]
Edwd. Putnam & Eliza Cheevir Deposition

(Essex County Court Archives, Salem Witchcraft Papers, I,39)

Samuel Parris, Nathaniel Ingersoll & Thomas Putnam Vs. Martha Cory

The Deposition of Sam: Parris aged about. 39. years, & Nathanael Ingersol aged about fifty & eight yeares & Thomas Putman aged about fourty yeares all of Salem--testifyeth & saith that severall of the bewitched persons were much afflicted at the examination of Martha Kory, wife to Giles Kory of Salem, #[& particu] before the honoured Magistrates.21.March.1691/2 & particularly that #[when] before her hands were held severall of them were bitten: & that some of the afflicted said there was a black man whispering in her ear, namely Mary Walcot and Abigail Williams both of which also were bit & pincht by her as they said

(Essex County Court Archives, Salem Witchcraft Papers, I,42)

Mercy Lewis & Elizabeth Hubbard Vs. Martha Cory

The following depositions by two of the afflicted girls relate to the various torments suffered by them in March including the time of the examination of Martha Cory on

"the Devil hath been raised"

the twenty-first. In a separate deposition attested to by Abigail Williams in May 1692 she also deposed "... that diverse times in the monthe of March last past particularly 14.20.21.& 23 dayes of the month ... she the said Abigail was much disquieted by the apparition of Martha Kory. ... "

The Deposistion of Mircy lewes agged about 19 years who testifieth and saith that I veryly beleve I was bewiched by gooddy Cory on the : 14 th of March 1691/92 for she then came to the house of Thomas putnam to se ann putnam whom I was atending and I was Immediatly taken whill gooddy Cory was their: and Ann putnam said shee se gooddy Cory bewich me: but I could not se parfitly who they ware that hurt me tell the 26 th of march and sence that I have often seen the Aperishtion of goody Cory com and afflect me by biting pinching and almost choaking me urging me vehemently to writ in hir book allso I was most dreadfully tortored whill martha Cory was in Examination being the 21 march and Mary Walcott and Elizabeth Hubburd said they saw the Apperishtion of Martha Cory tortor me: and I beleve in my heart that martha Cory is a most dreadfull wicth and yt she hath very often affleted me a severall others by hir acts of wicthcraft.

[Reverse]
Mercy Lewis against Martha Cory

(Massachusetts Historical Society, Salem Witchcraft Papers)

The Deposistion of Elizabeth Hubburd agged about 17 years who testifieth and saith that about the 15 th march 1691/2 I saw the Apperishtion of Martha Cory who did Immediatly hurt me and urged me to writ in hir book and so she continewed hurting of me by times tell the 21 march being the day of hir Examination: and then in the time of hir Examination she did torment me most dreadfully by biting pinching and almost choaking me the marks of which I shewed to severall and at the same time also I saw the Apperishtion of Martha Cory greviously afflect mircy lewes: and also severall times sence the Apperishtion of martha Cory has most greviously afflected me and urged me vehemently to writ in hir book. also on the day of hir Examination I saw martha Cory or hir Apperance most greviously tormet mary wolcott mercy lewes Abigail william and ann putnam and I beleve in my heart that martha Cory is a dreadfull wicth and that she hath very often affleted and tormented me and the afformentioned parsons by acts of wicthcraft

Jurat in Curia

(Document continued on next page)

The Documentary Evidence

Eliz: Hubbard: declared ye above written Evidence to be ye truth: before ye Jury of inquest upon oath: Augst 4:1692

[Reverse]
Eliz Hubbard against Martha Cory

(Massachusetts Historical Society, Salem Witchcraft Papers)

MONDAY - WEDNESDAY, MARCH 21-23, 1692

Ann Putnam, Sr. Vs. Rebecca Nurse

This continuation of a deposition by Ann Putnam, Sr., relates to the torments suffered by her during the several days prior to Rebecca Nurse's witchcraft examination. The deposition was sworn to before magistrates John Hathorne and Jonathan Corwin on May 31, 1692.

21:th march being the day of the Examinati of martha Cory: I had not many fitts tho I was very weak my strenth being as I thought almost gon: but on the:22 march 1691/92 the Apperishtion of Rebekah nurs did againe sett upon in a most dreadfull maner very early in the morning as soon as it was well light and now she appeared to me only in hir shift #[and night cap] and brought a litle Red book in hir hand urging me vehemently to writ in hir book and because I would not yeald to hir hellish temtations she threatened to tare my soule out of my body: blasphemously denying the blessed God and the power of the Lord Jesus Christ to save my soule and denying severall places of scripture which I tould hir of: to Repell hir hellish temtations and for near Two hours together at this time the Apperishtions of Rebekah Nurs did temp and tortor me before she left me as if indeed she would have kiled me: and allso the grates part of this day with but very little respitt: 23 march: I am againe affleted by the Apperishtions of Rebekah nurs: and martha Cory: but Cheafly by Rebekah nurs:

[Document continues]

(Essex Institute, Salem, Mass., Salem Witchcraft Papers, #22)

Israel Porter, Elizabeth Porter, Daniel Andrew & Peter Cloyce For Rebecca Nurse

This undated statement concerns a visit made to the Francis and Rebecca Nurse home sometime prior to March 23. The four visitors included Rebecca's sister Sarah's husband,

"the Devil hath been raised"

Peter Cloyce, as well as three prominent village inhabitants. They wanted to warn Rebecca that her name was being mentioned by some of the afflicted persons. Her reaction and sincerity were poignant.

We whos nams Are under writen being desiered to goe to goodman nurs his   49
hous to speeke with his wife and to tell her that several of the Aflicted persons mentioned her: and Acordingly we went and we found her in A weak
and Lowe condition in body as shee told us and had been sicke allmost A
weak and we asked how it was otherwis with her and shee said shee blest
god for it shee had more of his presents in this sickens then sometime shee
have had but not soe much as shee desiered: but shee would with the Apostle pres forward to the mark: and many other places of scriptur to the Like
purpos: and then of her owne Acord shee begane to speek of the Affliction
that was Amongst them and in perticuler of Mr Parris his family and howe
shee was greved for them though shee had not been to see them: by Reason
of fits that shee formerly use to have for people said it was Awfull to:behold:
but shee pittied them with: all her harte: and went to god for them: but shee
said shee heard that there was persons spoke of that wear as Innocent as shee
was shee belived and After much to this purpos: we told her we heard that
shee was spoken of allsoe: well she said if it be soe ye will of the Lord be done:
she sate still Awhille being as it wear Amazed: and then shee said well as to
this thing I am as Innocent as the child unborne but seurly shee said what
sine hath god found out in me unrepented of that he should Lay such an
Affliction upon me In my old Age: and Acording to our best observation
we could not decern that shee knewe what we came for before we tould her

Israel porter   To the substance
Elizabeth porter   of what is Above we if caled
                                                 there too: are Ready to testifie
                                                 on: oath
                                                    Daniell Andrew
                                                    Peter Cloys

(Essex Institute, Salem, Mass., Salem Witchcraft Papers, #16)

WEDNESDAY, MARCH 23, 1692

Rev. Lawson Visits the Thomas Putnam House

On Wednesday the 23 of March, I went to Thomas Putmans, on purpose
to see his Wife: I found her lying on the Bed, having had a sore fit a little
before, she spake to me, and said, she was glad to see me; her Husband and

she, both desired me to pray with her, while she was sensible; which I did, though the Apparition said, I should not go to Prayer. At the first beginning she attended; but after a little time, was taken with a fit: yet continued silent, and seemed to be Asleep: when Prayer was done, her Husband going to her, found her in a Fit; he took her off the Bed, to set her on his Knees; but at first she was so stiff, she could not be bended; but she afterwards set down; but quickly began to strive violently with her Arms and Leggs; she then began to Complain of, and as it were to Converse personally with, Goodw. N.[urse], saying, "Goodw. N. Be gone! Be gone! Be gone! are you not ashamed, a Woman of your Profession, to afflict a poor Creature so? what hurt did I ever do you in my life! you have but two years to live, and then the Devil will torment your Soul, for this your Name is blotted out of Gods Book, and it shall never be put in Gods Book again, be gone for shame, are you not afraid of that which is coming upon you? I Know, I know, what will make you afraid; the wrath of an Angry God, I am sure that will make you afraid; be gone, do not tourment me, I know what you would have (we judged she meant, her Soul) but it is out of your reach; it is Clothed with the white Robes of Christs Righteousness." After this, she seemed to dispute with the Apparition about a particular Text of Scripture. The Apparition seemed to deny it; (the Womans eyes being fast closed all this time) she said, She was sure there was such a Text; and she would tell it; and then the Shape would be gone, for said she, "I am sure you cannot stand before that Text!" then she was sorely Afflicted; her mouth drawn on one side, and her body strained for about a minute, and then said, "I will tell, I will tell; it is, it is, it is!" three or four times, and then was afflicted to hinder her from telling, at last she broke forth and said, "It is the third Chapter of the Revelations." I did something scruple the reading it, and did let my scruple appear, lest Satan should make any, Superstitious lie to improve the Word of the Eternal God. However, tho' not versed in these things, I judged I might do it this once for an Experiment. I began to read, and before I had near read through the first verse, she opened her eyes, and was well; this fit continued near half an hour. Her Husband and the Spectators told me, she had often been so relieved by reading Texts that she named, something pertinent to her Case; as Isa. 40. 1. Isa. 49.1. Isa. 50.1 and several others.

(Deodat Lawson, A Brief and True Narrative
[Boston, 1692] p. 5-6)

"the Devil hath been raised"

Warrant for the Apprehension of Rebecca Nurse

To the Marshall of Essex or his deputie

There Being Complaint this day made (before us by Edward putnam and 51
Jonathan putnam Yeoman both of Salem Village, Against Rebeca Nurce the
wife of francs Nurce of Salem Village for vehement Suspition, of haveing
Committed Sundry acts of Witchcraft and thereby haveing donne Much hurt
and Injury to the Bodys of Ann putnam the wife of Thomas putnam of Salem
Village Anna puttnam ye daufter of Said Thomas putnam and Abigail Williams &c

You are therefore in theire Majesties names hereby required to apprehend
and bring before us Rebeca Nurce the wife of francs Nurce of Salem Village, to Morrow aboute Eight of ye Clock in the forenoon at the house of
Lt Nathaniell Ingersoll in Salem Village, in order to her Examination Relateing
to the abovesd premises and hereof you are not to faile Salem March the 23d
1691/2

p us *John. Hathorne
Assists
*Jonathan Corwin

(Essex County Court Archives, Salem Witchcraft Papers, I, 70)

Warrant for the Apprehension of Dorcas Good

*William and Sarah Good's young daughter Dorcas, not above five years of age, had
also been cried out upon by some of the afflicted persons as having tormented them.*

To the Marshall of Essex or his Dept

You are in theire Majests names hereby required to bring before us Dorcas
Good the Daugter of Wm Good of Salem Village tomorrow morneing upon
suspition of acts of Witchcraft by her committed according to Complaints
made against her by Edwd putnam & Jonat putnam of Salem Village and
hereof faile not   Dated Salem.March 23d 1691/2

P us *John Hathorne
Assists.
*Jonathan. Corwin

March 23th:1691/2

(Document continued on next page)

The Documentary Evidence

I doe apoint mr Samll Brabrook to bee my lawffull Deputy, to serve this sumons and to make A true Returne   pr *George Herrick Marshall of Essex.

(Essex County Court Archives, Salem Witchcraft Papers, I, 61)

THURSDAY, MARCH 24, 1692

Marshall Herrick's Return of Rebecca Nurse's Apprehension

March 24th. 1691/2   I have apprehended ye body of Rebeca Nurse and brought her to ye house of Lut Nath: Ingersal where shee is in Custody pr *George Herrick   Marshall   Essex

[Reverse]

in ye Meeting house be Mary Walcott Marcy Lewis Eliz. Hubert all these accused goody Nurse then to her face yt she then hurt them &c and they saw besides ye others on Contra Side

(Essex County Court Archives, Salem Witchcraft Papers, I, 70)

Deputy Brabrook's Return of Dorcas Good's Apprehension

March 24th 1691/2   I have taken ye body of Dorcas Good and brought her to ye house of leut Nath: Ingersol and is in Custody there
                                *Sammuall brabrook Marshals Deputy

(Essex County Court Archives, Salem Witchcraft Papers, I, 61 reverse)

Rev. Lawson's Narrative of the Examinations of Rebecca Nurse & Dorcas Good

On Thursday the Twenty fourth of march, (being in course the Lecture Day, at the Village,) Goodwife N.[urse] was brought before the Magistrates Mr. Hathorne and Mr. Corwin, about Ten of Clock, in the Fore Noon, to be Examined in the Meeting House, the Reverend Mr. Hale, begun with Prayer, and the Warrant being read, she was required to give answer, Why she aflicted those persons? she pleaded her owne innocency with earnestness. Thomas Putman's Wife, Abigail Williams and Thomas Putmans daughter accused her that she appeared to them, and afflicted them in their fitts: but some of the other said, that they had seen her, but knew not that ever she

"the Devil hath been raised"

A BRIEF and TRUE

NARRATIVE

Of some Remarkable Passages Relating to sundry Persons
Afflicted by

VVitchcraft,

AT

SALEM VILLAGE

Which happened from the Nineteenth of *March,* to the
Fifth of *April,* 1692.

Collected by *Deodat Lawson.*

Boston, *Printed for* Benjamin Harris *and are to be Sold at his
Ship, over-against the* Old-Meeting-House. 1692.

*This title page is to the short pamphlet authored by former Salem Village minister Deodat
Lawson. The pamphlet concerned Lawson's observations of the early witchcraft outbreak in the
village.* Courtesy, Danvers Archival Center.

The Documentary Evidence

had hurt them; amongst which was Mary Walcut, who was presently after she had so declared bitten, and cryed out of her in the meeting-house; producing the Marks of teeth on her wrist. It was so disposed, that I had not leisure to attend the whole time of Examination, but both Magistrates and Ministers, told me, that the things alledged, by the afflicted, and defences made by her, were much after the same manner, as the former was. And her motions, did produce like effects as to, Biteing, Pinching, Bruising, Tormenting, at their Breasts, by her Leaning, and when, bended Back, were as if their Backs was broken. The afflicted persons said, the Black Man, whispered to her in the Assembly, and therefore she could not hear what the Magistrates said unto her. They said also that she did then ride by the Meeting-house, behind the Black Man. Thomas Putman's wife had a grievous Fit, in the time of Examination, to the very great Impairing of her strength, and wasting of her spirits, insomuch as she could hardly move hand, or foot, when she was carryed out. Others also were there grievously afflicted, so that there was once such an hideous scriech and noise, (which I heard as I walked, at a little distance from the Meeting house,) as did amaze me, and some that were within, told me the whole assembly was struck with consternation, and they were afraid, that those that sate next to them, were under the influence of Witchcraft. This woman also was that day committed to Salem Prison. The Magistrates and Ministers also did informe me, that they apprehended a child of Sarah G.[ood] and Examined it, being between 4 and 5 years of Age And as to matter of Fact, they did Unanimously affirm, that when this Child, did but cast its eye upon the afflicted persons, they were tormented, and they held her Head, and yet so many as her eye could fix upon were afflicted. Which they did several times make careful observation of: the afflicted complained, they had often been Bitten by this child, and produced the marks of a small set of teeth, accordingly, this was also committed to Salem Prison, the child looked hail, and well as well as other Children. I saw it at Lieut. Ingersols. After the commitment of Goodw. N. Tho: Putmans wife was much better, and had no violent fits at all from that 24th of March, to the 5th of April. Some others also said they had not seen her so frequently appear to them, to hurt them.

(Deodat Lawson, A Brief and True Narrative
[Boston, 1692] p. 6-7)

"the Devil hath been raised"

Examination of Rebecca Nurse

The examination of Rebekah Nurse at Salem Village
24.Mar. <u>1691/2</u>

Mr. Harthorn. What do you say (speaking to one afflicted) have you seen this Woman hurt you?
Yes, she beat me this morning
Abigial. Have you been hurt by this Woman?
Yes
Ann Putman in a grievous fit cryed out that she hurt her.
Goody Nurse, here are two An: Putman the child & Abigail Williams complains of your hurting them What do you say to it

N.   I can say before my Eternal father I am innocent, & God will clear my innocency
Here is never a one in the Assembly but desires it, but if you be guilty Pray God discover you.
Then Hen: Kenny rose up to speak
Goodm: Kenny what do you say
Then he entered his complaint & farther said that since this Nurse came into the house he was seizd twise with an amazd condition
Here are not only these but, here is ye wife of Mr. Tho. Putman who accuseth you by credible information & that both of tempting her to iniquity, & of greatly hurting her.

N.   I am innocent & clear & have not been able to get out of doors these 8. or 9. dayes.
Mr. Putman: give in what you have to say
Then Mr. Edward Putman gave in his relate
Is this true Goody Nurse
I never afflicted no child never in my life
You see these accuse you, is it true
No.
Are you an innocent person relating to this Witchcraft.
Here Tho: Putmans wife cryed out, Did you not bring the Black man with you, did you not bid me tempt God & dye—
How oft have you eat and drunk yr own damaon—
What do you say to them
Oh Lord help me, & spread out her hands, & the afflicted were greviously vexed

The Documentary Evidence

Do you not see what a solemn condition these are in? when your hands are loose the persons are afflicted.

Then Mary Walcot (who often heretofore said she had seen her, but never could say or did say that she either bit or pincht her, or hurt her) & also Eliz: Hubbard under the like circumstances both openly accused her of hurting them.

Here are these 2 grown persons now accuse you, wt say you?
Do not you see these afflicted persons, & hear them accuse you.
The Lord knows I have not hurt them: I am an innocent person
It is very awfull to all to see these agonies & you an old Professor thus charged with contracting with the Devil by the effects of it & yet to see you stand with dry eyes when there are so many whet –
You do not know my heart
You would do well if you are guilty to confess & give Glory to God
I am as clear as the child unborn
What uncertainty there may be in apparitions I know not, yet this with me strikes hard upon you that you are at this very present charged with familiar spirits: this is your bodily person they speak to: they say now they see these familiar spirits com to your bodily person, now what do you say to that
I have none Sir:
If you have confess & give glory to God I pray God clear you if you be innocent, & if you are guilty discover you And therefore give me an upright answer: have you any familiarity with these spirits?
No, I have none but with God alone.
How came you sick for there is an odd discourse of that in the mouths of many –
I am sick at my stumach –
Have you no wounds
I have none but old age
You do know whither you are guilty, & have familiarity with the Devil, & now when you are here present to see such a thing as these testify a black man whispering in your ear, & birds about you what do you say to it

"the Devil hath been raised"

It is all false I am clear

Possibly you may apprehend you are no witch, but have you not been led aside by temptations that way

I have not

What a sad thing it is that a church member here & now an other of Salem, should be thus accused and charged

Mrs Pope fell into a grievous fit, & cryed out a sad thing sure enough: And then many more fell into lamentable fits.

Tell us have not you had visible appearances more than what is common in nature?

I have none nor never had in my life

Do you think these suffer voluntary or involuntary

I cannot tell

That is strange every one can judge

I must be silent

They accuse you of hurting them, & if you think it is not unwillingly but by designe, you must look upon them as murderers

I cannot tell what to think of it

Afterwards when this was som what insisted on she said I do not think so: she did not understand aright what was said

Well then give an answer now, do you think these suffer against their wills or not

I do not think these suffer against their wills

Why did you never visit these afflicted persons

Because I was afraid I should have fits too

Note Upon the motion of her body fitts followed upon the com-plainants abundantly & very frequently

Is it not an unaccountable case that when #[they] you are examined these persons are afflicted?

I have got no body to look to but God

Again upon stirring her hands the afflicted persons were seized with violent fits of torture

Do you believe these afflicted persons are bewitcht

I do think they are

When this Witchcraft came upon the stage there was no sus-picion of Tituba (Mr. Parris's Indian woman) she profest much love to that child Betty Parris but it was her appari-tion did the mischief, & why should not you also be guilty, for your apparition doth hurt also.

The Documentary Evidence

57

Would you have me bely my self --
she held her Neck on one side, & accordingly so were the
afflicted taken
Then Authority requiring it Sam: Parris read what he had in
characters taken from Mr. Tho: Putmans wife in her fitts
What do you think of this
I cannot help it, the Devil may appear in my shape.

This a true account of the sume of her examination but by reason of geat
noyses by the afflicted & many speakers, many things are pretermitted

Memorandum

Nurse held her neck on one sid & Eliz: Hubbard (one of the sufferers) had
her neck set in that posture whereupon another Patient Abigail Williams cryed
out set up Goody Nurses head the maid's neck will be broke & when some
set up Nurses head Aaron Wey observed that Betty Hubbards was immediately righted.

Salem Village March 24.th 1691/2

The Revert Mr Samuell Parris being desired to take in wrighting ye Examination of Rebekah Nurse hath Returned itt as aforesaid

Upon heareing the aforesd and seeing what wee then did see together with
ye Charges of the persons then present—wee Committed Rebekah Nurse
ye wife of frans Nurce of Salem Village unto theire Majests Goale in Salem
as p a Mittimus then given out, in order to farther Examination

*John Hathorne

Assists

*Jonathan. Corwin

(Essex County Court Archives, Salem Witchcraft Papers, I, 72)

Expenses at Ingersoll's Ordinary

Upon Examination of goodwife Nurse
To ye Marshalls Horse Standing, Supper
Lodging one night and drink for his
attendance   . . . .   "   3   6
To Constable Herrick p Drink & Cake . . . .   "   "   6

"the Devil hath been raised"

To ye Majestrates Drink & Entertainemts
and horses wth ye Majestrats Horses . . . .   ”   5   ”

(Essex County Court Archives, Salem Witchcraft Papers, II,131)

Ann Putnam, Sr. Vs. Rebecca Nurse

The final portion of an Ann Putnam, Sr., deposition relating to her suffering during the examination of Rebecca Nurse. On May 31, 1692, this deposition was sworn to by Putnam.

24: march being the days of the examination of Rebekah Nurs: I was severall times afflected in the morning by the Apperishtion of Rebekah Nurs: but most dreadfully tortored by hir in the time of hir examination: in so much that The Honoured Majestraits gave my Husband leave to cary me out of the meeting house: and as soon as I was caryed out of the meeting house dores it pleased Allmighty God for his free grace and mircy sake to deliver me out of the paws of thos Roaring lions: and jaws of those tareing bears that ever sence that time they have not had power so to afflect me

[Reverse of document contains statements relating to incidents in May and June, 1692. They are not included here.]

(Essex Institute, Salem, Mass., Salem Witchcraft Papers, #22)

Samuel Parris, Nathaniel Ingersoll
& Thomas Putnam Vs. Rebecca Nurse

The Deposition of Sam: Parris aged about .39. years & Nathanael Ingersoll aged about fifty & eight yeares & Thomas Putman aged about fourty yeares all of Salem – – – – testifyeth & saith that Ann Putman Senr & her daughter Ann, & Mary Walcot & Abigail Williams were severall times & greviously tortured at the Examination of Rebekah Nurse wife to Francis Nurse of Salem before the Honoured Magistrates the. 24.March. 1691/2 & particularly that when her hands were at liberty some of the afflicted were pinched, & upon the motion of her head & fingers some of them were tortured; & farther that some of the afflicted then & there affirmed that they saw a black man whispering in her ear, & that they saw birds fluttering about her,

Jurat in Curia

(Document continued on next page)

The Documentary Evidence

[Reverse]

The Depotion of Sam: Parris &c agst Rebek: Nurse

60   *(Essex County Court Archives, Salem Witchcraft Papers, I, 79)*

Thomas Putnam & Edward Putnam Vs. Rebecca Nurse

The Deposition of Tho: Putman aged about 40. years & Edward Putman aged about. 38. years – – – – –

witnesseth & saith that having been several times present with Ann Putman junr in & after her fits & saw her much afflicted, being bitten, pinched, her limbs distorted, & pins thrust into her flesh, which she charged on Rebekah Nurse that she was the Acter thereof & that she saw her do it

The deponents farther testify that on the #[day of] 24.March—last past at the publick examination of said Nurse we saw the said Ann Putman Abigail Williams and Eliz. Hubbard often struck down upon the glance of the said Nurse eye—upon said Williams Putman & Hubbard several times & the said Putman Williams & Hubbard was then afflicted according to the various motions of said Nurse her body in time of examination as when said Nurse did clinch her hands, bite her lips, or hold her head aside the said Putman Hubbard & Williams was set in the same posture to her great torture & affliction.

                           ★Thomas putnam
                           ★Edward Putnam

                           Jurat in Curia

[Reverse]
Thomas Putman Edward Putman

(Essex County Court Archives, Salem Witchcraft Papers, I, 86)

Mary Walcott Vs. Rebecca Nurse

Mary Walcott gave oath to this deposition on June 3, 1692. It includes post-March information in the original deposition not duplicated here.

The Deposistion of Mary walcott aged about 17 years who testifieth and saith that on the 20 th march 1691/92 I saw the Apperishtion of Rebekah Nurs the wife of frances Nurs senr: but she did not hurt me tell the 24 march being

"the Devil hath been raised"

the day of hir examination but then the Apperishtion of Rebekah Nurs did most greviously torment me dureing the time of hir Examination: and also severall times sence she hath most greviously afflected me by biting pinching and almost choaking me urging me vehemently to writ in hir book or elce she would kill me:

[Document continues]

[Reverse]
Mary Walcott

(Essex County Court Archives, Salem Witchcraft Papers, I, 80)

Ann Putnam, Jr. Vs. Rebecca Nurse

As with the previous Walcott deposition, this one by Ann Putnam, Jr., was sworn to on June 3, 1692. The body of the deposition is written in one hand while the information at the conclusion relating to the oath is in another. This evidence was submitted in June during the Grand Jury inquest.

The Deposistion of Ann putnam junr who testifieth and saith that on the 13 th march 1691/92 I saw the Apperishtion of gooddy Nurs: and she did immediatly afflect me but I did not know what hir name was then: tho I knew whare she used to sitt in our Meeting house: but sence that she hath greviously afflected me by biting pinching and pricking me: urging me to writ in hir book and also on the 24 th of march being the day of hir examination I was greviously tortored by hir dureing the time of hir examination and also severall times sence and also dureing the time of hir examination I saw the Apperishtion of Rebekah nurs goe and hurt the bodys of Misry lewes mary wolcott Elizabeth Hubbrd and Abigaill Williams.

ann putnam junr: did one the oath which she hath taken this har evidens to be the truth. before us the : Juriers for Inquest this 3. dy of June: 1692

Jurat in Curia

[Reverse]
Ann puttnam
Goody Nurs

(Essex County Court Archives, Salem Witchcraft Papers, I, 81)

The Documentary Evidence

Elizabeth Hubbard Vs. Rebecca Nurse

The Deposistion of Elizabeteh Hubburd agged about 17 years who testifieth and saith that about the 20 th march 1692 I saw the Apperishtion of Rebekah Nurs the wife of frances Nurs senr senr tho she did not hurt me tell the 24 th march being the day of hir examination and then she did hurt me most geviously dureing the time of hir examination for if she did but look upon me she would strick me down or allmost choak me and also severall times sence the Apperishtion of Rebekah Nurs has most greviously afflected me by pinching pricking and almost choaking me urging me to writ in hir book and also on the day of hir examination I saw the Apperishtion of Rebeckah Nurs goe and hurt the bodys of Ann putnam senr and Mary Walcott and Abigail williams and Ann putnam Junr.

elizabeth hubard upon har oath she had taken did owne this testimony before us the Jariars of Inquest: this 3dy of June: 1692

[Reverse]
Eliz: Hubbard against Rebekah Nurs

(Essex County Court Archives, Salem Witchcraft Papers, I, 78)

Mary Walcott Vs. Dorcas Good

The deposition of mary walcott agged about 17 years who testifieth that about the 21: march 1691/92 I saw the Apperishtion of Dorothy good. sarah goods daughter com to me and bit me and pinch me and so she contineued afflecting me by times tell 24 march being the day of hir examination and then she did torment and afflect me most greviously dureing the time of hir examination and also severall times sence the Apperishtion of Dorothy good has afflected me by biting pinching and almost choaking me urging me to writ in hir book

[Reverse]

Mary Walcott agst
Dorothy. Good

(Essex County Court Archives, Salem Witchcraft Papers, I, 64)

Ann Putnam, Jr. Vs. Dorcas Good

The Deposistion of Ann putnam who testifieth and saith that on the 3th March 1691/92 I saw the Apperishtion of Dorythy good Sarah goods daugh-

"the Devil hath been raised"

ter who did Immediatly almost choak me and tortored me most greviously: and so she hath severall times sence tortored me by biting and pinching and almost choaking me tempting me also to writ in hir book and also on the day of hir examination being the 24 March 1691/92 the Apperishtion of Dorithy good did most greviously tortor me dureing the time of hir Examination and several times sence

[Reverse]

Ann. Putnam
Dorothy. Good

(Essex County Court Archives, Salem Witchcraft Papers, I, 63)

Giles Cory Evidence

This strange document, apparently in the handwriting of Salem minister Nicholas Noyes, recounts happenings which Giles Cory evidently believed to be obstructions put upon his activities and possible bewitchments to his animals. Cory was an 81-year-old farmer of a litigious and controversial background. He had married his third wife, Martha, in the mid 1680s. From allusions to his speaking at his wife's witchcraft examination and from this document, Giles was apparently not sure of Martha's beliefs or intentions. Still, this document does not accuse Martha of anything specific, and may not have been introduced as legal evidence during later proceedings.

Giles himself would be complained against on April 18 for afflicting several persons and would be arrested and examined. In September, after possibly protesting against the special witchcraft court by standing mute to their authority to try him, Cory was tortured to force his acquiescence to stand trial. Instead he would die under the torture of heavy weights. His wife would be executed on September 22, 1692.

The evidence of Giles Choree testifieth & saith yt Last satturday in the Evening. sitting by the fire my wife asked me to go to bed. I told I would go to prayr. & wn I went to prayer I could nott utter my desires wth any sense, not open my mouth to speake

2 My wife did perceive itt & came towards. me & said she was coming to me. After this in alittle space I did according to my measure attend the duty

---

Sometime last weake I fetcht an ox well out the woods. about noone, & he laying down in the yard I went to raise him to yoake him butt he could not rise butt dragd his hinder parts as if he had been hiptshott. butt after did rise.

63

I had a Catt sometimes last weeke strangly taken on the suddain. & did make me think she would have died presently. #[butt] my wife bid me knock her in the head. butt I did not. & since she is well.

Another time going to duties I was interrupted for aspace. butt afterward I was helpt according to my poore measure

My wife hath ben wont to sitt up after I went to bed, & I have perceived her to kneel down to the harth. as if she were at prayr, but heard nothing

#[At the Examination of Sarah] Good & others my wife was willing

March: 24th: 1691/2

(Essex County Court Archives, Salem Witchcraft Papers, I, 43)

Rev. Lawson's Sermon

Perhaps the most important function performed by a Puritan minister in his official duties was the preparation and delivery of sermons to his flock. Through the sermon, the main event in the congregational meeting service, the people were fed "spiritual milk." Such sermons would interpret the Bible, explain the meaning of the natural as well as the supernatural world, and serve as a guide for everyday living. The oral presentation of sermons also afforded the listeners intellectual stimulus. In agrarian towns and villages and in a late 17th century society where many inhabitants could not read or write, the weekly or twice weekly sermon and lecture days were typically looked upon as a welcome change to mundane existence. Though a sermon might last several hours, not a few of the listeners looked forward to inspirational words and spiritual renewal.

The Puritan meeting house itself was devoid of any outwardly religious symbols. The high pulpit with sounding board above was the focal point of the building. On a tasseled cushion on the pulpit desk rested the Holy Bible. Typically the congregation would be seated with women on one side of the building and men on the other, according to age and social status.

To the modern reader, printed sermons may appear tedious, yet their power rested upon oral delivery. The form of many Puritan sermons was built upon by a spiraling, repetitive logic which brought the listener from the minister's stated doctrine slowly through his various proposition examples until the application of the doctrine in the lives of the listeners would painstakingly be brought home to the congregation. Bible verses and anal-

"the Devil hath been raised"

ogies using things familiar to the congregation were heavily salted into the lecture.

Rev. Lawson's March 24, 1692, sermon to his former congregation and village which, " . . . God hath pleased to permit a sore and grievous affliction to befall. . . . " was presented, " . . . To give you the best assistance I could, to help you out in your distress." The thrust of Lawson's sermon was an attempt to understand and bring reason as to why the community was being so ferociously attacked by the "roaring Lyon Satan." Using numerous scriptural passages and examples, he displayed Satan's many powers of seduction and malignity and how God in testing the faith of His people had allowed Satan's chain more length.

The most specific portion of the sermon dealing with the village troubles lay in his application beginning with "Use I." To the vexing question of whether the shapes of innocent persons could be used by Satan to harm the afflicted ones, Lawson provided an ambiguous viewpoint. He knew that these afflictions were the " . . . effects of Diabolical malice and operations. . . . " and exhorted the authorities to pursue the instigators of these afflictions. He found no simple means of defense against witchcraft, nor an easy means of discovering witches. He also rejected the use of various popular white witchcraft methods to prevent attack. To Lawson the only true shield against Satan's malignity was faith in Christ and the exhortation to "PRAY, PRAY, PRAY."

Yet Lawson also gave his listeners a very mixed message. "I am this day Commanded to Call and Cry an Alarm unto you, ARM; ARM; ARM; handle your Arms. . . . " "Let us admit no parley, give no quarter. . . . " This and similar passages urged a vigorous discovery and prosecution of witches by the Church and secular authorities. In "Use III" he spoke to any in the congregation who had come in league with the Devil telling them of their eventual defeat.

His sermon, here printed in its entirety, was first published by Benjamin Harris of Boston in 1693. Though it is probably close in length and content to his oral presentation of 1692, undoubtedly some expansion and much editing were made in the printed version. To further explain his frame of reference, Lawson also included in his printed introductory remarks of 1693 an address to his original listeners and to his present readers. In this reprint, the original 1693 printed pagination is identified by numbers in brackets.

[t.p.] CHRIST'S FIDELITY
The only
Shield
Against
SATANS MALIGNITY.
ASSERTED in a
SERMON

Delivered at SALEM-VILLAGE, the 24th of March, 1692. Being Lecture-

The Documentary Evidence

day there, and a time of Public Examination, of some Suspected for WITCHCRAFT.

By Deodat Lawson, formerly Preacher of the Gospel there

Rev. 12. 12. We to the Inhabitants of the Earth, and of the Sea, for the Devil is come down unto you, having Great Wrath, because he knoweth that he hath but a short time.

Rom. 16. 20. And the God of Peace shall Bruise Satan under, your Feet shortly, &c.

Boston Printed, by B. Harris, & Sold by Nicholas Buttolph, next to Guttridg's Coffee-House.   1693.

[i] Licensed according to Order.

[ii] To the Worshipful
AND
Worthily Honoured

Bartholomew Gidney
John Hathorne
Jonathan Corwin Esqrs.
Together with the REVEREND
Mr. John Higginson Pastor,
AND
Mr. Nicholas Noyes Teacher
Of the Church of Christ at SALEM.

This discourse, concerning CHRISTS Prevailing intercession, against SATANS Malicious Operations: Being Delivered in a Congregation of that Vicinity, where most of them were present, as a Token of his Sincere Respect and Observance, is humbly Offered and Dedicated by

Deodat Lawson

[iii] Having Perused this Discourse, Entituled, *Christs Fidelity the only Shield, against Satans Malignity*. We are willing, to shew so much Respect, to the

"the Devil hath been raised"

Author, and his Friends; as to signify: That we Apprehend several Weighty, Profitable, and Seasonable Truths, are therein Soberly Explained; some of the Mysterious Methods, and Malicious Operations of Satan, modestly Discussed; the main Scope of this Excellent Subject, by Scripture and Argument Solidly Confirmed; And the whole Suitably applyed to All sorts of persons That the Blessing of the Lord that hath Chosen Jerusalem, may accompany it, to the Spiritual Benefit, of all that shall peruse it; and that the Author, may have much of the Grace and Spirit of Christ, to assist him in his Labours, and so become, an Instrument, of doing much Service For, and bringing Great Glory To the Name of God, in his Day, and Generation, is the Prayer of,

67

Your Servants for Christ's Sake
Increase Mather, Coll. Harv. Pres.
Charles Morton
James Allen
Samuel Willard
John Bailey
Cotton Mather

[iv] To all my Christian Friends and Acquaintance, the Inhabitants of Salem Village. Christian Friends.

The sermon here presented unto you, was delivered in your Audience; by that unworthy Instrument, who did formerly spend some years among you; in the work of the Ministry, though attended with manifold sinful failings and infirmities, for which I do implore the Pardoning Mercy of God in Jesus Christ, and entreat from you the Covering of Love. As this was prepared, for that Particular Occasion, when it was delivered amongst you; so the Publication of it, is to be Particularly recommended to your service.

My hearts desire and Continual Prayer, to God for you All is; that you may be saved in the day of the Lord Jesus Christ; and, accordingly, that all means He is using with you, by Mercies and Afflictions, Ordinances and Providences, may be Sanctified to the building you up in Grace and Holiness, and preparing you for the Kingdom of Glory. We are told by the Apostle (Acts 14.22), That through many Tribulations we must enter into the Kingdom of God. Now, since (besides your share in the Common Calamities, under the burden whereof this poor people are groaning at this time) the righteous and Holy God hath been pleased [v] to permit a sore and grievous affliction to befall you such as can hardly be said to be Common to men viz. By giving liberty to Satan, to range and rage amongst you, to the Torturing the Bodies, and Distracting the Minds of some of the visible Sheep and Lambs, of the Lord Jesus Christ. And (which is yet more astonishing) he who is THE

The Documentary Evidence

ACCUSER of the Brethren, endeavors to introduce as Criminal some of the visible Subjects of Christ's Kingdom, by whose sober and godly Conversation in times past, we could draw no other Conclusions than that they were real members of His Mystical body, representing them as the Instruments of his malice, against their Friends and Neighbors.

I thought meet thus to give you the best assistance I could, to help you out of your distresses. And since the wayes of the Lord, in his permissive, as well as Effective Providence, are unsearchable and his doings past finding out. And pious souls, are at a loss, what will be the Issue of these things, I Therefore bow my knees, unto the God and Father of our Lord Jesus Christ that he would cause all grace to abound to you, and in you, that your poor place may be delivered, from those breaking and ruining Calamities, which are threatened as the pernicious consequences of Satan's malicious Operations. And that you may not be left to bite and devour one another in your Sacred or Civil Society, in your Relations or Families; to the destroying much good, and [vi] promoting much evil among you; So as, in any kind, to weaken the hands, or discourage the Heart of your Reverend and Pious Pastor, whose family also, being so much under the influence of these troubles, Spiritual sympathy, cannot but stir you up, to assist him as at all times, so Especially at such a time as this: He (as well as his neighbors) being under such awful circumstances. As to this discourse; my humble desire, Endeavor is, that it may appear to be, according to the form of sound words, and in Expressions every way Intelligible to the meanest Capacities. It pleased God; of his free Grace, to give it some acceptation with those that heard it, and some that heard of it; desired me to Transcribe it, and afterwards to give way to the Printing of it. I present it therefore, to your Acceptance, and Commend it to the Divine Benediction; and that it may please the ALMIGHTY GOD, to manifest his Power, to putting an end, to your sorrows of this Nature, by Bruising Satan under your feet shortly. Causing these and all other YOUR and OUR troubles to work together for our good Now, and salvation in the day of the Lord; Is the unfeigned desire, and shall be the uncessant prayer of

Less than the least, of all those that serve,
in the Gospel of our Lord Jesus.

DEODAT LAWSON.

"the Devil hath been raised"

[1] CHRIST'S FIDELITY
The only
Shield
AGAINST
SATAN'S MALIGNITY.

Zach. 3:2. And the LORD said unto SATAN, the LORD Rebuke thee, O SATAN; even the LORD that hath Chosen Jerusalem; Rebuke thee: Is not this a Brand pluckt out of the Fire?

IT seemed good to the Great and Glorious God, the Infinite and Eternal ELOHIM in the beginning, to Create the Heavens and the Earth; and together with and in the Third Heavens, a numberless [2] number of glorious Angels; that were Ordained to do his Pleasure, and they his Commands. To these he appointed (as a tryal of their obedience) a Ministration in this lower world, for the good of the Children of Men, and especially of the Heirs of Salvation. But a number of these Intelligent Spirits, being unwilling (as some Learned conceive) to yield their Service to man, of so much an inferiour nature to themselves being made of Earth: They Rebelled against the Will of their Soveraign Lord and Creator; For which their horrid Transgression, they were by the Righteous Judgment of God, thrust down from that Glorious Place, which was once Appointed to be their own Habitation, into the Lake of Eternal Perdition, there to be Reserved in Chains of Darkness, to the Judgment of the Great Day, Jude 6. SATAN himself then, and all his accursed Legions being Fallen into a miserable and irrecoverable Estate, are filled with Envy at the Malice against, all Mankind; and do set themselves by all ways and means, to work their Ruine and Destruction for ever: Opposing to the utmost, all Persons and Things, Appointed by the Lord Jesus Christ, as Means or Instruments of their Comfort here, or Salvation hereafter. Hence when Joshua (the type of JESUS) stood to Minister, as High Priest before the Lord, to make Atonemement for the People of his Covonant; SATAN stands at his Right hand, [3] to withstand and oppose him in his Ministration: which the Blessed Jesus (the Antitype of Joshua) taking notice of, he doth according to his Sovereign and Irresistible Power and Authority Command Deliverances to his Chosen Ones, by Stilling the Clamour and Suppressing the Power and Malice of SATAN, their Grand Adversary and Implacable Opposer, as in the Words now before us; And the Lord said unto SATAN, the LORD Rebuke thee, O SATAN, &c.

The Documentary Evidence

THESE Words are part of the Prophecy of Zechariah, whose Name by Interpretation, signifies the Remembrance or Memory of the Lord, and his Title agrees to the very Nature of this Prophecy; which was to put them in mind, what GOD had done for them, in delivering them from Captivity, and what they had done against him by Iniquity; that so they might be awakened unto Reformation of what was amiss. He was the Second Prophet, that came from the Lord to the People of Israel after their Return from the Babylonish Captivity. He was Contemporary and Colleague with Haggai, beginning to Prophecy but two Months after him, and backing what the other had said, more briefly, with more full and mysterious Testimonies; especially as to the Coming of the Messiah, &c. He Warns [4] them of the Amazing Revolutions, were coming upon them, in the Destruction of Jerusalem, and the Second Temple by the Romans, and Foretells the Rejection of the Jews, for their Sins, and especially, for Rejecting of the MESSIAH, who was to be Born among them according to the Flesh. The Prophecy contains then, Exhortations to true Repentance, dispersed throughout the Prophecy: Predictions of many Blessings and Mercies to the Faithful, relating to the Times of the Gospel, viz. The Coming of the LORD JESUS, the Calling of the Gentiles, and the Protection of his Church to the end of the World, notwithstanding all the Rage and Fury of his and their Enemies; together with severe Comminations against the Enemies of the Jews, and against the Impenitent among themselves; Intermingling Encouragements to Joshua, and all Leaders, both in Civil and Sacred Order, to be Faithful in the Discharge of Duty incumbent on them in all respects as the matter might require. These are the principal matters in the whole Prophecy.

In this Chapter, we have an account of Zechariahs Fourth Vision, concerning the Restoration and Establishment of the Priesthood, and Temple-Worship; and the Comforts Redounding to the Church from those Administrations; [5] Typically by Joshua the Brand, Spiritually and Mystically by JESUS the Branch.

Particularly, First we have the Conflict of the Angel of the Lord, that is Christ, against SATAN on behalf of Joshua, whom, the Mischievous (yet seemingly zealous) Devil, (transforming into an Angel of light) objected against, and despised, by reason of his filty garments; verse, 2, 3.

Secondly, SATAN being rebuked for his malice, the cause of his objection is removed, by taking away the filthy garments, and gieving him change of raiment; verse 4. And in order to his New Inauguration, or Enstallment in the Priesthood, there is bestowed on him, those ornaments which might Represent him, full of Splendour, and fitly qualified for that Office, verse 5.

Upon his Installment, the Angel of the Lord gives him a renewed Charge,

"the Devil hath been raised"

in a Solemn Protestation of the Continuance of his Office, and that he would be with him, and assist him in all Administrations, that were according to his own Institution, verse 6, 7.

Thirdly, We have GOD the FATHER, Revealing the Lord Jesus Christ, the Great and True High Priest.

First, Under the Title and Metaphor of the BRANCH, Verse 8.

Secondly, of a STONE with Eyes, being full of Providence and Wisdom for the Church Verse 9. Adjoyning the Special Effects of his [6] Coming, in Taking away Iniquity, latter end of Verse 9. And in Propagation, and Enlargement of his Kingdom and Interest, under the Gospel; Verse 10.

Here then, In the first Verse, We have the Representation of Joshua the High-Priest, or Great Priest, as the Hebrew, who was so by Descent, a great Officer in the Church, however mean he was in his Garb, and being a Publick Person, Represented the whole Church, And as he Conducted the People out of Babylon, and Rebuilt the Temple, was a Type of Christ, both in his Name and Office. (2) We have the posture of this Joshua; standing before the Angel of the Lord, the Angel of the Covenant, as he is elsewhere called. Now Joshua is brought in Standing (I) as a Servant, to show Inferiority as sitting, denotes Dignity, and Superiority; As a Servant deriving Authority, in his Office; from his Lord; As a Servant manifesting all Readiness, and Reverence in Obedience. As a Servant, to be by his Lord directed, as also under his Eye, for Support and Protection. Or,

2. Standing, as a guilty Person; As one unworthy to be imployed, in such Eminent Service; And as a Publique Person, had much to answer for the sins of the People, as well as his own.

3. Here is the Opposition Joshua met with, And SATAN the Adversary; whose malice appears, [7] against all good men, and good things in the world.

4. We have the Posture, and Order of SATAN in Opposing, and accusing of Joshua; Standing at his Right Hand the Right Hand is the place of the accuser that being.

1. The Weapon Hand.

2. The Working Hand. Satan the accuser or opposer there, takes his advantagious station.

5. We have the end of Satans so standing; viz. To resist him, to oppose his Execution of the Priests Office, the words in the Hebrew signify the withstander stood to withstand him, both to accuse, and oppose him.

In this second verse we have the LORD appearing in the vindication of Joshua, from the malicious accusation of Satan, according to his Covenant Mercy, and Special Favour shewed to him, and the People in delivering them from the Babylonish Captivity; Particularly Here we Note.

The Documentary Evidence

1. The Person speaking, the LORD, that is Jesus Christ, set forth by a Title of Glorious Soveraignty and Power, the LORD-REDEEMER, and Restorer of Mercy, to His Covenant People. The LORD-MEDIATOR, King and Head of His Church; He before whom, Joshua but now stood, as a SOVER-EIGN LORD, appears for him, as a Glorious Advocate, and Intercessor. [8] 2. We have The Person Spoken to, and that is Satan the ADVERSARY and Enemy, as the Divel ever was and the Notation of the Title here given to him holds forth. (3.) The Testimony of the Blessed Jesus, against the cursed Satan, the Enemy of Gods Covanant-People; The Lord Rebuke thee, O Satan, &c.

Where Note we, First, The Glorious Name, and Soveraign Authority, he uses for the Repelling of Satan, and Repressing his Malice, and Opposition, Viz. The Dreadful Name, of GOD the FATHER, the Great and Everlasting JEHOVAH. (2) The Soveraign and Powerful Manner of his Checking Satan, and that is, The Lord Rebuke thee, O Satan, he doth not stand to dispute the matter with him, but silenceth him at once, and the reduplication of the Rebuke points out to us (1.) Satans Earnestness in his Opposition; he stands in need of Rebukes, again and again, before he would yield and begone. (2) CHRIST'S Pitty, Tenderness, and Fidelity, in opposition to Satans Impudence and Importunity: Thirdly, We have the Rebuke armed and strengthened, by Arguments drawn from the Covenant of GOD, with Joshua and the People, in that Expression The God that hath chosen Jerusalem. (4) There is also Argument drawn, from that Special Salvation of which Joshua and the People had so lately been made partakers; (qs.d.) It is [9] but a vain thing for thee, O Satan, to move me against them, I know their faults, but I will now admit no further accusations, being resolved to perfect my Mercy to them, Is not this a Brand pluckt out of the Fire? The Hebrew Word rendred Brand, signifies Light and Sparkling on Fire, so that it would have been utterly burnt up, if the Lord had not been exceeding Merciful; and therefore nothing but Diabolical Cruelty, could put it into the Fire again, the like Expression we have, Amos 4.11. Ye are as a Brand pluckt out of the Burning, The Sum is here then; I have (qs. d.) but now graciously delivered them, and I will not by any of thy Malicious Clamours, be moved to Reject or Afflict them.

The Doctrine then is:

That the LORD JESUS CHRIST, is the only Prevalent Intercessor with GOD the FATHER, for the relief of those that are in Covenant with him,

"the Devil hath been raised"

& are made partakers of his special mercy; when they are under the most threatning and amazing distresses; that by therage and malice of Satan they can be exposed unto.

The whole Explication, and Confirmation of this Doctrine, will be dispatched, in the Illustration of these Propositions contained therein. [10]

PROPOSITION I.

Satan is the ADVERSARY and Enemy. He is the Original, the Fountain of malice, the Instigator of all contrariety, Malignity and Enmity; It is to be observed, this Title is here given to the Devil in our Text, and Context, on account of the Malicious Opposition, he made to Joshua as a Type of Christ, and representative of the People, for it is noted by Cricks the Hebrew word Satan signifies the most Universal Opposition both in words and deeds; & is a Radical Noun, derived from the Verb, which is in the close of the foregoing verse, rendred Resist, Oppose, or Withstand. Hence it is read frequently, Adversary, importing the same with the Greek Word 'ANTIDIKOS, used 1 Pet. 5.8. which signifies not barely Adversary, but Adversary in Cause, Suit or Action; The Scope then of this Proposition is couched under the Name or Epithet here given to the Devil, which is SATAN, the Adversary, or ARCH-ENEMY: And this Title is given him, in two eminent cases, by our Saviour himself, as in the Parable of the good Seed and Tares; Mat. 13.28. An Enemy hath done this, which our Lord himself declares, verse 39. in Opening the Parable, is the Devil. Again, Luk. 10.19. Over all the Power of the Enemy, which is Interpre- [11] ted of the Devil, or Unclean Spirits, Vers. 20 In this Rejoyce not that the Spirits are subject to you, but rather &c.

In a word, what was foretold concerning Ishmael, is in the most absolute sense true of him, Gen. 16.12. His Hand is against every Man, and every Mans Hand is (or should be) against him. Such an Universal and Implacable Adversary and Enemy is this Satan. But to Instance briefly in the Objects of his Enmity.

1. First He is Gods Enemy. He sets himself against the Infinite and Eternal GOD, All Satans designes and Operations; do strike and level, at the very being of God; he would dethrone and Un-God him, if it were possible. He fell from Gods favour at first, by rebellion, and hence by his righteous Judgement, was doomed to continue, under the power of irreconcilable enmity, against him for ever. He is an Enemy to all the Divine Attributes, and most glorious Persons in all their holy designs and operations. To all the Divine Attributes, Negative, Positive, Relative, and Endeavors by Blasphemous

The Documentary Evidence

denying them to Eclipse the glory of them; he was a lyar in and from the beginning, against the Truth and Holyness of GOD; Gen. 3.1. Yea hath GOD said &c. He puts them, upon scrupling the truth of the threatning and in the fourth verse, down right denies it, ye shall not surely dy &c. Herein also he reflected upon the Holyness of God, [12] by which he was engaged in that threatning, to advance his own glory; viz. The glory of his justice, by punishing mans transgression with Dying the Death as is denounced, Gen. 2.17. Then shalt surely dy, or dy the Death.

Thus the Unclean lying Satan, set himself against these Essential, and Inseperable Attributes, of the Blessed God: and in the same manner, doth he Eclipse the rest, so far as he is permitted to do it. Again, he is an Enemy to all the most glorious Persons in the God Head; FATHER, SON, and HOLY GHOST, in their joynt Determinations, and Eternal Decrees, concerning the Redemption, and Salvation of sinners; by and under the Mediator; and he is an Enemy to them in their Distinct Operations, in a way of Efficiency, for the promoting that which is Holy, and Just, and Good. To GOD the FATHER in Managing his Eternal Purposes of Grace, to Sinners by and in the New Covenant, and manifesting his Electing Love unto them, which is primarily and properly ascribed to him, 2 Thes. 2.13. As also, Ephes. 1.3,4,5. Of these Purposes, Designs and Resolutions, Satan mightily opposeth the Execution: As in this Instance of Joshua; GOD the FATHER, had a Decree of Mercy to him, and to his Covenant People Represented by him; Satan stands in Opposition to that Gracious Resolution. He is an Enemy to GOD the SON, to God made [13] Man, and the more, because he was Made Flesh, and shewed such Favour to Mankind, as to Tabernacle among them; John 1.14. And indeed, this Humiliation of the SON of GOD being made Man gave Satan advantage to shew and exercise his Enmity against him, (i.e.) as he was the Seed of the Woman, for as he was the SON of GOD, he could not any way come at him, being God over all Blessed for ever, Rom. 9.5. But when once Incarnate, and become an Inhabitant of this Lower World, where Satan Ranges to and fro continually; then he Spits his Venemous Malice against him, To cut him off by Herods bloody Decree, Mat. 2.16. To Over-throw his Obedience, and draw him to Sin; Mat. 4 to 11. To Destroy Him, by stirring up Judas to Betray him into the Hands of his Enemies, Luke 22.3. Satan Entred into Judas, & c. Again, he is the Enemy of the HOLY GHOST, as he is the Spirit of Grace, Heb. 10.29. The Spirit of Truth John 14.17. The Spirit of Holiness, or Holy Spirit, Eph. 4.30. And his being so called, imports the Holiness of his Nature, and Operations, in opposition to the Unclean Spirit, and his Operations. Hence Amanias is said to Lye against the HOLY GHOST, or Spirit of Truth, Acts 5.3. And indeed, this Unclean Spirit, or

"the Devil hath been raised"

Grand Fomentor of Spiritual Wickedness, is ever doing all he can, to Oppose and [14] do Despight unto the Holy Spirit of Grace, Heb. 10.29. By stirring up men to Resist him Acts 7.51. Thus Satan is an Enemy of GOD-CREATOR, to GOD-REDEEMER, to GOD-SANCTIFIER, in all their Operations, and Designs of Grace.

2. Satan is the GRAND Enemy of all mankind. He is full of Enmity, against the Woman and all her Seed, as Eve was the Mother of all living; Gen. 3.15. And I will put enmity betwixt thee and the woman &c.

Now Enmity, denotes a principle of Irreconcilable Hatred, an Innate Contrariety, which vents itself in all manner of Endeavour, to prevent the good, and promote the hurt, ruine and destruction of the Object. This Enmity of Satan, appears in the Names given him in Scripture, relating to man, as the Object of his Malice; He is called THE Accuser, even of the Brethren, Rev. 12.10, THE Tempter, Mat. 4.3. The Devourer, I Pet. 5.8. The Destroyer, hence the Eastern Antichrist, is so named in two Languages, Abaddon in the Hebrew, and Apollyon in the Greek, Rev. 9.11. because he acts in his horrible Destructions and Devastations of People and Kingdoms as the inspired Instrument substitute and representative of Satan the Grand Destroyer. It appears also, by Allusions made in the Sacred Pages, to Creatures that are a dread to man. He is called a Serpent, Gen. 3.13. The Old Serpent [15] Rev. 20.2. A Dragon, Rev. 12.13. A Lyon, I Pet. 5.8. Now put all these three together, that Satan hath the subtilty of the Serpent, the malice of the Dragon, and strength of the Lion, and suppose all these to be improved to the utmost vigour, of Angelical Activity; and we must believe him to be a most Formidable Enemy. He is such, did set upon, and was too hard for our First Parents, striking at the Stock and Root of all Mankind, in order to the certain confusion of the whole Progeny and Posterity: which Hellish Design had undoubtedly succeeded to full effect, had not the promise of the MESSIAH been Revealed to Lost Man, to lay hold of for his Restoring to a State of Reconciliation, and consequently to Eternal Salvation. The Sum is, Satan being doomed to the Chains of Eternal Darkness, for his Treason against his Creator, and Spight against Man, his Fellow-Creature; swells with cursed Enmity, against the children of men, yea, and the adopted children of GOD, so long as they are in this world; & being a spiritual Enemy, he is the more formidable, because an UNEQUAL match, for poor mortal flesh: For though by his fall, he lost his Angelical Holyness, yet he did not loose his Angelical nature, so that his Enmity must needs be Exceeding fierce, and Penetrateing, and although his Powers are much debased, from what they were in his State of integrity, yet do they vastly exceed, the most Elevated Powers [16] of any meer mortal whatsoever. But

Particularly here; First, He is the Enemy of the SOULS of men. And indeed, this is that he drives at, in all his designs, and operations, to catch devour and destroy SOULS; Hence when he draws wretched mortals, to Contract with him; He bargains with them that after the time of his service to them, he will have their Souls, viz. Intending to Torment them for ever.

He is a Spirit, and hence strikes at the spiritual part the most Excellent (Constituent) part of man. Primarily disturbing, and Interrupting the Animal and Vital Spirits, he maliciously Operates upon, the more Common Powers of the Soul, by strange and frightful Representations to the Fancy, or Imagination, and by violent Tortures of the body, often threatning to extinguish life; as hath been observed, in those that are afflicted amongst us. And not only so, but he vents his malice, in Diabolical Operations, on the more sublime and distinguishing faculties, of the Rational Soul, raising Mists of Darkness, and ignorance, in the Understanding. Ephes. 4.18. 2 Cor. 4.4: Stirring up, the innate Rebellion of the will, though he cannot force it unto sin. Introducing Universal Ataxy, and inordinacy, in the Passions, both Love and Hatred, the Cardinal or Radical affections, with all other that accompany or flow from them; Hence we read of Hating God, who ought above all to be loved; Rom. 1 [17] 30. And loving the world (i e) the Pleasure, Treasures, and Honours thereof, in such a degree as is inconsistent, with the love of the chief good; I John 2.15. James 4.4. And although it must be acknowledged, that there is a Corrupt Principle in Fallen Man; yet it is Satan, that frequently moves it unto act, and all he intends thereby is the captivating the whole Soul, and by consequence the Whole Man, to Disobedience of the Command of GOD; that by his Holy, and Righteous Judgment, his Wrath might be Revealed to the utmost, against the Souls and Bodies of Impenitent Sinners, Cursing them to Everlasting Burnings, Prepared for the Devil and his Angels, Mat. 25.41. And thus he would destroy all Souls, did not Divine Grace prevent.

Secondly, Satan is the ENEMY of the BODIES of Men. The Soul being the better part, is the principal object of his Malice, but together with that (as in Instrument by which it Exerteth its Powers in the State of Union) the Body is often sorely afflicted by him, when he cannot obtain leave to go any further. And here

1. Sometimes he brings Distress upon the Bodies of Men, by malignant Operations in, and Diabolical Impressions on, the Spirituous Principle or Vehicle of life & Motion. This we have set before us in the case of the Possessed, Mark 9.18. and [18] wheresoever he taketh him, he teareth him, and he foameth, and gnasheth with his Teeth, &c., Now although Actual Possessions, were most frequent and observable, while our SAVIOUR was on

"the Devil hath been raised"

the Earth, and it seems to be so much permitted in that time, that the Eternal Power and GOD HEAD, of the Lord Jesus might appear, in the subduing Satan, and Suppressing his Tyranny over the Souls and Bodies of the Children of Men: Yet there are certainly some Lower Operations of Satan, (whereof there are sundry Examples among us) which the Bodies of Men and Women, are liable unto. And whosoever, hath carefully observed these things, must needs be Convinced, that the Motions of the Persons Afflicted, both as to the Manner, and as to the violence of them, are the meer effects of Diabolical Malice and Operations, and that it cannot rationally be imagined, to proceed from any other cause whatsoever.

2. Sometimes by Moving and Exasperating the Corrupt Particles of the Blood, & vitiated Humours of the Body, he doth (by God's Permission) Smite the Bodies of Men, with Grievous, Pestitential and Loathsome Disease; Of this JOB was a special Instance, Job 2.7. So Satan went and smote Job with sore Boiles, &c. It is not expressed, what Disease it was, with which the Devil smote Job; but certainly it Seized [19] him, with the utmost degree of Malignity and Loathsomeness, that natural causes, under the influence of Diabolical Malice, could produce; and we may rationally conceive that never any man, had that Disease or those Boiles (as Job had them) who outlived the Tormenting Pains, and Malignity thereof. Neither can we deny, but that Satan may (by Divine Permission) spread the Contagious Attomes of Epidemical Diseases, in the Aiery Region (the Territory assigned to him) who is Prince of the Power of the Air, Eph. 2.2) And make them Penetrate, so as to render them the more Afflictive and Destructive to the Bodies of such as are Infected by them. This he did by Permission (not only for Tryal as in Jobs case) but also for the Punishment of Sinners; hence we read of his being employed sometimes by the Great God, as the Executioner of his just Revenges, in the Destruction of his and his Peoples Enemies; and thus he was among the Egyptians when the Lord plagued them, Psal.78.49, 50. By sending Evil Angels among them. He spared not their Souls from Death, but gave them over to the Pestilence. Besides, I may not insist here How Satan by wicked men his Instruments brings outward Calamities, Sorrows, Pains, and Punishments on the Bodies even of the Children of God; of whom as the Apostle declares the [20] World was not worthy, Heb. 11.37, 38. They Wandred in Sheep-skins and Goat-skins, in Dens and Caves of the Earth, &c. by reason of the malicious Persecutions of wicked Tyrants, the Instruments of Satan, and who doubtless were harried on by his Instigations. And surely what is said concerning Casting into Prison, is likewise true of other Afflictions, as Scourgings, or any Corporal Punishments for Righteousness sake. That though men are the Actors, yet it is the Devil, that shall Cast some into Prison,

The Documentary Evidence

Rev. 2.10. He is the principal Instigator, in all such Designs for the hurting the Bodies of men, when not permitted to proceed further, being willing to do all the mischief that he can, when he cannot do so much as he would: But

Thirdly, Satan vents his Malice against the very LIVES of men, to cut them off and destroy them. He is the Prince of Death, that hath the Power of Death, Heb. 2.14. He is the DESTROYER of all Life, both Spiritual and Corporal. All his Designs against the Souls and Bodies of men, terminate here, even in the Weakening or Extinguishing of Life, and when he touches the life of the Body, he aims at the Life of the Soul. He it was that stirred up Cain, to Commit the first Murder, in the World, when he slew Abel his Brother, for [21] which he is said to be of the Wicked One; I Job 2.12. (i.e.) Acting from the same principle of Enmity: as if he were his very Spawn and Offspring. He it was that Raised a wind, that smote the House where Jobs Sons and Daughters were, and slew them all, Job 1.19. having permission so to do, verse 12. This same Adversary it was, that stirred up David to Number the People, that so by displeasing GOD, 70000 men might be cut off by the Pestilence; I Chron. 21.1. 2 Sam. 24.15. This Design against the Lives of Men, the GRAND Destroyer hath been carrying on, from the beginning, by stirring up Wars, Tumults, Insurrections, Commotions and Confusions, amongst People, Nations and Kingdoms, by which means multitudes of multitudes have fallen in the valley of Destruction, and gone down to the Congregation of the Dead; the Devil hath begotten Pride, Pride hath Created Wars, and Wars promoted Slaughter, and Destructions; so that it is the true Mark and Character of Satans Kingdom, that it is Established, Supported, and Propogated by Malice, Enmity, Wars, Blood, Slaughter, and Destruction of Mankind.

PROPOSITION II.

That Satan makes it his business to improve [22] all Opportunities and Advantages, to Exercise his Malice upon the Children of Men. He is an indefatigable, as well as an implacable Enemy: Thus he was willing to represent himself, as appears by his answer given to the GREAT GOD, when he inquired of him, Job 2.2. Whence comest thou? Satan said from going to and fro in the earth, &c. (i.e.) Traversing the Earth, to spie out what mischief he could do, against the Inhabitants thereof. This is the Argument used by the Apostle Peter, I Pet. 5.8. Be sober, (i.e.) be in a Holy Frame, to Attend all Duty; Be vigilant, (i.e.) be careful to avoid all that Sin which might betray you, Because your Adversary the Devil goes about as a Roaring Lion, seek-

"the Devil hath been raised"

ing whom he may Devour; here note we his strength, a Lyon; his Malice, A Roaring Lion; his Industry, he goes about; his End and Design seeking whom he may devour: and he exerts his malice, either (1) Immediately, or (2) Mediately; Of each of these briefly.

1. Immediately and directly, Operating in, and upon the object by his own power and influence. And indeed his Angelical Activity is such, as doth render him capable to Operate far beyond Humane Power of Resistance, without any Instrument whatsoever, whensoever [23] he hath obtained the Divine Permission, and this he doth

1. Sometimes by sudden injections, or suggestions working upon the corrupt principle, or Original Depravity that is in man. Thus Satan is said to have fired the heart of Annanias to Lye against the Holy Ghost, Acts 5.3.

2. Sometimes by false Representations to the Eyes, or only to the minds of men, concerning things delightful to the Senses: Of this kind was the Representation of the Kingdomes of the World to our LORD Jesus Christ, Mat. 4.8. Some think it was in a Vision, or Illusion, some by pointing at the four quarters and in words relating the glory thereof; Doctor Taylor judgeth the Devil offered the Images, and Representations of them all, sensibly and actually, in a strange manner, making their Images appear to his Senses, and not by vision or illusion, which did not so well agree to the perfection of Christ's mind. But Christ did indeed, see the Images and most glorious Representations of the World and the Kingdoms thereof. And the better to perswade him, that he saw the things indeed, he set him on an exceeding High Mountain; I do the rather conceive this to be the manner, because men by art can Represent to the Senses in a Glass, the [24] Lively Image of a person or thing, and Satan certainly can do it much more; and besides, it seems hardly safe to believe; that the Devil was capable, to impose upon the pure and sinless imagination of our LORD JESUS CHRIST, by any Illusion whatsoever.

3. Sometimes by Entring into, and Possessing the Soul of the Man; bringing him unto full Submission, and entire Resignation to his Hellish Designs; thus it is said, Satan entred into Judas, Luk. 22.3. that is Totally Enslaved him to his Authority and direction. In this manner he Captivates the whole Soul In all its faculties by seven Spirits (i.e.) Fullness of Devils, Luk. 11.26. And this may be, in those that are not Bodily Possessed, and indeed is in a sort, in all Unregenerate SINNERS, as 2 Timothy 2. 26. Who are taken Captive by him at his Will; The Greek Word there used, signifies to Hunt and Catch alive. The man with all his Faculties and Powers, are at the Devils Beck; and Devoted to his Service.

Secondly, Mediately by imploying some of mankind or other creatures, and he frequently useth other persons or things, that his Designs may be the more undiscernable. Thus he used the Serpent in the first Temptation, Gen. 3.1. Now when he useth Mankind, he seemeth to [25] bring in what he intends, in a way of Familiar Converse with us Mortals, that he may not be suspected at the bottome of all. Hence he Contracts and Indents with Witches and Wizzards, that they shall be the Instruments by whom he may more secretly Affect, and Afflict the Bodies and Minds of others, and if he can prevail, upon those that make a Visible Profession, it may be the better. Covert to his Diabolical Enterprizes: And may the more readily pervert others to Consenting unto his subjection. Thus in Tempters to any Wickedness, but in reference to the present occasion, especially in Witches, Sorcerers, Diviners, &c. So far as we can look into those Hellish Mysteries, and guess at the Administration of that Kingdom of Darkness, we may learn that Witches make Witches, by perswading one the other to Subscribe to a Book, or Articles, &c. And the Devil, having them in this subjection, by their Consent, he will use their Bodies and Minds, Shapes and Representations, to Affright and Afflict others, at his pleasure, for the Propagation of his Infernal Kingdom, and accomplishing his Devised Mischiefs, to the Souls, Bodies and Lives of the Children of men; yea, and of the Children of GOD too, so far as permitted and is possible. [26]

PROPOSITION III.

The Covenant People of God, and those that would Devote themselves intirely to his Service, are the special objects of SATANS Rage and Fury.

He is the malicious Enemy of the Church of God, and of every Member thereof; and that on account of the Kingdom of Christ that is established, and the Ordinances of the LORD JESUS that are celebrated there; and the benefits that acrue to the Souls of men, by those blessed Institutions, for the Translating of them, from the Power of Satan unto the Subjection of the Lord Jesus Christ; the Redeemer of his People, and Head of his Church; hence when the Church is Resembled to a Woman, for Beauty of Holy Profession, clothed with the Sun, (i.e.) adorned with all Sanctifying Gifts and Saving Graces of the Spirit of GOD, shining with utmost brightness, of the Faith and Order of the Gospel, Rev. 12.1. To a Woman, for Tenderness and Weakness. Yea, &c to a Woman, for Fruitfulness, being with Child and ready to be Delivered, verse 2. Then do we find, the Implacable Adversary of Mankind Represented by a Great Red Dragon, verse 3. (i.e.) most formidable, both for his Power, a Great Dragon, and for his venomous Rage and Fu- [27] ry, A Red Dragon; and he is set forth, pouring out his Malice against her, in a fearful manner, by a Flood out of his mouth, verse 15. And here we may note two things.

"the Devil hath been raised"

First, That the more solemnly, any Person or People are Devoted to God, and thence do shine with Lustre of Holiness, both of Heart and Life, the more vehemently doth he oppose, malign, and Persecute them. That which makes him so malicious against the Children of GOD, is his accursed Contrariety, to the Image of GOD that is on them, and the Principle of Holiness that is in them. So that the more Beauty of Holiness, they hold forth in their Conversation, the more violently and outragiously doth he Oppose them: A special Instance of this, we have in Job, concerning whom the Searcher of Hearts, did (before his afflictions) give this Testimony, that he feared God, and eschewed evil, Job 1.8. Upon the notice whereof, Satan set himself against him, to interrupt him in, and divert him from, that Sincerity and Universality of Obedience, by obtaining permission to bring Crosses and Afflictions upon him, in his Estate and Children, chap. 1. And finding him to be constant in this Resolution, to Serve GOD Uprightly, according to the Testimnoy of GOD himself, chap. 2, 3. He pleads for a farther Permission, against his Person, chap. 2.5. And in the management of [28] his Designs, he did Transform himself into an Angel of Light, as the Apostle saith, 2 Cor. 11.14 (i.e.) pretend to as much Holiness in outward appearance, as the best; hence when the Sons of GOD, viz. the Angels, the Eldest Sons of GOD by Creation, came to present themselves before the Lord, (i.e.) to pay their Homage unto, and to receive the Commands of their Soveraign LORD, Satan came also among them, Job. 1.6. Thus also by Seducers, and False Teachers; 2 Cor. 11.13. he insinuates into the Society of the Adopted Children of GOD, in their most Solemn Aproaches to him, in Sacred Ordinances; endeavouring to look so like the true Saints, and Ministers of Christ, that if it were possible, he would deceive the very Elect, Mat. 24.24. by his subtilty; for it is certain, he never works more like the Prince of Darkness, than when he looks most like an Angel of Light, and when he most pretends to Holiness, he then doth most secretly, and by consequence most surely undermine it, and those that most Excel in the Exercise thereof.

Secondly, That the mere eminent Service, or Office any person is employed IN, or called to the discharge OF, for the glory of GOD, and the good of his Church, the more violently doth Satan resist, withstand or oppose him.

In this Context, we have Joshua who was Ordained to be the High Priest of GOD, a Repre- [29] sentative of the whole People, whose Office it was, to Offer Sacrifice for their sins, and to Enter into the Holy-place once a year, with the Blood of Atonement, Exod. 30.10 (being therein also a Type of Christ, the Great High-Priest of his People) He stood before the Angel, or Messenger of the Covenant of the LORD to attend his Duty, and discharge his Office; and presently the Devil or Calumniator, stands up to accuse, and

Satan, or the Withstander to resist him; yea, such was the Subtilty, Impudence and Enmity of the Old Serpent, called the Devil and Satan, (all engaged against our Lord Jesus Christ, the Antitype of Joshua,) that no sooner, was he explicitely Ordained, to the work he came into the World for, Mat. 3.17. but immediately Satan sets upon him to hinder him, and (if it had been possible) to make void the whole Design, Mat. 4.1. to the 11 Thus also we find Paul, The Apostle of our Lord Jesus Christ, (who was so Laborious, and indefatigable, in the Work of the Gospel, 1 Cor. 15.10. complaining of Satans putting Impediments or Discouragements in his way of coming to the Thessalonians, I Thes. 2.18. Wherefore we would have come unto you (even I Paul) once and again, but Satan hindred us: partly by Persecutions, raised against him, and the Lying in wait of the Jews, mentioned, Acts 20.19. and again, chap. 23.16. as a Discouragement to him, partly by Raising Troubles in other Churches, and thereby [30] finding Paul other business, as an Impediment to his Serving them. Thus Satan still is, and will be, the Opposer of the Faithful and Fervent Officers of the Church, to the end of the World, and so I pass to the next Proposition.

PROPOSITION IV.

That in all Satans Malicious Designs, and Operations, he is absolutely Bounded and Limited, by the Power and Pleasure of the Great and Everlasting GOD, the LORD JEHOVAH.

That is the Title given to God the Father in our Text, and although many times particularly applyed to GOD the FATHER, yet is comprehensive of all the Persons in the God-head; and especially, relating to the Execution of the Eternal Purposes of Grace, and Good Will to the Elect, for Opera Trintatis ad Extra, sunt indivisa & indistincta. Polar Syn. Here then are two of the Persons in the Ever Blessed Trinity, mentioned, each under the Title of JEHOVAH in the Hebrew; whereby we are confirmed in the Doctrine of the Trinity; By JEHOVAH, the LORD the SON, making use of the Soveraign Name and Authority, of Jehovah the FATHER, The Lord Rebuke thee O Satan, the Lord that hath Chosen Jerusalem Rebuke thee. [31] Now Election, Is Primarily ascribed, to the Eternal purpose, and Soveraign Pleasure, of GOD the Father In concurrence with GOD the Son & GOD the Holy Ghost, These Glorious Divine Persons, Coequal, Coessential, and Coeternal do hold Satan, in the chain of their absolute power and soveraignty being able at their pleasure, with a word of rebuke, to remand and restrain, yea totally to vanquish and suppress him, in his most outragious efforts of malice, against the Children of men, or servants of the MOST HIGH GOD. This

"the Devil hath been raised"

Published in 1874, this engraving represents the Salem Village Meeting House used by the villagers from 1673 to 1701. The structure was 34 feet long, 28 feet deep and 16 feet high to the front and rear plate. It was in this building that all of the March 1692 witch examinations took place and that Rev. Deodat Lawson preached his important March 24th sermon, Christ's Fidelity the Only Shield Against Satan's Malignity. *Courtesy, Danvers Archival Center.*

The Documentary Evidence

is presented to us in that Expression used, in our Text, The LORD REBUKE thee the Hebrew word GAGNAR used here, signifies to rebuke, not only in word but in Deed; Cum potestate Objurgare, to rebuke with power, so as totally to subdue, and suppress, thus it is used, Ps. 9 : 6. Thou hast rebuked the heathen, (i.e.) suppressed their power, and rage, even to their utter destruction, as in the next words, thou hast destroyed the wicked, and put out their name for ever, the words then, The Lord Rebuke thee, Import.

First Authority of Office, to reprove and rebuke, Titus is directed, Ch 1 18. Rebuke them sharply (i.e.) by vertue of thine Office Power and Authority thus their Lord and master, Rebuked the Heat and Rashness of his Disciples, Luke 9. 54, 55. But he turned and rebuked them and said ye know not what manner of spirit ye are of.

Secondly Rebukeing imports, putting to shame in [32] sense of weakness in argueing, or disputeing, Jude: 9. brought not raileing accusation; but made the Grand Railer ashamed by saying the LORD Rebuke thee, or confound thee in thy Argument.

And (Thirdly) it imports Checking and putting to silence. Luk. 19.39. Master Rebuke thy Disciples (i.e.) put them to silence, Thus it belongs to the Soveraignty, of the blessed Jehovah, One God in Three Persons with authority to Rebuke Satan, to Shame him in his accusations, and to Silence his clamours, against the servants of God. And that will appear, if we consider three things,

(First) The Great God the Eternal Jehovah, did at first Create him by his Power, He made him in a Glorious state of Happiness, and perfection of Holyness, in the beginning of time; when the innumerable company of Angels were made in and with the highest heavens, to do his pleasure Ps. 103.20, 21. And although, the Apostate Angels, that fell by rebellion are reserved in Chains &c. Jude ver. 6. Yet our Saviour tells the Devil Math. 4.10. Thou shalt worship the Lord thy God &c. Therein not only testifying his own Son like subjection to God his Father, and stedfast, resolution, to exalt his glory, against all manner of temptations, but also thereby, put- [33] ting Satan in mind, that even He & all other creatures, are bound to worship GOD, their Soveraign Lord and Maker and thence that the Devil ought to worship the Lord Jesus who was Truly and Essentially God his Creator. For surely he is even the Devils God by Creation, in which he was made a glorious Angel, but he made himself by transgression an horrible Devil.

(Secondly) The Soveraign Power, of the Great God to rebuke Satan, appears, In that he doth manage and over-rule, all his motions and Operations, to serve his most Holy Ends, and to advance his own glory in the winding up. Angelical natures are very active, and as the blessed Angels, are very diligent in serving and glorifying GOD, and ministring for the good of the heirs of salvation, Hebr. 1.14. So the cursed Devils, are full of subtile contrivances, malicious designs, and Diabolical operations, for the dishonour of GOD, the ruine of Mankind, and injuring the Heirs of Promise, to the uttermost of their Permission and Ability.

But what the wise man saith, wisely and truely concerning the Devices of man, is every way true of the Designs of Satan, Prov. 19:21. There are many devices in a mans heart, but the Counsel of the Lord it shall stand, (i.e.) totally to defeat the accomplishment of them, [34] or to over-rule the issues, effects and consequences of them to his own Glory. Thus the GREAT GOD, doth many times outdo Satans Politicks, and over-shottes him in his own bow, making that which he designed, as meanes to Prevent the good of the Church, appear to be a most proper medium to promote the benefit thereof, according to his Blessed will and Counsel, who can say concerning his own most Holy Design; and be as good as his word, in despight of Men and Divels, Isa. 46.10. My counsel shall stand, And I will do all my pleasure. This will appear, if we consider the pernicious designs, and malicious methods of Satan, in order to the Curcifixion of Our LORD JESUS, and the end he aimed at in his being cut off; and how in a stupendious manner; all was overruled, to accomplish Gods Eternal Purposes, in the Salvation of his Elect.

Briefly then, The Devil finding nothing in him) (as our Saviour saith, John. 14.30.) On which to fix any temptation, whereby he might stain him in his Holyness; or pervert him from his Obedience; but was totally overcome, and routed, in a Single conflict, with the Captain of our Salvation, Math. 4: 1, to, 11. He is resolved to prosecute another design, even the taking away his bodily life, in order whereunto He entred into Judas, Named Iscariot one of the Twelve. Luk. 22.

[35] 3. Who presently went and set himself to take opportunity, to betray him, Ver. 6. Then Satan stirred up, the Envy of the people, to deliver him to the Judgment, Math. 27.18. Brought in Two false Witnesses against him; Math. 26.60 Moved Herod, and Pontius Pilate Gentiles, to condemn him, and therein gratify the wicked people. of Israel, that were gathered together, Acts 4.27. And (to compleat the Diabolical Tragedy) Instigated the people, with wicked hands to Crucify him. Acts 2.23. And after his Buryal, they endeavour to prevent his Rising again, or removal out of the Sepulcher (as they pretended) by setting a guard about it, rolling a great stone upon it, and sealing it to make it unalterable; Math. 27.66. &c.

SATAN then had thus far gained the Point, & prevailed in his Hellish designs, against the life of the Man CHRIST JESUS; yet in all this process he had neither broken the Chaine by which the GREAT GOD holds him, nor could he (in, the least) overstraine one linke thereof; nor yet deviate one inch from the methods determined, and traced out, by the Purpose of the Eternal God in any one step or intreague, of this whole affaire: but in spight of all the Malice, Power, and Policy, of EARTH and HELL, it came to pass in every particular passage thereof, As the Hand of GOD disposed, in the Course of his Providence: According as his Counsel fore-determined should be done. Acts 4:27, 28. As also, Acts 2.23 [36] Hitherto we may observe, how Satans plot and project, seemed to be agreeable, (though against his will,) to the purpose, and Eternal Counsel of the blessed GOD: but in the ends and issues proposed, Behold how vastly (even Toto Celo) they differ! For instance, Satans Design herein was to cut off the hopes of the sons of men, as to Redemption and Salvation by the Man Christ Jesus, I. Tim 2:5 That so the benefits of the New Covenant, of which he was the ONE, and onely MEDIATOR, might utterly faile, and poor miserable man, might again fall, Fearfully, Fatally, and Irecoverably, into the hands of the LIVING GOD, Heb: 10, 31. And by the Infinite weight, of his vindictive Justice be crushed down to the Nethermost Hell: But on the other hand, GODS designs was far otherwise, even by the Deep Humiliation, and death of the Man Christ on the Cross, to produce such Effects as these, Namely that Man's Redemption, might be wrought out and Finished, John 19, 30. Peace made by the blood of his cross, betwixt an offended God, and sinful man. Ephes: 2: 14, 16, Sinners Redeemed from the Curse of the Law, by Christ's being made a curse for them, Gal. 3:13: And he made heirs of the blessing, ver. 14 A number of lost Soules, bought with a price from the Bondage of Satan, and Power of Sin, to be Instruments of Glorifying God, in their Bodies and Spirits which are Gods, I Cor. 6.20. [37] In a word; that the Eternal Power and God-Head of the LORD JESUS, (the Blessed Seed of the Woman, according to his Humane Nature) might appear in a fatal wounding and Bruising the head of the Old Serpent, Gen. 3.15. And a final Destruction of Death, and him that had the Power of Death, that is the Devil, Heb. 2.14. And no less Eminent, is the Soveraign Wisdom and Power of God, in Over-ruling this Tragical Scene of Diabolical Malice, in the glorious Consequences thereof, viz. Loosing the Pains of Death, by which it was impossible, the LORD JESUS should be held, Acts 2.24. Raising him from the Dead, verse 32. That having Conquered Death, Hell, and Satan; and Spoiled Principalities and Powers, openly Triumphing over them, Col. 2.16. He might appear to be the Author of Eternal Salvation, to all them that obey him, Heb. 5.9. And having humbled himself to death, even the Death of the Cross, Phil. 2.8. Might by GOD the FATHER, be highly Exalted, verse 11. And ascending on high, might Lead Captivity Captive, Psal. 68.18. Ephes. 4.8. And set down at the Right

"the Devil hath been raised"

hand of the Majesty on High, Col. 3.1. Far above all Principalities and Powers, Ephes. 1.21. Expecting, until all his Enemies be made his Foot-stool, Heb. 10.13. Until the day be come, in which he shall appear, in Power and great Glory, Mat. 24.30. To Judge the Quick and the [38] Dead, at his Appearance and his Kingdom, 2 Tim 4.1; Thus Thus; did the Ever Blessed God, Over-rule the Grand Project of the Old Serpent against the Saviour, and Salvation of his Elect, bringing his mischievous Devices, upon his own pate, to his utter amazement and Confession for ever. And since the Salvation of us All, is so much concerned therein, this may excuse my so free and large dilating upon Description thereof. Thus is Satan under the limitations of Gods Soveraignty in all his Operations which yet farther appears.

Thirdly, In that God will Judge and Sentence him at last, unto Eternal Punishment. Satan is now but Gods Instrument, as all other Creatures are; and it is the Property of an Instrument, to be absolutely subservient to the Pleasure of the principal Agent, or Efficient when therefore the GREAT GOD hath used him for a while, to Serve his own most Holy Designs, in the world, by the trying of his People, and the Judicial Blinding, and hardening of obstinate and impenitent Sinners unto their Eternal Destruction: When the day is come, in which he hath Appointed to Judge the World by Jesus Christ, Acts 17.31. Then shall that Old Serpent, called the Devil and Satan, be Judged, Sentenced, and Confined to those Everlasting Torments Prepared for him, and together with him, for all such miserable and [39] accursed Souls as have here been Deluded, and Ensnared by him. As appears by that dreadful Definitive Sentence, that shall then be Pronounced, by the GREAT KING, in the day of his wrath, and Revelation of his Power Mat 25:41. Go ye Cursed into Everlasting burnings Prepared for the Devil and his Angels. If therefore GOD Created him; Over-rules all his Operations; And shall at last Judge him to Eternal Destruction; then it will follow, he is alwayes absolutely bounded, and limited, by the same Soveraignty of GOD, which sets bounds to the Sea permitting it so far, Hitherto shalt thou go, and prohibiting it from going any farther, and here shall thy proud Waves be stayed, Job 48:11. The like limitations Satan had, in his permission concerning Job, as in Chap. 1.12 & 2:6. And he could in no degree, exceed the limits of Gods Power and Pleasure, notwithstanding all his Malicious Inclinations thereunto.

V. PROPOSITION

That Whensoever, God hath declared a person or people, to be in Covenant with him, as the Objects of his special mercy and favour, he will assuredly and shortly, suppress the malice of Satan, however violently engaged against them.

The Documentary Evidence

[40] To Explaine this Proposition, we may consider the Arguments used in the Text, to Repress Satan's importunity and Magnify God's Mercy, which are Twofold,

First; God's Free-Love, set on them from Eternity, is that expression, The LORD that hath chosen Jerusalem. &c

Secondly HIS particular favour, in delivering Joshua and them, from the Babylonish Captivity. Is not this a Brand pluckt out of the Fire? Of each of these a few words.

First; Gods free love from Eternity, placed on his Covenant people. The Lord that hath chosen Jerusalem &c. God at the first, chose the seed of Abraham, Isaac and Jacob, to be a people to himself, above all the nations of the earth, Psal. 105.6. And avenched them to be His peculiar people, Deut. 26.16. He chose the land of Judea, to be the place of their abode, and there he chose the City Jerusalem, or the vision of peace, as the name signifies, in which his people might enjoy peace and quietness; after their travels, toils and troubles in the wilderness, where the Thrones of Judgment were established, Psal. 122.5. Where also the Temple was builded, & the Worship and Ordinances of GOD, Celebrated, and the tokens of Gods presence were placed. So that audience, and acceptance of prayers, might be expected, when offered towards this City and House, I Kings 8.44. Hence by a Metonymie of the City, put for [41] the inhabitants, it notes the people of Jerusalem, and by a Senecdoche of the part for the whole, implies that whole people which was in Covenant with GOD in those days, which did also figuratively represent, the Evangelical Church, the Heavenly Jerusalem, Heb. 12.22. Now Choosing is an act of freedom and Liberty in God; and a Testimony of Love and Mercy, to such as are chosen; By which he is inclined to help them in Misery.

Secondly HIS particular favour, in delivering Joshua and them, from the Babylonish Captivity is not this a brand &c. Where GOD hath begun to shew special favour, he will compleat it, in opposition to Earth and Hell. As he said so the Lords people find it, God is not a man that he should lye, Numbers 23.19 (i.e.) as to his promise, nor that he should fail in his Providence, to carry on those works, in which he hath made such blessed beginnings, is not this a brand pluckt out &c (i.e.) with an holy pitty rescued, when all on a light fire, now CHIRST is brought in, using this argument in his Intercession for his people, who in imitation of him may also use it for themselves, and it seems thus to be framed (qs.d.) KNOW O Satan, GOD the FATHER, hath begun to own Joshua and the People, in their deliverance in part, and that may encourage them to expect all that remains, for the LORD will [42] perfect what concerns them, and will not forsake the works of his own hands, because his mercies endure for ever, Psal. 138.8. The force of argument then,

"the Devil hath been raised"

for clearing the Proposition lyes in these two affections.

First, GOD in choosing of and covenanting with a Person or People, doth engage all his Glorious Attributes, for their good as the matter doth require. When he Declareth he will be their GOD, all his Sufficiency and Efficiency, is for them, (i.e.) to the utmost of what he hath Engaged by Covenant: hence his Negative, Positive, and Relative Attributes, do Recommend him as a proper Object of Faith, for Present help to his People in time of Trouble, Psal. 46.1. So that humble Reminding him of his Covenant, doth in its own Nature prevail with him to exert His Wisdom, Power, Goodness, Truth and Faithfulness, &c. in a proportionable degree, to Relieve the Distressed, as their occasion doth or may require: For He Remembred his Covenant, and Repented according to the multitude of his Mercies, Psal. 106.45.

Secondly, Where GOD hath given some Experience of his Mercy, it is to be used as argument to prevail with Him, for what we may further stand in need of. Thus in the Text, Joshua is as a Brand pluckt out of the Fire, and therefore may depend on it, to be Established in the Priesthood, and owned accordingly. Thus [43] then the scope of the Proposition is cleared up, viz. When God hath taken a person or people into Covenant, and shewed them special Favour, The Gates of Hell (as our Savior saith, Math. 16.18) shall never prevail against them. Lastly,

PROPOSITION VI.

The Great GOD, doth manage all his Designs of Mercy to his People, under the Gospel Dispensation, in and through the Mediator. The very Tenure of the Gospel Covenant is such; and the Termes thereof, are so Methodized, as to introduce a necessity of depending on a Mediator. The whole Transaction of the Gospel Covenant, betwixt the GREAT GOD, and Fallen Man, is by the Mediator; hence it is on better Termes, than the Covenant of Works, Heb. 8.6. Under the New Covenant, all Addresses to God, are by the Mediator, Heb. 4.15, 16. and all Communications of Grace from God, are by the Mediator, Joh. 1.16. Here then three things are briefly to be considered.

First, JESUS CHRIST is appointed, according to the method of the Covenant of Grace, to be the Only Mediator betwixt God and Man, 1 Tim. 2.5. For there is ONE GOD, and ONE MEDIATOR, betwixt GOD and Man, the Man-Christ- [44] Jesus. And He is, the Mediator of the New Covenant, Heb. 12.24. To his Mediatorial Office, is to be referred; His Intercession with GOD the FATHER, for all Good to his Elect; which he ever Liveth to Discharge, Heb. 7.25. By Him our Prayers Ascend to GOD, Heb. 4.14. By Him

The Documentary Evidence

all Answers of Grace from GOD Descend to us. Hence he promiseth, What-soever ye shall ask the Father in my Name, he will give it, Joh. 16.23.

Secondly, In the Management of this Office, He is invested with Kingly Power. He is a KING for Dignity, Psal. 2.6. A KING for Authority of Government: KING OF KINGS and LORD OF LORDS, Rev. 19.16. A King for Judgment, All Judgment is Committed unto Him, John 5.22. And it shall finally be Managed by him, Mat. 25.34. & 41.

Thirdly, It is one special Administration of CHRISTS Mediatorial King-dom, to Oppose, Suppress, and Destroy, the Kingdom and Power of Satan, that Grand Enemy of the Souls, and Salvation of men. Betwixt CHRISTS Kingdom, and Satans Kingdom, there is a direct Contrariety and Opposi-tion: Now Contraries do mutually endeavor to Overcome each other, and bring them to nought. Hence when CHRISTS Kingdom goes up, Satans must go down; On this special Errand, our Savior is said to come into the World: For this [45] the Son of God was manifested, that he might destroy the works of the Devil, 1 John 3.8. He was Incarnate, not only to Oppose his most secret Insinuations and Temptations; but to Over-power his most violent motions, and hostile Invasions, when he ruffles in the Titles of the God of this World; 2 Cor. 4.4. And the Prince of this World, who is by CHRIST Dismantled of his Dignity, and Cast out of all his Power and Dominion, which he had over the Children of men, John 12.31. The reason is, by CHRIST'S Execu-tion of His Kingly Office in Heaven, Satans Power is Suppressed, and the Prince of this World is judged, John 16.8. (i.e.) Condemned to Lose all his Authority, that His Kingdom may be no more; such then was and is the Divine Authority and Power of CHRIST-MEDIATOR; that he could have Rebuked, and totally Vanquished Satan by his own Power, Who is over all God blessed for ever, Rom. 9.5. But was pleased rather, to Magnify his Medi-atorial Capacity, presenting it to us, as a blessed Rule to direct us in our Addresses to God; The Name and Merits of the LORD JESUS, being so acceptable with the FATHER, because every way corresponding with his Designs of Grace to the Souls of men Revealed in the Gospel.

[46] The APPLICATION of this Doctrine to ourselves remains now to be Attended.

USE I.

And First, Let it be for solemn WARNING, and awakening, to all of us that are before the Lord at this time, and to all other of this whole people, who shall come to the knowledge, of these direful Operations of Satan, which the HOLY GOD hath permitted in the midst of us.

"the Devil hath been raised"

The LORD doth terrible things amongst us, by lengthening the Chain of the Roaring Lyon, in an Extraordinary manner; so that the Devil is come down in great wrath, Rev. 12.12. Endeavouring to set up his Kingdom, and by Racking Torments on the Bodies, and Affrighting Representations to the Minds of many amongst us, to Force and Fright them, to become his subjects. I may well say then, in the words of the Prophet; Micah, 6.9. The Lords voice cryeth to the City, and to the Country also, with an unusual and amazing loudness, and the Man of Wisdom (or Substance) will see his Name: Hear Ye the Rod, and who hath appointed it. Surely it warns us, to awaken out of all sleep, of Security or Stupidity; to arise, and take our Bibles, turn to, and learn that lesson, not by [47] Rote only, but by Heart. I Pet. 5.8. Be SOBER, be VIGILANT; because your adversary the Devil, goes about as a ROARING LYON seeking whom amongst you he may distress, delude, and devour. And let this warning have suitable Impressions on us all.

First, according to our Spiritual State, respecting our Regeneracy, or Unregeneracy: And therefore.

1. Let Regenerate Souls, that are in good hope of their Interest in GOD, and his Covenant, stir up themselves to Confirm and Improve, that Interest to the uttermost. Under shaking dispensations, we should take the faster hold of GOD by Faith, and cleave the closer to him, that Satan may not, by any of his Devices or Operations, draw us from our stedfastness, of hope, and dependence, on the God of our Salvation. We would hope we are Interested in the Everlasting Covenant of GOD, and delivered from the Raging Tyranny of the Roaring Lyon. It is good to be sure, and too sure we cannot be at any time, much less at such a time as this: That it may appear before Angels and Men, that we are chosen unto Salvation, by the GOD of Jerusalem, & are accordingly devoted to him, and to his service in an Unvoilable Covenant, against which the gates of Hell shall never have any power. And the clearing up that we are in Covenant with GOD, is a Soveraign Antidote, a- [48] gainst all attempts of Satan, to bring us into Covenant with him, or Subjection to him. And in order to this let us be Awakened.

First, To put our selves, upon faithful and thorow Tryal and examination, what hath bin amiss. We all, even the best of us, have by sin a hand and share, in Provoking God thus to let Satan loose, in an unusual manner, WHO can say he is clean? This is a time then, for Solemn-self-examination.

In this time of sore affliction, there should be great Searchings of heart, as there was for the Divisions of Reuben; Judges 5 : 19. GOD is a GOD of Wisdome, A Righteous & Holy GOD, and he never afflicts the people of his Covenant without a Cause, and that Cause is always Just: We should go, as far as we can in the search, by the light of conscience, conducted by the Rule of the word, and when we can go no farther, we should pray the prayer of Job : chap, 10, 2. Do not condemn me; show me wherefore thou Contendest with me. Yet was he Upright, and (even in God's account;) One that feared GOD, and eschewed evil, Ch 1 : 8.) The Like prayer David makes, Ps; 139 : 23, 24. Search me O GOD, and know my Heart, try me and know my thoughts. And see if there be any wicked way in me &c. These malicious operations of Satan, are the sorest afflictions can befal a person or people. And if [49] under the Consideration of Grievous Calamities, upon the People of GOD, the Nations round about, will inquire with amazement after the Cause: Then surely the People themselves, ought strictly to Examine, as Deut. 29.24. What meaneth the Heat of this great Anger? And to the making this Improvement of remarkable Afflictions, we are directed by the Example of the Church, Lam. 3.40. Let us Search and Try our Ways, and Turn again unto the Lord. Which leads to the second thing.

2. Add then to the former, True and unfeigned Reformation, of whatsoever appears to be the Provoking Evils, we fall into. He or they that to Serious Examination, (which must be supposed to include Hearty Confession of what hath been amiss) Adds thorow Reformation, may only hope to obtain Pardoning Mercy at the Hand of God, Prov. 28.13 And may it not be said, even to the Purest Churches, as he said to them, 2 Chron. 28.10. but are there not with you, even with you Sins against the LORD your God. And certainly, no Provokings are so abhorred of the Lord, as those of his Sons and Daughters, Deut. 32.19. This Returning and Reforming then, is the Duty Required of, and Pressed upon Israel, or the Visible Covenant People of God, when by sin they had departed from him, Hosea 14.1. O ISRAEL, Return unto the Lord thy God, for [50] thou hast fallen by thine Iniquity. Hence the neglect of this Returning, in those that are under many and great Afflictions, is very displeasing unto God, Amos 4.11. And ye were as a Fire-brand pluckt out of the Burning, yet have ye not returned unto me, saith the Lord. Insomuch, that obstinate persisting, in the neglect of it, after frequent Warnings, provokes the Lord, to punish those that are guilty thereof, seven and seven times more, Lev. 26. 23, 24. If we would then, avoid the displeasure, and obtain the Covenant Favour of GOD, we must both in Profession, and practice, fall in with the Example, of the formerly Dagenerous, but afterwards Reformed Ephraim, Jer. 31.18, 19. Turn thou me, and I shall be turned; for thou art the Lord my God. Surely after that I was Turned, I Repented, and after that I was Instructed, I smote upon my Thigh, &c. Then, and not till then, will the Bowels of the LORD, be turned within him, and his Repentings kindled together for us. Now that our Reformation may be unto Divine Acceptation, it must be,

"the Devil hath been raised"

First Personal and particular (in universalibus latst dolus) We commonly say, that which is every Bodies work, is no Bodies work. Every one is guilty, in the Provocation, and therefore every one should apply themselves to Reformation. Every one of us should set our selves to do our own Duty, and Repent of our own Sin. [51] There is an inclination in the best, to Charge the Sins of others, as the procuring cause of GODS Judgments and to reflect severely on the Pride, Lukewarmness, Covetousness, Contention, Intemperance, and Uneven Conversation of others; but we can hardly be brought, to smite upon our own Breast, and say, What have I done? Unless we be, in particular Charged, and Convicted, as David was by the Prophet Nathan, in the 2 Sam. 12.7. Thou art the man. Thou art he (qs.d.) that art concerned in this Provocation by thy Transgression.

Secondly, Reformation, (by which we may clear up, that we are the Covenant People of God) must be Universal. We must turn from all and every sin which hath been Committed, and apply our selves to the discharge of every Duty, which hath been neglected. We must have no sinful Reserves, as he, 2 Kings 5.18. In this thing pardon thy Servant, &c. He was Convicted it was a Sin, that needed Pardon, and yet would fain be Excused in the Commission thereof. Thus Junius, and Trem. and the Dutch Annotators Translate it, and Pisc. Interprets it of his desire to continue in that Office, which he could not with good Conscience discharge. Though some Learned and Judicious understand it as a craving of pardon for what he had therein done amiss in time past. In short so far as we are guil- [52] ty of Reservations in our Reformation so far will there remain a Cloud upon the Evidences of our covenant Interest in GOD that hath Chosen Jerusalem. This to Regenerate Souls. Secondly then

Let Unregenerate sinners, be warned and awakned, to get out of that miserable state of sin, and consequently of subjection to Satan, (That Tyrannical, Implacable, and Indefatigable, Enemy of souls) in which you are. O break off your sins by repentance, and your Iniquities by a saving closure with the LORD JESUS CHRIST, for Justification, Sanctification & Salvation, That ye may be delivered, from the power, and dominion of Satan, under which you are ensnared, to do his will, although utterly cross to the will of GOD, and may be translated, into the Kingdom of the Lord Jesus; the Dear Son of God, and Blessed Saviour of the souls of men Col: 1.13. Being by infinite mercy, recovered out of the snare of the Devil, who are (now) taken Captive by him at his will. 2 Tim: 2,16. Awake, Awake then, I beseech you, and remain no longer under the Dominion of that Prince of Cruelty and malice, whose Tyrannical Fury, we see thus exerted, against the Bodies and Minds of these afflicted persons. Surely no Sinner in this Congregation, who is sensible of his Bondage to Satan, that cruel (and worse than Egyptian) Task-mas- [53] ter, and Tyrant, can be willing, to continue quietly, in subjection to him one day or hour longer. Thus much in respect of the Spiritual State of men.

Secondly This warning is directed to all manner of persons, according to their condition of life, both in civil and sacred Order: Both High and Low, Rich and Poor, Old and Young, Bond and Free. O let the observation, of these amazing dispensations of GODS unusual and strange providence, quicken us to our Duty at such a time as this, in our respective Places and Stations, Relations, and Capacities. The GREAT GOD, hath done such things amongst us, as do make the ears of those that hear them to tingle; Jer. 1, 3. and serious soules, are at a loss to what these things may grow; and what we shall find to be the end, of this dreadfull visitation, in the permission whereof the provoked GOD as a Lyon hath roared; who can but Fear? The LORD hath spoken, who can but Prophecy? Amos 3:8. The Loud Trumpet of God, in this thundring providence, is Blown in the City, and the Echo of it, is heard throughout the Country, surely then, the People must, and ought to be afraid, Amos 3:6.

USE II.

Let it be for DEEP HUMILIATION, to [54] the people of this place which is in special under the influence of this Fearful Judgment of GOD. The Lord doth at this day, manage a great controversy with you, to the astonishment of your selves and others. You are therefore, to be deeply humbled, and sit in the dust Considering.

First, The signal hand of God, in singling out this place, this poor Village, for the first seat of Satans Tyranny, and to make it (as 'twere) the Rendezvous of Devils, where they Muster their infernal forces appearing to the afflicted, as coming Armed, to carry on their malicious designs, against the Bodies, and if God in mercy prevent not, against the Souls of many in this place. Great Afflictions, attended with Remarkable circumstances, do surely call for, more then ordinary degrees of Humiliation.

But Secondly be Humbled also, That so many Members of this Church, of the LORD JESUS CHRIST, should be under the influences of Satans malice, in these his Operations; some as the Objects of his Tyranny, on their Bodies to that degree of distress, which none can be sensible of, but those that see and feel it, who are in the mean time also, sorely distressed in their minds, by frightful Representations, made by the Devils unto them. Other professors, & visible Members of this Church, are under the awful accusa-

"the Devil hath been raised"

tions, and imputations, of being the Instruments of Satan [55] in his mischievous actings. It cannot but be matter of deep humiliation, to such as are Innocent, that the Righteous and Holy GOD, should permit them to be named, in such pernicious and unheard of practices, and not only so, but that HE who cannot but do right, should suffer the stain of suspected Guilt, to be as it were Rubbed on, and Soaked in, by many sore and amazing circumstances; and it is matter of foul abasement, to all that are in the Bond of GODS Holy Covenant in this place, that Satans seat should be amongst them, where he attempts to set up his Kingdom, in Opposition to Christs Kingdom, and to take some of the Visible Subjects of our LORD JESUS, and use at least their shapes and appearances, instrumentally, to Afflict and Torture, other Visible Subjects of the same Kingdom. Surely his design is, that CHRISTS Kingdom, may be divided against it self, that being thereby weakned, he may the better take Opportunity to set up his own accursed powers and Dominions. It calls aloud then, to all in this place, in the Name of the Blessed JESUS and words of his Holy Apostle; I Pet. 5 : 6. Humble yourselves, under the mighty hand of God, thus lift up in the midst of you, and he shall exalt, save, and deliver you, in due time. [56]

95

USE III.

It is matter of TERROR, Amazement, and Astonishment, to all such wretched Souls (if there be any here in the Congregation, (and God of his Infinite mercy grant that none of you may ever be found such) as have given up their Names, and Souls, to the Devil: who by Covenant explicite or implicite, have bound themselves to be his Slaves and Drudges, consenting to be instruments, in whose shapes, he may Torment and Afflict their Fellow Creatures (even of their own kind,) to the amazing and astonishing of the standers by.

I would hope, I might have spared this Use, but I desire (by Divine assistance) to declare the whole Counsel of God; and if it come not as Conviction where it is so, it may serve for Warning, that it may never be so: For it is a most dreadful thing to consider, that any should change the service of GOD, for the service of the Devil, the worship of the Blessed GOD for the worship of the cursed Enemy, of GOD and Man. But Oh! (which is yet a Thousand times worse) how shall I name it? If any that are in the Visible Covenant of God, should break that covenant, and make a League with Satan, if any that have set down and eat at CHRISTS Table should so lift up their Heel against him, [57] as to have Fellowship at the Table of Devils; and (as it hath been represented to some of the Afflicted) Eat of the Bread, and Drink

*The Documentary Evidence**The Documentary Evidence*

of the Wine, that Satan hath mingled. Surely if this be so, the Poet is in the right; Audax omnia perpeti, Gens Humana ruit, per vetitum nefas. Audacious Mortals are grown to a fearful height of Impiety. And we must cry out in Scripture Language, and that Emphatical Apostrophe of the Prophet Jeremy; chap. 2.12. Be astonished O ye Heavens at this, and be horribly afraid; be ye very Desolate, saith the Lord. Now Terrors may justly seiz upon those, that have so done, on these accounts.

First, All Mankind is now (as well by Gods Authority, as their own Interest) set against you. You have proclaimed your selves Mortal Enemies to all men, and they cannot but mortally hate and abominate you. If you are in League with the DESTROYER, what is said of Ishmael is true, not only of Satan, but also of you, Gen.16.12. His Hand will be against every man and every mans hand against him: So every mans hand is, and will be against you, to accuse, condemn, destroy and cut you off from the Land of the Living, The Enmity that God in just Judgment placed, betwixt the Old Serpent and the Woman, and betwixt her Seed, and his Seed, Gen.3. 15. is improved to the height a- [58] gainst you, as you Stand, Look and Act, like your Father and King the Devil.

2. If you have been guilty of such Impiety, The Prayers of the People of God, are against you on that account. It is their Duty to Pray daily, that Satans Kingdom may be Suppressed, Weakened, brought down, and at last totally destroyed; hence that all Abetters, Subjects, Defenders, and Promoters thereof, may be utterly Crushed and Confounded. They are constrained, to Suppress that Kindness and Compassion, that in their Sacred Addresses, they once bare unto you (as those of their own kind, and framed out of the same mould). Praying with one consent, as the Royal Prophet did against his malicious Enemies (the Instruments of Satan) Psal. 109.6. Set thou a wicked man over him, and let Satan stand at his Right-hand (i.e.) to withstand all that is for his good, and promote all that is for his hurt, and ver. 7. When he is Judged, let him be condemned, and let his Prayer become Sin. What a miserable condition must they be in, who have all the Faithful, that have Interest in Heaven thus engaged against them? But

Thirdly, If this seems a light thing KNOW, That if you are in Covenant with the Devil, the Intercession of the BLESSED JESUS is against you, for your Contract with his Grand Implacable Enemy. His Prayer is for the Subdu- [59] ing of Satans Power and Kingdom, and the utter Confounding of all his Instruments. He is Exalted at the Right hand of GOD, to make Intercession for his Elect, as also expecting, till all his Enemies (and such are all the Sworn Subjects and Vassals of Satan) be made his Footstool (i.e.) put to shame, and Everlasting Contempt, Psal. 110.1. Heb. 10.13. Hence in the Text,

"the Devil hath been raised"

He Intercedes with GOD the FATHER for Joshua and the People, against Satan and all his Powers and Instruments. And the LORD (i.e.) The INTERCESSOR) said unto Satan, the Lord Rebuke thee, &c.

Lastly, If it be so, Then the GREAT GOD is set against you. The Omnipotent JEHOVAH One God in three Persons, FATHER, SON, and HOLY GHOST in Their Several distinct Operations, and all Their Divine Attributes, are ingaged against you: as it hath been already noted, they are against Satan: even so because you are his Ofspring, Officers, Instruments, of mischiefs, cruelty; murther &c. Against you. You justify the Old Subjection, made by our first Parents in the Transgression, of themselves (and for theirs) to the Dominion of Satan, and shew, that if it were to be done again you would do the same. Therefore KNOW YEE, that are guilty of such Monstrous Iniquity, That since you are the People, that have no more understanding, than to forsake the Covenant of your God, to enter [60] into Covenant with Satan: He that made you, will not save you, and he that formed you will show you no favour, Isa. 27.11. And so you are utterly undone for ever, unless by the Infinite Power and Mercy of GOD, you are rescued out of the horrible Pit, and snare of THE Destroyer. Be assured, that although you should now Evade, the Condemnation of mans Judgment, and escape a violent death by the Hand of Justice: Yet unless God shall give you Repentance, (which we heartily pray for) there is a day coming, when the Secrets of all Hearts shall be Revealed by JESUS CHRIST, Rom. 2.16. Then, Then your sin will find you out; and you shall be punished with Everlasting Destraction, from the Presence of the LORD, and Doomed to those Endless, Easeless and Remediless Torments, Prepared for the Devil and his Angels, Mat. 25.41

The Reverend Mr. Simmes, some time since Minister of this Country, coming into Prison to a Condemed Witch; though he knew her not, yet she took knowledge of him, and said, O Mr. Simmes, I remember a Text you Preached on in England Twenty Four Years since, from those words, Your sin will find you out, for I find it to be true in mine own case.

USE IV.

Let it be for CAUTION to all of us that are [61] before the Lord: As ever we would prevaile with God, to prevent the spreading of this sore affliction, and to rebuke Satan for us; Let us take heed of sideing with, or giving place unto, the Divel Ephes. 4 : 27 Neither give place to the Devil, yield no subjection to him no not for an hour Thus we may be said to do in general, when we give way voluntarily, to the Commission of any sin, he that Committeth sin (i:e) sinneth sciens volens, wittingly, and willingly, is of the Divel, 1 John 3 : 8. (i.e.) Joynet with him in his rebellion against GOD, hence the more there is, of a Man's will in any sin, the more he is rendred like Satan, who willeth nothing but sin from the beginning. Ibid. And it gratifies the Devil, because the man appears captivated by that sin, hence so far as the Regenerate fall into known sin, they please the Devil, and are (in a sort) guilty of yielding to him, and siding with him.

And we do especially, give place to him by these sins.

First, By giving way unto sinful and unruly Passions, such as Envy, Malice, or Hatred of our Neighbours and Brethren. These Devil like, corrupted passions, are contrary unto, and do endanger the letting out of, the life of grace and Holyness; and letting in Satan and his Temptations, yea he generally, comes into the soul at these Doors, to captivate any person to the horrid sin of Covenanting with him. These are greedy and insatiable Passi- [62] ons, that strike at the being as well as the good of the Object, and to gratify these, many have been Overcome by Satans temptations, so that (as the wise man saith in another case He hath wounded; yea many strong men have been slain by him, Prov: 7: 26. And as for you of this place, you may do well Seriously to Examine, whether the LORD hath not in Righteous Judgment sent this Fire of his Holy displeasure, to put out some Fires of Contention, that have been amongst you by which the Fruits of the Spirit Gal. 5.22. Have been (as I may say) much Blasted, and the Fruits of the Flesh Cherished to maturity, so as to threaten the Choaking of all that is good, with the Principles thereof; through the Malice of your Adversary the Devil, who is now come down among you, with open mouth as a Roaring Lyon to devour you: by setting you one against another with earnestness, He sows discord amongst bretheren (both in Civil and Sacred Order Prov. 6, 19. Stirring them up to bite and devour one another, that they may be consumed one of another, Gal: 5.15. Upon this ground the Apostle brings in this Caution Ephes. 4.26. Let not the Sun go down upon your wrath, Neither give place to the Devil. Inveterate Anger and Ill–will, makes way for the Devil, and gives place to him. And the same we do

Secondly, By using indirect means to prevent or remove this affliction; and trying unwarrantable [63] projects, to reveal Secrets, or discover future events. When persons have been under long exercise, those about them are very desirous, to relieve them out of, or prevent those grievous fits, of Diabolical tortures, with which they are distressed. And hence do not consider the Efficacy or Tendency of those things they use. I call such indirect means, as being duely observed, cannot be found to have any Natural or Physical virtue in them, to produce the Desired Effect of themselves: Nor yet have

"the Devil hath been raised"

any warrant from the word of GOD, which if they had; ought to be believed and depended upon, to produce the Effect for which they were Instituted; tho' never so mean in their own nature. Because the Power of the GREAT GOD, is engaged, to uphold the decisive influence of his own instituted means, as we find in the bitter water which caused the curse, Num: 5 : 17. which was onely compounded, of Holy Water (or common water set apart unto sacred use) and the dust of the floor of the sanctuary: This we may imagine had not any physical influence in its own nature, proportionable, to such a solemn effect or consequence, as was in that case appointed thereunto; It must then depend, wholly and onely, on the Divine Institution of it, to be for the Cursing, or Clearing, of the woman as she was in the sight of GOD, Guilty or not Guilty; as we read ver. 27 and 28. viz. if Guilty her Belly should Swell, and her Thigh should Rot, if [64] clear, she should be free (i.e.) from any hurt and should Conceive Seed. But seeing we find no means instituted of God, to make Tryal of Witches, or to Charm away Witchcraft, (both which are a kind of Witchcraft) we are to expect Effects in the ordinary course of Providence, suitable to the natural vertue of Causes, and means used accordingly; but what is otherwise, must be of the Nature of Inchantments; these indirect means, are such as, Burning the Afflicted Persons Hair; parings of Nails, stopping up and boyling the Urine. Their Scratching the Accused, or otherwise fetching Blood of them, with many more, which I forbear to mention, least unwary persons should be inclined to try these Diabolical Feats. But as to the Effect, this is plainly found, a Giving place to the Devil, for he giving way to it, and Ceasing to Afflict, upon the use of it, brings such projects into Esteem, and Gaines to his own Devices (for I can call them no better) too much Credit and Observance: For hence such as use them, finding him flee thereupon, are encouraged to the frequent use of them, and are (as a Learned Writer saith) made Witches, by endeavouring, to defend themselves against Witchcraft, and using the Devils Shield, against the Devils Sword, or (as I may allude) going down to the Philistines, to have those Weapons sharpened and pointed, with which we [65] intend to Fight against them.

In a word, is it because there is not a GOD in the midst of us, able to Rebuke and Vanquish Satan, in all his Operations: If there be, then away with whatsoever hath not Scripture Precept or President for its Warrantee. And let us use those Weapons, which are not Carnal, but Mighty through God, to the pulling down strong Holds, Etc. 2 Cor. 10.4. Thus may we put to the worse, those Principalities and Powers of Darkness which do in such a fearful manner, wrestle and Contend with us at this time, Ephes. 6.12.

But I must not conclude this particular, without testifing against some other practises amongst us Condemned by the Rule of God, and writings of learned and judicious men as yielding to, and tampring with the Divel, Viz the sieve and scyssers; the Bible and Key; The white of an Egge in a Glass; The horse shooe nailed on the threshold; A stone hung over the Rack in a stable with many more: which I would not make known to any, that are ignorant of them; because they are no better than Conjurations, and if in the use of them Discoveryes are made; or Effects produced, to the gratifying their sinful Curiosity in any degree, it must be from the Devil, and not from GOD; who never instituted any such ways, by and in which, to discover secret things or future Events to the Children of Men. [66] Hence such as by these Experiments, adventure to play or the hole of the aspe, and approach unto the Den of the Dragons; are in great Danger to become a prey unto Satans malice, being (or ever they are aware seduced by his subtilty into an intire subjection to his Infernal powers, so as last to be Destroyed by him, and cast with him into the Lake that burneth with Fire and Brim stone for ever.

Thirdly, Give no place to the Devil by Rash Censuring of others, without sufficient grounds, or false accusing any willingly. This is indeed to be like the Devil, who hath the Title Diabolical in the Greek, because he is a Calumniator, or False Accuser. Hence when we read of such false Accusers in the Latter Days, they are in the Original called (Diabon) Calumniateres, 2 Tim. 3.3. It is a time of Temptation amongst you such as never was before: Let me intreat you not to be lavish or severe in reflecting on the Malice or Envy of your Neighbours, by whom any of you have been accused lest while you falsely charge one another viz. The Relations of the Afflicted, and Relations of the Accused; the Grand Accuser (who loves to Fish in Troubled Water) should take advantage upon you. Look to Sin the procuring cause, GOD in Justice of Soveraign Efficient, and Satan THE Enemy, principal Instrument, both in afflicting some and accusing others: And if Innocent Persons [67] suspected, it is to be ascribed to GODS pleasure supreamly permitting, and Satans Malice subordinately troubling, by Representation of such to the Afflicting of others, even of which as have all the while, we have reason to believe, (especially some of them) no kind of Ill will, or disrespect, unto those that have been complained of by them. This giving place to the Devil avoid, for it will have uncomfortable and pernicious influence, upon the Affairs of this place, by letting out Peace, and bringing in Confusion and every evil work which we heartily pray, God in mercy to prevent. Fourthly and Lastly,

Then we give place to the Devil, When we are guilty of unbelief of God, and his Power, promise and Providence; for our benefit and relief under our troubles. Unbelief betrayed our first Parents, to the first sin. The Devil in the serpent, first moved them to question the truth of the Threatning, and

"the Devil hath been raised"

so they came to deny it Gen. 3.1 and 4. yielding to the God of this world, the Author and main Fomenter of Unbelief, by and in which he reignes over the children of perdition, 2 Cor. 4.4. Unbelief is a mother sin, & there are many sins, to which men could not be drawn, were it not for Unbelief of the Threatnings, denounced in the word of GOD against that sin, which they do so boldly perpetrate and of the Promise made unto the contrary Duty, which they do so a- [68] bominably neglect. Indeed Unbeleif of the truth of God's promise, or Efficacy of His providence, extending towards us (these being Inseparable attributes of the Blessed God) brings in question whether he is or hath a being. For he can as soon cease to Be as to be most Powerful, most Faithful, most Gracious, and Bountiful, which are all Attributes relating to his Providence, and this is to go away from GOD For he that cometh to GOD, must believe that he is Heb. 11 : 6. Hence the Apostle, Cautions even the brethren, that they may not be guilty of it, Heb 3: 12. Take heed Brethren lest there be in any of you, an evil heart of Unbelief, Departing from the Living God. Intimating, that so far as the best fall into Unbelief, they go from God, and so far must needs give place to the Divel. For there are but these two Rulers, over all men in the world, and all that leave the one go to the other. But to proceed.

USE V

Let it be for EXHORTATION and direction, to this whole Assembly, and to all others that shall come to the knowledge of these amazeing dispensations, Here then give me leave, to press those special Dutyes, which all persons are concerned to put in practice, at such a time as this.

1. Be we Exhorted and directed, to Excercise True Spiritual sympathy with, and Compassion towards, those poor afflicted persons, that are by Divine Permission, under the Direful Influences of Satan's malice [69] Deep sense of all these things, and being heartily affected with them, makes way for, and stirs up unto, those other dutys which are now incumbent on us. I fear we are not enough affected, with this solemn providence, unless it be those few that have seen these fearful things who by their eyes, have had their hearts affected accordingly. There is a Divine Precept enjoyning the practice of this Duty, Heb. 13.3. Remember them that suffer Adversity, as being your selves also in the Body; (i.e.) being of the same mould; in the same mortal and frail Estate; and therefore liable to the same Affliction, if the Holy GOD should please to permit Satan to bring it upon us: Let us then be deeply sensible, and as the Elect of God, put on Bowels of Mercy, towards those in misery, Col. 3.12. Oh Pitty, Pitty them, for the Hand of the LORD hath touched

The Documentary Evidence

them, and the Malice of Devils hath fallen upon them.

Secondly, Let us be sure to take unto us and PUT ON, the whole Armour of God, and every piece of it, let none be wanting. Let us labour to be in the Exercise, and Practice, of the whole Company of Sanctifying Graces, and Religious Duties. This Important Duty is pressed, and the particular pieces, of that Armour recited, Eph. 6.11. and 13 to the 18. Satan is Representing his Infernal Forces, and the Devils seem to come Armed, mustering amongst us. I am this [70] day Commanded to call and Cry an Alarm unto you, ARM; ARM; ARM; handle your Arms, see that you are fixed and in a readiness, as faithful Souldiers under the Captain of our Salvation, that by the Shield of FAITH, ye and we All may Resist the Fiery Darts of the Wicked. And may be Faithful unto Death, in our Spiritual Warfare, so shall we assuredly Receive the Crown of Life, Rev. 2.10.

Thirdly, Let us be watchful, to take all advantages and strenuously to improve all means (unto which the word directs us) for the managing of our spiritual conflict, with the Powers of Darkness. Let us admit no parley, give no quarter, let none of Satans Forces or Furies, be more vigilant to hurt us than we are to resist & repress them in the NAME and by the Spirit, Grace, and Strength, of Our LORD JESUS CHRIST. Let us watch the first motions of the Enemy, for if we let him get within us, he will certainly be too hard for us. Let us take the Apostles Counsel; James 4 : 7. Resist the Devil and he will flee from you. but qs.d. if you yield to him by Flight, he will pursue you, to the very Death. Avoid therefore all fellowship with him, under any of his insinuating presences, and let us Wrestle, vigorously, against Principalities and Powers, &c. Ephes. 6. 12, Let us make sure, that in nothing we give them advantage against us, seeing (through Grace) we are not Ignorant of Satans devices 2. Cor. 1. 11. [71]

Fourthly, Let us Ply the Throne of Grace, in the Name and Merit, of Our Blessed Mediator. With our Frequent, Faithful, and Fervent Prayers. Let us be Frequent in the Duty, taking all possible Opportunities. Publick, Private and Secret, to Pour out our Supplications, to the GOD of our Salvation, Prayer is the most proper, and potent Antidote, against the old Serpent's Venemous Operations. When Legions of Devils, do come down amongst us; Multitudes of Prayers should go up to God; for suitable Grace and Strength, to defend us, from being deceived, and destroyed by them in that case of the Apostle Paul, when he was under the violent Assaults of a Messenger of Satan. He doubled and trebled his Ordinary Devotions; For this I besought the Lord thrice, that It might depart from me. 2. Cor. 12.8.

Again let us be faithful in Prayer. The life of Prayer, lyes in the Exercise of Faith therein It is to the Prayer of Faith that the Promise of Answer is made;

"the Devil hath been raised"

by Him in whom all the Promises, are Yea and Amen; Math: 21.21. Whatsoever ye ask believing in my Name, ye shall receive it. Be sides It is said the prayer of Faith, shall save the Sick; James 5. 15. (i.e.) Whatsoever kind of sickness it is, under which they labour. Faith in Prayer, engageth the glorious Intercessor on our behalf, according to his promise, and thereby makes way for us to be accepted with the FATHER, in all our requests, Faith in CHRIST [72] Excercised in prayer, is the Token, of Gods Covenant, with his Elect under the Gospel, As the bow in the Clouds, was the token of his Covenant with the world, in the dayes of Noah; Gen. 9. 12, 13. And through Christ it is prevalent, for him the Father heareth always, Joh: 11.42. And therefore us also through him For He hath made us accepted, in the Beloved; Ephe 1.6.

103

Yet once more, Let ours be Fervent prayers; even with our whole heart, Psal. 119.10. for such Prayer (only) hath the promise, of finding God and his Salvation. Then shall ye find me, when ye seek me with all your heart, Jer. 29.13. Hence David pronounceth all those blessed, that thus seek the LORD Ps. 119.2. This is when we do Rouze up our Soul, with all its faculties unto Prayer, as the Psalmist doth unto praise, Psal. 103. 1. 2. When our whole Soul in all its affections are poured out before the Lord as Hannah 1 Sam. 1. 15. This prayer is like to speed, we say amongst men, Out timmide rogat, docet negare; he that begs faintly, may expect a denyal. And in this case Justly; the Apostle James tell us, Let not such a man as is Faint, Weak, Doubting In prayer, Expect any thing of the LORD, James 1 : 7. yet on the other hand, the same Apostle assures us the Effectual fervent prayer, of a Righteous man AVAILETH MUCH Chap 5 : 16. This Faithful and Fervent Prayer, frequently put in [73] practice, is the most Powerful Exorcisme, to drive away Devils; some of which, will not stir without it, Mark9.29. This Kind can come forth by nothing, but by Prayer and Fasting.

Let us then use this Weapon; It hath a kind of Omnipotency, because it interesteth us, in the help of THE OMNIPOTENT: Satan the worst of all our Enemies, is called in Scripture a DRAGON, to note his Malice; a SERPENT to note his Subtilty; a LYON to note his Strength. But none of all these can stand before Prayer, The most inveterate Malice, (as that of Haman) Sinks under the Prayer of Esther; chap. 4.16. The deepest policy (the counsel of Achitophel) Withers before the Prayer of David. 2 Sam.15. 31. And the vastest Army (an Host of a Thousand Thousand Ethiopians) Ran away like so many Cowards, before the prayer of Asa. 2 Chron. 14. 11, 12.

What therefore I say unto one, I say unto all, in this Important Case; PRAY, PRAY, PRAY.

Fifthly and Lastly; To Our HONOURED MAGISTRATES, here present this day, to inquire into these things; Give me leave much Honoured; to offer One word, to your Consideration, Do all that in you Lyes, to Check and Rebuke Satan; Endeavouring by all wayes and meanes, that are according to the Rule of GOD to discover his In- [74] struments in these Horrid Operations: You are Concerned in the Civil Government of this People, being invested with Power, by their Sacred MAJESTIES; under this Glorious JESUS, (the King and Governour of his Church) for the Supporting, of CHRIST'S Kingdome, against all Oppositions of Satans Kingdom, and his Instruments. Being Ordained of GOD to such a station, Rom. 13.1. We entreat you, bear not the sword in vain, as Ver. 4. But approve your selves, a Terrour of, and Punishment to, evil doers; and a Praise to them that do well. I Pet. 2. 14. Ever remembering, that ye Judge not for men, but for the Lord; 2 Chron. 15.6. and as his promise is so our Prayer shall be for you without Ceasing, that he would be with you in the Judgment, As he that can and will, Direct, Assist, and Reward you. Follow the Example, of the Upright Job, Chap. 29. 16. Be a Father to the poor; to these poor Afflicted persons, (in pittiful and painful, endeavours to help them) and the Cause that seems to be so dark, as you know not how to determine it, do your utmost in the use of all regular means to search it out. And if after all, it still remains too hard for you, carry it unto GOD by Christ as the Israelites were ordered, to do theirs by Moses; Deut. 1. 17. For the Judgment is Gods, and the cause that is too hard for you, bring unto me, and I will hear it. [75]

104

USE VI.

The Sixth and Last USE, is in two words of Comfort, to bear up the fainting Souls of those that are Personally under, or Relatively Concerned in, these direfull Operations, of the GRAND Enemy of Mankind.

First, there is Comfort for you, in that ye are the visible Covenant People of GOD. In General, this whole People of New England, As to the maine bulk of them (or in and by their Godly Leaders, who engage themselves & all under them, both in Civil & Sacred Order) are in Covenant with GOD, and have many times (as such) been signally owned by Him; notwithstanding all their Defections and Degeneracies. Besides, there are many that have been both Explicitely, and Implicitely; Visibly and Really Devoted themselves to God: And are indeed of the Number Chosen by the GOD of Jerusalem; True Citizens of that Jerusalem that is above, which is the Mother of us all, Gal. 4.26. Yea, some of those, that are under these Afflictions, may plead these Priviledges, to prevail with the LORD, to Rebuke Satan, and Deliver them and theirs, from these his malicious and woful Oppressions. Add to this, that

"the Devil hath been raised"

there are scarce any, who are under the influence, of this Affliction, but are also under the Solemn Obligation, of a Baptismal Covenant, which in its own nature, ob- [76] ligeth them, to be for God, and is a valid Argument to plead with GOD to be for them, and against Satan. Put all these together, and surely we shall not cast away our Confidence in GOD, for deliverance from these sore Calamities. For we are all his people on one account or other : And the LORD will not forsake his people, because it hath pleased him to make you his People, I Sam.12. 22 But Secondly,

2. There is Comfort, in Considering, that the LORD JESUS the Captaine of our Salvation, hath already overcome the Devil, CHRIST that Blessed Seed of the woman, hath given this cursed old Serpent, called the Devil, and Satan, a mortal, and incurable, Bruise on the head, Gen 3 : 15. He was too hard for him in a Single conflict Matth 4 : Beg : He opposed his Power and King-dom in the Possessed; He suffered not the Devils To speak, Because they knew him Mark 11 : 34. He compleated his Victory, by his Death on the Cross, and Destroyed his Dominion, Hebr 2 : 14. That through Death he might destroy Death, and him that had the Powers of Death, that is the DEVIL; and by and after His Resurection, made shew openly unto the world, that he had sported Principalities; and Powers, Triumphing over them Col 2: 15. Hence, if we are by Faith united to him, his victory is an earnest and and praelibation of our Conquest at last. All Satans struglings now, are but those of a Conquered enemy; [77] to a believer: And although He may give a Child of God, great Exercise, in his way to the Kingdom, such as may often bring him to his knees, in earnest prayers, to God for more Grace, yet it may be truly said of him, which was Prophetically said of God, Gen 49 : 19 A Troop shall overcome him, but he shall overcome at the last. The Exaltation also, of Our LORD JESUS, doth assure us, that we shall be Exalted, to the throne of Glory with him, Rev 3 : 21. Comfort we then, one another with these words That the God of Peace, Even JESUS the Prince of Peace, will Totally & Finally, Bruise Satan under our feet, and that shortly, Rom. 16.20. It will be but a Little, Little while, before we shall enter into, and take Pos-session of, that place, into which shall in no wise enter, any thing that defileth, neither worketh abomination, or maketh a Lye, Rev. 21. 27. where we shall sin no more, sorrow no more, Nor the Spiritual Wickedness, afflict us any more for ever.

To conclude; The Lord is known by the Judgments which he Executes in the midst of us. The Dispensations of his providence, appear to be Unsearchable, and his doings past finding out. He seems to have allowed Satan, to afflict many of our people, and that thereupon he is come down in Great wrath, threatning the Destruction of the Bodyes and (if the Infinite

The Documentary Evidence

mercy of GOD prevent not) of the Souls of many in this place. Yet [78] may we say in the midst of the terrible things which he doth in righteousness; He alone is the GOD of our Salvation, who represents himself, as the Saviour of all that are in a low and distressed Condition, because he is good, and His mercy endureth for ever.

Let us then Return, & Repent, rent our hearts, and not our Garments. Who can tell, if the Lord will Return in mercy unto us? And by his Spirit lift up a Standard, against the GRAND Enemy, who threatens to come in like a Flood, among us, and overthrow all that is Holy, and Just, and Good. It is no small comfort, to consider, that Job's exercise of Patience, had its beginning from the Devil; but we have seen the End to be from the LORD. James 5. 11. That we also, may find by experience, the same Blessed Issue, of our present distresses, by Satan's Malice. Let us Repent of every Sin, that hath been Committed; and Labour to practice, every Duty which hath been Neglected. And when we are Humbled, and Proved for our good in the latter end: Then we shall assuredly, and speedily find, that the Kingly Power of Our LORD and SAVIOUR, shall be Magnifyed, in delivering his Poor Sheep and Lambs, out of the Jaws, and Paws, of the Roaring Lyon.

Then will JESUS the Blessed Antitype of [79]
Joshua, the Redeemer, and Chooser of Jerusa-
lem, Quell, Suppress, and utterly Vanquish, this
Adversary of ours, with Irresistible
Power and Authority, according to
our Text. And the Lord said unto
Satan, the Lord Rebuke thee O
Satan, Even the LORD that hath
Chosen Jerusalem, Rebuke
thee: is not his a
Brand pluckt out of
the FIRE?

F   I   N   I   S.

(Deodat Lawson, Christs Fidelity the Only Shield
Against Satans Malignity [Boston, 1693] p. 1-79)

"the Devil hath been raised"

FRIDAY, MARCH 25, 1692

Samuel Sibley Vs. John Procter

This revealing document shows that all did not believe the afflicted persons to be bewitched. John Procter, Sr., about 60 years of age, was a yeoman and licensed tavern keeper in Salem Farmes, located just southerly of the Salem Village boundary. His maid-servant, Mary Warren, had become one of the afflicted persons. In this later sworn state-ment written in the hand of Rev. Parris, Sibley recalls Procter being very specific the day following the Nurse examination in his non-belief of the accusers and how they should be treated. By early April 1692 Procter's wife, Elizabeth, and then Procter himself were accused of practicing witchcraft.

John would later be tried. Found guilty he was hanged August 19, 1692. His wife was also condemned by the court, but as she was pregnant, her execution would be stayed until she gave birth. The time was postponed long enough for the witchcraft delusion to run its course, and she was thus spared the fate of her husband.

The morning after ye examination of Goody Nurse. Sam: Sibly met John Proctor about Mr Phillips wo called to said Sibly as he was going to sd Phillips & askt how ye folks did at the village He answered he heard they were very bad last night but he had heard nothing this morning Proctor replyed he was going to fetch home his jade he left her there last night & had rather given 40d than let her come up Sd. Sibly askt why he talkd so Proctor replyed if they were let alone so we should all be Devils & witches quickly they should rather be had to the Whipping post but he would fetch his jade Home & thresh the Devil out of her & more to the like purpose crying hang them, hang them. And also added that when she was first taken with fits he kept her close to the Wheel & threatened to thresh her, & then she had no more fits till the next day he was gone forth, & then she must have her fits again firsooth &.

Jurat in Curia

Procter ownes he meant Mary Warren

attest.   *St. Sewall. Cler

[Reverse]

Sam Sibleys Evidence

(Essex County Court Archives, Salem Witchcraft Papers, I, 52)

The Documentary Evidence

Edward Putnam Vs. Rebecca Nurse

The deposistion of Edward Putman aged about 38 years ho testifieth and saith apon the 25 Day of march 1692 ann Putnam Juner was bitten by rebakah nurs as she said and about 2 of the clok the same day she was strock with her Chane the mark being in a kind of a round ring and 3 stroaks a Cros the ring she had 6 blos with a Chane in the space of half an ouer and she had one remarkable one with 6 stroaks a Cros her arme I saw the mark boath of bite and Chane.

Jurat in Curia

(Essex County Court Archives, Salem Witchcraft Papers, I,75)

Rev. Lawson's Narrative

Rev. Parris removed his 9-year-old daughter Betty from the environment of the village witch frenzy by sending her to live for a time in the Salem household of merchant and county official Stephen Sewall. In this account, Sewall later told Rev. Lawson how the girl continued to suffer fits in his household, though her afflictions gradually diminished. Betty Parris was not involved in the remainder of the legal proceedings, though Sewall was later in 1692 appointed clerk of the Special Court of Oyer and Terminer which tried the witchcraft cases.

On the 25th of March, (as Capt. Stephen Sewal, of Salem, did afterwards inform me) Eliza. Paris, had sore Fits, at his house, which much troubled himself, and his wife, so as he told me they were almost discouraged. She related, that the great Black Man came to her, and told her, if she would be ruled by him, she should have, whatsoever she desired, and go to a Golden City. She relating this to Mrs. Sewall, she told the child, is was the Divel, and he was a Lyar from the Beginning, and bid her tell him so, if he came again: which she did accordingly, at the next coming to her, in her fits.

(Deodat Lawson, A Brief and True Narrative
[Boston, 1692] p. 7)

SATURDAY, MARCH 26, 1692

Mercy Lewis Vs. Elizabeth Procter

Mercy Lewis swore to this deposition on June 30, 1692. It includes post-March information not duplicated here.

"the Devil hath been raised"

The Deposistion of Mircy lewes aged about 19 years who testifieth and that on the 26th march 1692 I saw the Apperishtion of Elizabeth proctor the wife of Jno proctor senr.: and she did most greviously tortor me by biting and pinching me most greviously urging me to writ in hir book

[Document continues]

[Reverse]

Mircy lewes against Elizabeth proctor

(Essex County Court Archives, Salem Witchcraft Papers, I, 99)

Rev. Lawson's Narrative

Lawson reports how the two Salem magistrates and a Salem minister examined little Dorcas Good.

On the 26th of March, Mr. Hathorne, Mr. Corwin, and Mr. Higison, were at the Prison-Keepers House, to Examine the Child, and it told them there, it had a little Snake that used to Suck on the lowest Joynt of it Fore-Finger; and when they inquired where, pointing to other places, it told them, not there, but there, pointing on the Lowest point of the Fore-Finger; where they Observed, a deep Red Spot, about the Bigness of a Flea-bite, they asked who gave it that Snake? whether the great Black man, it said no, its Mother gave it.

(Deodat Lawson, A Brief and True Narrative *[Boston, 1692] p. 7-8)*

SUNDAY, MARCH 27, 1692

Rev. Lawson's Narrative

Though dated April 3, this account by Lawson of the Parris sermon based on the text from John 6:70 actually took place on March 27. This particular sacrament day at the Salem Village meeting house was highly unusual and emotionally charged. Present in the congregation was Sarah Cloyce, a covenant member of the village church and sister of the recently accused and jailed Rebecca Nurse. When Parris named his text, "Christ knows how many Devils there are in his church," Cloyce saw the obvious innuendo and chose not to listen to these uncharitable and condemning words. In a strong gesture of protest Cloyce stormed from the meeting house, the door slamming behind her. Such righteous yet foolhardy action was not lost on some of the afflicted people who soon in their fits saw Cloyce participating in the Devil's sabbat. On April 8 warrants were

The Documentary Evidence

sworn out against Cloyce, along with Elizabeth Procter, on suspicion of witchcraft.

The third of April, the Lords-Day, being Sacrament-day, at the Village, Goodw. C. upon Mr. Parris's naming his Text, John 6, 70. *One of them is a Devil,* the said Goodw. C. went immediately out of the Meeting-House, and flung the door after her violently, to the amazement of the Congregation: She was afterward seen by some in their Fits, who said, "O Goodw. C. I did not think to see you here!" (and being at their Red bread and drink) said to her, "Is this a time to receive the Sacrament, you ran-away on the Lords-Day, & scorned to receive it in the Meeting-House, and, Is this a time to receive it? I wonder at you!" This is the summ of what I either saw my self, or did receive Information from persons of undoubted Reputation and Credit.

(Deodat Lawson, A Brief and True Narrative
[Boston, 1692] p. 8)

Rev. Parris' Sermon

Like most of his ministerial contemporaries, Rev. Parris put down his sermon text and notes, if not the entire sermon, on paper. One of Parris' notebooks, a small 5⅓" by 3½" bound volume, has been preserved and includes 291 pages of meticulous, easily readable notes which he could expound upon in a sermon lasting as long as three hours or more. This book contains notes for some fifty-two sermons delivered by Parris at the village between 1689 and 1694. Two of Parris's sermons dealing with witchcraft are included in this volume under March 27 and May 8, 1692, though from a reference in the book, "see these sermons in loose papers," we know that other material, not presently extant, was also produced by Parris.

In his sermon notes for March 27 Parris defined "Devils" not only as witches in league with the devil himself, but also as any notorious sinners. The thrust of his sermon, however, was inflammatory. He publicly doubted that the Devil would be allowed by God to use the form of an innocent person to afflict others. Coupled with his forceful pronouncement that within the church are both "Devils as well as Saints," Parris questioned the generally held belief that covenant membership in the church intimated righteousness. He also, however, made the caution that there are certain sins that make us Devils including, "A slanderer or an accuser of the godly." It must be remembered that this is not the full sermon as delivered and that much that Parris said and instructed concerning this topic is now unrecorded.

Christ knows how many Devils there are in his Churches, & who they are.

27 Mar. 1691/2 Sacrament day.

"the Devil hath been raised"

Occasioned by dreadfull Witchcraft broke out here a few weeks past, & one Member of this Church, & another of Salem upon public examination by Civil Authority vehemently suspected for Shee-Witches, & upon it commited

6.John.70

Have not I chosen you twelve, & one of you is a Devil. This chap. consist of .3. principal parts.
1. Part consists of a declaration of Christs miraculous feeding of 5000. with 5. loaves & 2 small fishes. 1–15. v.
2. Part treats of Christs miraculous walking upon the Sea. 15–22. v.
3. Last part consists of Christs Sermon to the Capernaites 22. v. ad finem concerning the Heavenly or truly vivifical [vivified] bread. This part consist of sundry particles. viz.
1. The occasion of this sermon. 22. 23. 24. 25. v.
2. The Sermon it self. 26–59. v.
3. Last: The event of this sermon. 59 ad finem
  Now this event consists of
1. The offence of many. 59. v etc.
2. A Reprehension of their error from whence this their, offence arose: in which Reprehension he shows them that it was not the eating of his flesh carnally but spiritually that he spake of. 61 etc.
3. Christs complaint of the incredulity of many 64. 65. v
4. An other event which was worse than the former, namely the total departure of several of his disciples from him. 66. v. Whereupon note
1. Our Lord takes occasion to ask his Disciples whither they also would desert him. 67. v.
2. Peter in the name of the rest answers by confessing #[both] the excellency both of Christs Doctrine & his Person. 68. 69. v.
3. Last: This confession Christ so approves of, that in the mean while he doth admonish them, that there is an Hypocrite among them, a Devil among them 79. 71. verses. Have not I chosen you 12. & one of you is a Devil. i.e. I have chosen 12. of you to familiarity with me, to be my Apostles, & for all one of you is a Devil.
Doctr:[ine] Our Lord Jesus Christ knows how many Devils there are in his Churches & who they are.
1. There are Devils as well as Saints in Christs Church.
2. Christ knows how many of these Devils there are.
3. Last: Christ knows who these Devils are.

The Documentary Evidence

1. Prop:[osition] There are Devils as well as Saints in the Church of Christ:
Here 3 things may be spoken to
1. Show you what is meant here by Devils

2. That there are such Devils in the Church
3. Last: That there are also some Saints in such Churches
1. What is meant here by Devils. One of you is a Devil. An:[swer] By Devil
is ordinarily meant any wickard Angel or Spirit: Sometimes it is put for the
Prince or head of the evil spirits, or fallen Angels. Sometimes it is used for
vile & wicked persons, the worst of such, who for their villany & impiety
do most resemble Devils & wicked Spirits. Thus Christ in our text calls Judas
a Devil, for his great likeness to the Devil. One of you is a Devil i.e. a Devil
for quality & disposition: not a Devil for Nature, for he was a man etc. but
a Devil for likeness & operation . 8. John. 38. 41. 44. Ye are of your Father
the Devil
2. There are such Devils in the Church: Not only sinners but notorious
sinners; sinners more like to the Devil than others. So here in Christs little Church. Text. This also Christ teacheth us in the Parable of the Taxes
13. Matth. 38. Where Christ tells us that such are the children of the wicked
one. i.e. of the Devil.
Reason: Because Hypocrites are the very worse of men corruptio optimi est
pessima. Hypocrites are the sons and heirs of the Devil, the free-holders of
hell; whereas other sinners are but Tenants. When Satan repossesseth a soul
he becomes more vile & sinfull 11. Luke. 24. 25. 26. As the Goaler layes
load of iron on him that hath escaped. None are. worse than those that have
been good, & are naught: & might be good, but will be naught.
3. Last: There are also true Saints in the Church. The Church consists of
good; & bad: as a Garden that has weeds as well as flowers: & as a field that
has wheat as well as Tares. Hince the Gosple is compared to a net that taketh
good & bad. 13. Matt. 47. 48. 49. 50. Here are good men to be found, yea
ye very best; & here are bad men to be found, yea ye very worst: Such as
shall have the highest seat in glory; & such also as shall be cast into the lowest
& fiercest flames of misery. Saints & Devils. Like Jeremiahs Basket of figs.
24. Jer. 1–4.
2. Prop:[osition] Christ knows how many of these Devils there are in his
Churches. As in our text there was one among the twelve. And so in our
Churches God knows how many Devils there are: Whither 1 . 2 . 3 . or
4 in 12. How many Devils, how many Saints. He that knows whom he has
chosen. 13. John. 18. he also knows who they are that have not chosen
him, but prefer farms & merchandize above him, & above his ordinances.
2 Tim. 4 10

"the Devil hath been raised"

3. Prop:[osition] Last: Christ knows who these Devils are. There is one among you said Christ to the twelve: Well who is that? Why it is Judas. Why so Christ knows how many Devils among us: Whither one or ten, or 20 & also who they are: He knows us perfectly; & he knows those of us that are in the Church, that we are either Saints or Devils; True believers, or Hypocrites & dissembling Judass that would sell Christ & his kingdom to gratify a lust. We do not think we are such 2. Reg [Kings] 8. 12.13.

1. Use. Let none then build their hopes of Salvation meerly upon this, that they are Church-members This you & I may be, & yet Devils for all that 8. Matth. 11. 12. Many shall come from the East & West, & shall sit down etc. And however we may pass here a true difference shall be made shortly etc.

2. Use. Let none then be stumbled at Religion because too often there are Devils found among the Saints. You see here was a true Church, sincere converts, & sound believers, & yet here was a Devil among them.

3. Use. Terror to Hypocrites, who Profess much love to Christ, but indeed are in league with their lusts, which they prefer above Christ. Oh remember that you are Devils in Christs account. Christ is lightly esteemed of you, & you are vilely accounted of by Christ. Oh if there be any such among us, forbear to come this day to the Lords Table, least Satan enter more powerfully into you. Least whilst the bread be between your teeth, the wrath of the Lord come pouring down upon you. 78. Ps[alms] 30. 31

4. Use Exhort in two branches

1. To be deeply humbled for the appearances of Devils among our Churches. If the Church of Corrinth were called to mourn because of one incestuous person among them. 1 Cor. 5. initio how much more may N.E. Churches mourn that such as work witchcraft, or are vehemently suspected so to do should be found among them.

2. To be much in prayer that God would deliver our Churches from Devils. That God would not suffer Devils in the guise of Saints to associate with us. One sinner destroys much good; how much more one Devil. Pray we also that not one true Saint may suffer as a Devil, either in name or body. The Devil would represent the best Saints as Devils if he could, but it is not easy to imagine that his power is of such extant, to the hazard of the Church.

5. Use. Last: Examine we our selves well, what we are: What we Church members are: We are either Saints, or Devils, the Scripture gives us no medium. The Apostle tells us we are to examine ourselves. 2 Cor. 13. 5. Oh it is a dreadful thing to be a Devil, & yet to sit down at the Lords Table. 1. Cor. 10. 21. Such incur the hottest of Gods wrath, as follows 22 v. Now if we would not be Devils we must give ourselves wholly up to Christ, & not suffer the predominancy of one lust, & particularly that lust of covetous-

113

ness, which is made so light of, & which so sadly prevails in these perilous times: why this one lust made Judas a Devil. 12. Joh. 6. 26. Matth. 15. And no doubt it has made more Devils than one. For a little pelf, men sell Christ to his enemies, & their Souls to the Devil. But there are certain sins that make us Devils, see that we be not such

1. A liar or murderer. 8. Joh. 44.
2. A slanderer or an accuser of the godly
3. A tempter to sin
4. An opposer of godliness, as Elymas. 13. Acts. 8 etc.
5. Envious persons as Witches
6. A Drunkard. 1 Sam. 1. 15. 16.
7. Last. A proud person.

Finis textus

(Connecticut Historical Society, Rev. Samuel Parris Manuscript Sermon Book, p. 147-151)

Parris Records the Witchcraft Outbreak in the Church Record Book

In this lengthy entry in the Salem Village church record book, Rev. Parris makes notation of what he believes to be the key event in unleashing witchcraft within the village. Sometime earlier in the month, church member Mary Sibley had instructed Parris's slave, John Indian, to make a witch cake to discover what was vexing the neighborhood children. The cake, made from meal and the children's urine, was apparently fed to a dog, and the animal's reaction would supposedly help reveal the guilty ones. Parris regarded this incident as calling upon diabolical means to aid in discovering witches, and sister Sibley was severely chastised for her "going to the Devil." She confessed her error and her sorrow to the church, and Parris seemed to have in this incident an acknowledged bench mark event upon which to blame the witchcraft outbreak.

27. March. Sab. <u>1692</u> Sacrament day

After the common Auditory was dismissed, & before the Church communion at the Lords Table, the following testimony against the Error of our Sister Mary Sibly, who had given direction to my Indian man in an un warrantable way to find out Witches, was read by the Pastor.

It is altogether undenyable that our Great & Blessed God, for wise & holy ends hath suffered many persons, in several families, of this little Village, to be greivously vexed, & tortured in body, & to be deeply tempted, to the endangering of the destruction of their souls; all these amazing feats (well

"the Devil hath been raised"

-tion of their souls; & all these amazing feats (well known to many of us) to be done by witchcraft, & Diabolical operations. It is also well known that when these calamities first began, which was in my own family, the affliction was several weeks before such Hellish operations, as Witchcraft was suspected. Nay it never brake forth to any considerable light, untill Diabolical means was used by the making of a cake by my Indian man, who had his direction from this our sister Mary Sibly. Since wth Apparitions have been plenty, & exceeding much mischief hath followed. But by this means (it seems) the Devil hath been raised amongst us, & his Rage is vehement & terrible, & when he shall be silenc'd the Lord only knows. But now that this our sister should be instrumental to such distress, is a great grief to my self, & our godly Honoured & Reverend Neighbours, who have had the knowledge of it. Neverthelsss, I do truly hope, & belive that this our sister doth truly fear the Lord, & am well satisfyed from her, that what she did, she did it ignorantly, from what she had heard of this nature from other ignorant, or worse persons. Yet we are in duty bound, to protest against such actions, as being indeed a going to the Devil, for help against the Devil; we having no such directions from Nature, or Gods word, it must therefore be, & is, accounted by godly Protestants, who write or speak of such matters as Diabolical, & therefore calls this our sister to deep humiliation for what she has done; & of us to be watchfull against Satans wiles & Devices.

Therefore, as we in duty, as a church of Christ are deeply bound, to protest against it, as most directly contrary to the Gospell, yet in as much, as this our sister did it in ignorance as she professeth, & we belive, we can continue her in our holy fellowship, upon her serious promise of future better advisedness and caution, & acknowledging that she is indeed sorrowfull for her rashness herein.

Rev. Samuel Parris noted the witchcraft outbreak in this church record book entry for March 27, 1692. Page 11 of the volume included Parris's declaration that " . . . the Devil hath been raised amongst us. . . . "   *Courtesy, Danvers Archival Center.*

The Documentary Evidence

known to many of us) to be done by witchcraft, & Diabolical operations. It is also well known that when these calamities first began, which was in my own family, the affliction was several weeks before such Hellish operations, as Witchcraft was suspected. Nay it never brake forth to any considerable light, untill Diabolical means was used, by the making of a cake by my Indian man, who had his direction from this our Sister Mary Sibly: since wch Apparitions have been plenty, & exceeding much mischief hath followed. But by this means (it seems) the Devil hath been raised amongst us, & his Rage is vehement & terrible, & when he shall be #[allay'd] silenc'd the Lord only knows. But now that this our sister should be instrumental to such distress, is a great grief to my self, & our godly Honoured & Reverend neighbours, who have had the knowledge of it. Nevertheless, I do truly hope, & believe, that this our sister doth truly fear the Lord, & am well satisfied from her, that what she did, she did it ignorantly, from what she had heard of this nature from other ignorant, or worse, persons. Yet we are in duty bound, to protest against such actions, as being indeed a going to the Devil, for help against the Devil; we having no such directions from Nature, or Gods word, it must therefore be, & is, accounted by godly Protestants, who write or speak of such matters as Diabolical, & therefore calls this our sister to deep humiliation for what she has done; & all of us to be watchfull against Satans wiles & Devices.

Therefore, as we in duty, as a Church of Christ are deeply bound, to protest against it, as most directly contrary to the Gosple, yet in as much, as this our sister did it in ignorance as she professeth, & we believe, we can continue her in our holy fellowship, upon her serious promise of future better advisedness and caution, & acknowledging that she is indeed sorrowfull for her rashness herein.

Brethren, If this be your mind that this iniquity should be thus born witness against, manifest it by your usual signe of lifting up your hands.

The Brethren voted generally, or universally: None made any exceptions.

Sister Sibley, If you are convinced that you herein did sinfully & are sorry for it: Let us hear it from our own mouth.

She did manifest to satisfaction her error & grief for it. Brethren. If herein you have received satisfaction, testify it by lifting up of your hands.

A general vote passed: no exception made.

Note

25. March. 1691/2 I discoursed said sister in my study about her grand error abovesaid, & also then read to her what I had written as above to read

"the Devil hath been raised"

to the Church, & said Sister Sibly assented to the same with tears & sorrow-
ful confession.

*(Church Record Book, p. 10-11, from the First Church
of Danvers, Congregational, deposit collection of the Danvers
Archival Center)*

MONDAY, MARCH 28, 1692

John Tarbell & Samuel Nurse for Rebecca Nurse

*Rebecca Nurse's son-in-law tells of a visit to the Thomas Putnam house during which
he learns that the afflicted women of the household are unclear as to who first identified
the apparition hurting Ann Putnam, Jr., as that of Rebecca Nurse.*

John tarball being at the house of thomas putnams upon the: 28 day of this
instant march being the yeare 1692 upon descource of many things i asked
them some questions and among others i asked this question wheter the garle
that was afflicted did first speack of of goody nurs before others mentioned
her to her they said she told them she saw the apperishton of apale fast woman
that sat in her granmothers seat but did not know her name: then i replyed
and said but who was it that told her that it was good nurs: mercy lewes said
it was goody putnam that said it was goody nurse: goody putnam said it was
mercy lewes that told her: thus they turned it upone one an other saying it
was you & it was you that told her: this was be fore any was afflicted at thomas
putnams beside his daughter that they told his daughter it was goody nurs
samuel nurs doth testifie to all above written

[Reverse]

John Tarball

(Essex County Court Archives, Salem Witchcraft Papers, I, 87)

MONDAY, MARCH 28, 1692

Testimony of William Rayment, Jr. & Daniel Elliott

*These three undated documents concern an incident at Ingersoll's Tavern. Two of
the documents, virtually identical in content though recorded by a different hand, relate
the experience of William Rayment, Jr., while the third document contains the testimony
of Daniel Elliott, who adds details and dates the occurrence as having taken place on*

The Documentary Evidence

March 28. These two young men testified that at least one of the unnamed afflicted persons began crying out at the tavern that the spectre of Elizabeth Procter was present. When reproached by Hannah Ingersoll, the afflicted girl made light of her accusations claiming "she did it for sport." Her name having been bandied about for several weeks, Elizabeth Procter was subsequently arrested and examined on April 11, 1692.

The testimony of William Rayment aged 26 years or there about testifieth and saith that I being at the hous of Leftnt Ingarsols some time in the Later end of march; there discoursing conserning the examyning of severall persons suspected for wiches: I was saying that I hard that goody procter was to be examyned to morrow to which goody Ingarsoll replyed she did not beleve it for she heard nothing of it: som of the afflicted persons being present one of them or more cryd out there goody procter there goody procter and old #[which] witch Ile have her hang goody Ingersoll sharply reproved them then they semed to make a jest of it

(Essex County Court Archives, Salem Witchcraft Papers, I, 98)

The testimony of william Rayment aged 26 years or there abouts testifieth & saith that I being at the house of leftint Ingesone some time in the later end of march: there discoursing conserning. the examying of severall person suspected for witches: I was saying that I hard that goody procter was to be examyned to morrow to which goody ingersone replyed she did not beleve it for she heard nothing of it: some of The afflicted persons being present one of them or more cryed out there is goody procter there is goody procter and old wich Ile have har hang-goody ingerson Sharply reproved them: then they semed to make a Jest of it

[Reverse]
Wm. Rayment.

(Essex Institute, Salem, Mass., Salem Witchcraft Papers,
Fowler Collection)

the testimony of Daniel elet aged 27 years or thear abouts who testifieth & saith that I being at the hous of leutennant ingasone one the 28 of march in the year: 1692 thear being preasent one of the aflicted persons which cryed out and said thears goody procter William raiment juner being theare present told the garle he beleved she lyed for he saw nothing then goody ingerson told the garl she told aly for thear was nothing: then the garl said that she did it for sport they must have some sport

(Essex County Court Archives, Salem Witchcraft Papers, I, 109)

"the Devil hath been raised"

TUESDAY, MARCH 29, 1692

Testimony of Samuel Barton & John Houghton

the testimony of Samuel Barton aged 28 years or therabouts who testifieth and saith that I being at Thomas putnams a helping to tend the aflickted folks i heard them talking who the Children Complained of an I heard them teel mercy lewes that she Cryed out of goody procter and mercy lewes said that she did not Cry out of goody procter nor nobody she said she did say thear she is but did not teel them who and Thomas putnam & his wife & others told her that she Cryed out of goody procter and marcy lewes said if she did it was when she was out in her head for she said she saw nobody this being the 29 of march in the year 1691/2

John Houghton aged 23 testifieth and saith I this Deponent was present at the same tyme above written and I heard Thomas Putnam, and his wife sayd that mercy Lewis saw or named the wife of John Procter in her fitt and we heard the sayd mercy Lewis affirme that she never sayd that ever she saw her

(Essex County Court Archives, Salem Witchcraft Papers, I, 107)

THURSDAY, MARCH 31, 1692

Lawson's Narrative

The 31 of March there was a Publick Fast kept at Salem on account of these Afflicted Persons. And Abigail Williams said, that the Witches had a Sacrament that day at an house in the Village, and that they had Red Bread and Red Drink.

(Deodat Lawson, A Brief and True Narrative *[Boston, 1692] p. 8)*

The Documentary Evidence

Appendices

Demographics of 1692 Salem Village

An examination of the documentary evidence from March 1692, as reproduced in the main section of this book, will reveal approximately sixty names of Salem Village men, women and children who were involved as accuser, accused or witness in the various proceedings and events. From obvious gaps within these surviving records, it appears highly probable that there were others who were also directly involved, but whose involvement in these early days now is not known. A further examination of the retained witchcraft legal records for the months following March would dramatically display that more and more villagers were drawn in a substantive manner into the witchcraft frenzy occurring around them.

When one looks at a former era or culture and attempts to reconstruct the physical make-up of that society, the researcher begins to sense that there is a missing presence of many people within the historical record who just do not get written up within the traditional sources. Just as today, during our intense decennial census, homeless people and large numbers of minorities are not fully discovered and counted, so too, but to an even greater extent, significant numbers of inhabitants of former, less technocratic societies are often lost to history. Rev. Parris's slave, Tituba, one of the most important characters in the drama of 1692 Salem Village, would have been completely unknown in the traditional historical record if it had not been for her prominent role in the witchcraft proceedings. Too often the researcher can underestimate or misunderstand the breadth of historic events if he does not gather and consider all the possible types of primary sources available.

As the Salem Village of 1692 has been such a popular topic for both scholars and the general public, any documentary inquiry into the subject should be founded on a general understanding of the size and status of this village, thereby putting it into the context of late 17th-century Massachusetts society. The peculiarities of the legal and social status of Salem Village have been the subject of much previous work including helpful information from the first volume of Charles W. Upham's classic 1867 tome, *Salem Witchcraft*. In more recent times, Paul Boyer and Stephen Nissenbaum's 1974 book, *Salem Possessed: The Social Origins of Witchcraft* uncovered previously unexplored sources and took a fresh look at the evidence to explain the village society and its what might be called "psychotic relationship" with Salem town.

The editor of this volume believes it important to provide the user with a brief overview of the make-up of the Salem Village population. Therefore this appendix section will outline some general characteristics of the village in 1692. The material is taken from his *A Demographic Study of Salem Village in 1692* originally compiled in 1971.

Beginning in the 1960's, demographic studies of American colonial society have been the subject of some significant scholarship. John Demos, Kenneth Lockridge and Philip Greven, among others, have examined the society of several 17th-century Massachusetts communities. The definition of demography, "the statistical study of the characteristics of a population," might conjure up a dry, dehumanizing culling through vital records; but as these and other researchers have shown, such inquiry into the raw statistics of life allows us to better understand the common man and his effect upon society as a whole.

The editor's 1971 attempt to reconstruct the 1692 Salem Village population utilized numerous and varied sources. Included were the Salem Village church record book, the village record book, depositions and other papers filed during the witch trials, family genealogy volumes, a map of 1692 Salem Village compiled in 1866 by William P. Upham, articles by Sidney Perley concerning land history in 1700 Salem Village, information from the Quarterly Court files, and local histories.

Some information including servants, kin living within the household, and transients in the village was under-recorded in 1692, and subsequently unrecorded. Yet by glancing at the conclusions arrived at from the available and compiled statistics, the reader will note certain interesting and significant bits of information about the village society, and will gain thereby a clearer picture of the people of Salem Village and their society of 1692.

The Salem Village of 1692 as constituted in its legally, though nebulously, described bounds, contained a population of approximately 525 to 550 people living in some 90 households. The most prevalent village occupation was that of yeoman with 60% of the householders engaged in farming, while an additional 9% combined both agriculture and a trade. Twenty percent of the villagers engaged in trades providing such essential commodities as clothing (weaver, cordwainer, tailor), tableware and storage vessels (dish turner, traymaker, potter, cooper), tools (blacksmith, cooper, plowright, wheelwright), and structures (carpenter, glazier, sawyer, housewright, brickmaker, bricklayer). Four taverns or ordinaries operated within the village bounds, and two men pursued the trade of maltster. Four percent of the householders were widows, while laborers and seamen were represented by a little over 1% each. The average size of 86 households of which we have fairly complete information was about 6 persons per household. Forty-five households contained six or more people and constituted 75% of the total village population. Those household heads between the ages of 31 and 40 years had the most people in their households, with 15 of the 22 in this age bracket having 6 or more persons living in their homes.

The marital status of the heads of households indicated 80% were married, while 6% were bachelors and 10% were widowed. Of the total village population in 1692, 31% were married. The figures concerning the number of related kin who lived in households is undoubtedly under-recorded as such information, especially for an individual year, is relatively hard to acquire. This study found, nonetheless, 31 verifiable kin living in 11 households, indicating a total of at least 12% of the households with resident relatives other than children and spouses.

Information concerning only 9 servants was found, this information gathered chiefly from witchcraft legal records. There were many sources listing bondsmen and other servants as having lived in various Salem Village families during the period of 1670 through 1710, but most of them could not be included in this study since their servitude period was unknown, and since it could not be positively shown that they were in the Salem Village families during 1692. Thus this area of the statistics is also under-recorded. It is interesting to note, however, the diversity of the 9 known servants. Their ages range from that of a small child of undetermined age to one woman aged 48. They included Blacks and Indian slaves, bonded servants, and a servant/kinswoman.

Of the known Salem Village population, almost 250 people, or 47.5% of the

"the Devil hath been raised"

inhabitants, were made up of persons under age 16. Males constituted approximately 52% of the total population and females 48%.

The average age of the Salem Villagers in 1692 could be computed with only 416 known ages, or some 80% of the population. Since those whose ages were specifically known tended to be children, the statistics favored an earlier average age than if all the ages were known. With this in mind, the computed average age for males was 21 and for females was 17.

The average age at marriage for persons living in Salem Village in 1692 was 25 years for males and 21 years for females; and the average age of wives at the birth of their first child was 23 years. Of those married or widowed persons living in the Village in 1692, 13% of them had been married at least twice, and 2% of them had been married three times.

After computing the number of children householders had had up to 1692, including those who had either died or removed from the village, it was found that 5.8 children per married household was the average. Twenty-two households, or 24% of the known households, were then examined in order to determine the total number of children born to these families during the wives' total fertile period. These figures showed that on the average, 9 children were born to each of the 22 households. It should be recognized, however, that this statistic might not conform to the average married couple, since the families used in reaching this statistic tended to be fairly stable and well-to-do, had their records available in printed family genealogies, and continued to maintain both spouses during the entire fertile period, or remarried fairly rapidly after the death of one spouse. The time span between births for a sampling of 17 women living in Salem Village was one child about every 25 months. The birth rate for 1692 Salem Village was 36.6 children per thousand population, while two sets of fraternal twins inhabited the village in 1692. Five couples were married in 1692 and at least one household moved into the village during that year.

Though obvious, it should be pointed out that Salem Village was not a closed society, as many persons from surrounding towns took an active part in village life. Many of them owned land in the village, but through a slip in boundary lines, lived outside the village. Many of these people, especially those living in Salem Farms, Topsfield, Rowley Village, and Beverly, had close ties with their Salem Village neighbors; and many of them were related to Salem Village families and attended church and military drill at the village.

Concerning the interrelationship of the village families, 15 separate family names were responsible for 54 households and 62% of the entire population. The most frequent family name, Putnam, represented 11 distinct households, including a total of some 66 persons. When coupled with families interrelated through marriage, it becomes obvious that the village society, like many similar communities, had a vast and complex familial interrelationship. In the village the Nurse family, through the marriage of three daughters, represented 5 households of 34 people, while the Porter family was represented by 22 people for 4% of the population.

Even a cursory examination of the statistics of the Salem Village society reveals that this community, like its 17th-century neighbors, was far more rich and complex than a mere reading of documentary records would indicate.

(Information extracted from Richard B. Trask, A Demographic Study of Salem Village in 1692, *a Northeastern University Master's Thesis, June 1971)*

Appendices

Biographical Notes

Over sixty persons are represented or mentioned in the surviving March 1692 witchcraft related papers. The following are brief descriptions of each of these persons so that the reader will have a better understanding of the events and those who were involved in them:

Allen, William
A young bachelor and cooper by trade, Allen married Elizabeth Small in 1695.

Andrew, Daniel
Born in Watertown in 1643, Andrew moved to Salem by 1669. He was a successful brick-layer/plasterer and in 1677 settled in the north part of Salem Village near Wenham with his wife Sarah, the daughter of John and sister of Israel Porter. Andrew owned a considerable estate and retained many ties to Salem Town. Having earlier served as a Salem representative to the General Court, Andrew was elected Salem Town Selectman in 1691. A non-Parris supporter, Andrew was one of the five new Village Committeemen elected in October 1691. In May 1692, shortly after his re-election as Salem Town Selectman, a warrant was sworn out for Andrew's arrest as a witch suspect. He temporarily went into hiding and thus escaped arrest. He died of smallpox in 1702.

Baker, Jonathan
The son of Cornelius and Hannah (Wood-bury), Baker was baptized in 1669. He resided in Beverly.

Barton, Samuel
Born about 1664, Barton had lived in Salem Village from at least 1690 when he had been taxed for the support of Rev. Parris. His name is not found on the 1694 rate list.

Bibber (Vibber), Sarah
The wife of John Bibber of Wenham, Mrs. Bibber was born about 1656. The family lived at various times with other Salem Village families, and in several post-March 1692 depositions Goodwife Bibber was described as an "unruly, turbulent spirit" and "double-tongued" person.

Braybrook, Samuel
A weaver by trade, Braybrook was born in the 1640s. He was widowed in 1689.

Cheever, Ezekiel, Jr.
Son of noted Boston schoolteacher Ezekiel, Sr., Cheever was born in 1655 and married Abigail Lippingwell in 1680. He resided in Salem until 1684 when he moved to the Lothrop estate that he had inherited in the western part of the village near Hathorne Hill. Cheever was a tailor and had become a covenant member of the village church at its founding in 1689.

Cloyce, Peter
Born in 1639 and from York, Maine, Cloyce in 1692 was a yeoman living in the northerly portion of Salem Village on the Daniel Andrew estate. He lost his first wife, Hannah, in 1680 and married Sarah Bridges in 1681. Peter was an original 1689 covenant member of the village church. Following his wife's arrest in 1692, he became a vocal opponent against Rev. Parris. After his wife's release from jail, the family moved, resettling by 1701 in modern-day Framingham, Massachusetts, where he died in 1708.

Cloyce, Sarah
Born to William and Joanna (Blessing) Towne about 1641, Cloyce was a sister to Rebecca Nurse and Mary Esty, both of whom were executed for practicing witchcraft later in 1692. First married to Edmund Bridges of Topsfield with whom she had produced five children, Sarah upon his death married Peter Cloyce. Sarah and Peter together had three children, and she became a covenant member of the village church in January 1690. In April 1692 Sarah was accused of witchcraft and jailed for many months. She died in 1703.

Corwin, Jonathan
Born in Salem in 1640 to Captain George and his wife Elizabeth, Corwin was a successful merchant and retailer of liquors. A former deputy in the General Court for several years, Corwin in 1692 was a member of the Court of Assistants serving in the colony's highest

"the Devil hath been raised"

judicial and legislative body. A member of the Salem First Church, he and Salem magistrate John Hathorne presided at many of the preliminary witchcraft hearings. Later in 1692 following the resignation of Nathaniel Saltonstall as a justice of the Court of Oyer and Terminer, Corwin was appointed to replace him. He died in 1718.

Cory, Giles

Born in England about 1611, Cory lived in Salem until about 1659 when he moved to what is now West Peabody. Owning a large tract of land, Cory possessed a bad reputation and was known to live a "scandellous life." In 1675 he pummeled a farm worker named Jacob Goodale, who shortly thereafter died. Accused of being a cause in Goodale's death, Cory paid a heavy fine. Cory buried two wives before marrying Martha Rich in about 1685. In 1691 he joined the Salem church and in 1692, following the imprisoning of his wife, he was also accused of witchcraft and arrested on April 19, 1692. Standing mute and refusing to acknowledge a trial before the special Court of Oyer and Terminer, Cory was subjected to "peine forte et dure," a torture of having heavy weights placed upon his body until he acquiesced. He refused to yield and died under this torture on September 18, 1692, a day after his Salem church excommunicated him.

Cory, Martha

Probably born in the late 1620s, Martha Cory had first been married to a man named Rich prior to her marriage to Giles Cory. She was accepted into membership in the village church in April 1690, and had a reputation of being a pious, intelligent but somewhat overbearing woman. After her March 1692 arrest she was tried in September. Following her excommunication from the village church on September 14 and the death of her husband on September 18, Martha Cory was hanged on the twenty-second of September. In 1703 her excommunication was revoked by the village church.

Crosby (Crossly), Henry

In 1683 Crosby married Deliverance Cory, daughter of Giles and his first wife Margaret Cory. Crosby gave evidence during his father-in-law's third wife's examination in March 1692. Though the documentation of this evidence is not extant, it appears not to have been positive for Martha Cory.

Dunnell (Dwinell), Michael

Most probably the son of Michael and Mary of Topsfield, Michael Jr. was born in 1670 and died in Topsfield in 1761.

Elliott, Daniel

Born about 1665, Elliott married Hannah Cloyce, daughter of Peter Cloyce and his first wife Hannah in 1686.

Good, Dorcas

Born ca. 1687-88 the daughter of William and Sarah Good, Dorcas Good was the youngest person to be cried out upon during the witchcraft delusion and subsequently she spent over seven months in jail. That the child suffered during her incarceration is beyond doubt. In 1710 her father said of her, " . . . being chain'd in the dungeon [she] was so hardly used and terrifyed that she hath ever since been very chargeable haveing little or no reason to govern herself."

Good, Sarah

Born in 1653 to well-to-do innkeeper John Solart, Sarah Good's life was a struggle. Her father's estate was enmeshed in litigation after his death in 1672, and when finally settled, she was left with virtually nothing. Her first marriage to a poor, indentured servant named Daniel Poole, ended with his death in 1686 and with his estate in debt. After her marriage to William Good, the couple was forced to make good on her former husband's debts, and this left them in near poverty. Sarah was known to beg for food and lodging in Salem Village for her family which in 1692 included at least two young children. Her sullen manner and mutterings at those who did not help her and her perceived curses upon them made her an unwelcome and suspicious neighbor. Following her arrest and eventual trial, Good was hanged on July 19, 1692, but not before her "suckling child dyed in prison." This infant daughter had been born in December 1691.

Good, William

Early on Good was described as a weaver and later as a laborer. His background is unknown. He and his wife were inhabitants of Salem Village in 1692 and for a time had lived with the Samuel Abbey family, though turned out after a time "for quietness's sake." William was still living in 1712.

Goodale, An ancient woman

Most probably Margaret Lazenby who was born in the early 1600s and was the second wife of Robert Goodale. Goodale by his first wife, Catharine, produced several children including a son, Jacob, the man Giles Cory was accused of beating to death in 1675.

Griggs, William, Sr.

Self-described in 1693 as aged and a physician, Griggs did not live in the Salem Village area much before 1690, when he is recorded on a parish tax list. By February 1692 Griggs was living near Long Hill, the present Folly Hill, which was in close proximity to the ill-defined Salem Village and Beverly border. Upon the doctor's death in 1697 an inventory was made of his estate. Listed among other possessions were "9 fissick bookes."

Hale, Rev. John

A Charlestown, Massachusetts, native born in 1636 and graduated from Harvard in 1657, Hale was invited about 1664 to preach at Bass River, which in 1667 became the town of Beverly. Following the death of his first wife in 1684, Hale married Sarah Noyes, a cousin of Rev. Nicholas Noyes of Salem. Hale remained as pastor of the Beverly church until his death in 1700.

Hathorne, John

Born in 1641 to an influential Salem family, Hathorne was a merchant who also attained high military rank. He held various offices, including deputy to the General Court, member of the Court of Assistants, and Councillor. Although not formally trained in law, but possessing practical experience, Hathorne presided over local legal cases as a magistrate. He died in 1717.

Herrick, Joseph

Born in 1644 the son of Henry Herrick, Herrick saw service during the King Philip's War and was thereafter referred to as "Corporal." He lived near the village and Beverly border on Alford or Cherry Hill. Herrick served as a constable for Salem in 1692 and brought in several accused witches for examination. Later that year he signed a petition attesting to the good character of Rebecca Nurse. He died in 1718.

Herrick, Mary

Born an Endecott, Mary was the second wife of Joseph Herrick, marrying him in 1678. She died in 1706.

Higginson, Rev. John

The son of Francis and born in England in 1616, Higginson arrived in New England in 1629. In 1659 he came to Salem and was ordained the next year, remaining that town's minister until his death in 1708.

Holten (Houghton), John

Born to Joseph and Sarah (Ingersoll) Holten ca. 1667, Holten was a cooper by trade. He married Mary Star in 1688 and about 1692 built a house in the center of Salem Village a short distance southerly of Ingersoll's ordinary. He died in 1721.

Hubbard, Elizabeth

The 17-year-old unmarried great niece of Rachel (Hubbard) Griggs, second wife of village physician William Griggs, Hubbard lived with and was a helper to this elderly couple.

Hutchinson, Joseph

The son of early settler Richard Hutchinson, Hutchinson was born in North Muskham, England, in 1633. A yeoman with a homestead near the village center, Hutchinson gave the inhabitants an acre of land in 1672 for the construction of its meeting house. He and his second wife Lydia Buxton, the widow of Joseph Small, both signed the petition in support of Rebecca Nurse in later 1692.

Indian, John

Referred to as "my Indian man," by Samuel Parris, John Indian was the husband of Parris's other slave, Tituba. Virtually nothing is known of this man who also did work next door to the parsonage at Nathaniel Ingersoll's ordinary. Following the commitment of Tituba to jail in April, John Indian, undoubtedly as a means of self-preservation, became "afflicted" and gave testimony against Sarah Cloyce and Elizabeth Procter. In late May while working at Ingersoll's, John Indian showed a visiting couple named Cary several scars upon his body which he claimed were caused by witchcraft. Shortly thereafter he and a number of girls accused Elizabeth Cary of witchcraft. This is the last existing document referring to the slave.

"the Devil hath been raised"

Ingersoll, Nathaniel

The son of Richard, Ingersoll was born in 1633. At the age of 11, upon his father's death, he was taken into Governor John Endecott's family for four years, helping out and learning as he lived at "Orchard Farm." Inheriting his father's estate, Ingersoll married and built a dwelling near the center of the village. He served as lieutenant in the local training band, ultimately deeding to the inhabitants the lot of land near the center of the village used for training purposes. The first deacon of the village church, Ingersoll operated a licensed victualing house at the convergence of two major roads near the watch house and at close proximity to the meeting house. This tavern, or ordinary, served as a meeting place for numerous public functions, both civil and religious. Ingersoll died in 1719.

Ingersoll, Hannah

The wife of Nathaniel, Mrs. Ingersoll was born Hannah Collins in Lynn in 1637. The Ingersolls had only one child, a daughter Sarah, born 1662. They also adopted as their own, Benjamin, the son of Joseph Hutchinson. Born in 1668, Hutchinson married in 1689 and lived closeby.

Kenney, Henry

Most probably Henry, Sr., he was born ca. 1624. Kenney settled in Salem Village about 1648 and served as a soldier in 1654 at the capture of St. John. He was a yeoman and died after 1705. A son, Henry, Jr., was born in 1669 and was living on his father's homestead in 1692, a year after marrying Priscilla Lewis.

Lawson, Rev. Deodat

Following the unhappy departure of George Burroughs as minister of Salem Village, in 1684 English-born minister Deodat Lawson was offered and took this ministerial post. In 1686 after several years of relative peace, a group in the village pressured for the creation of a covenant church and the ordination of Lawson. The resulting controversy caused Lawson to separate from the village at the end of his 1688 contractual term. He had lost his wife and at least one child while inhabiting the village parsonage. Following his return visit to the Salem Village in March 1692, Lawson eventually traveled back to England where, according to some sources, his last days ended sadly and in destitution.

Lewis, Mercy

A 17-year-old servant girl living in the Thomas Putnam household, Lewis was born about 1675 in the Casco, Maine area. Upon her parents' deaths at the hands of Indians, she resided in Maine with Rev. George Burroughs for a time, later to find a temporary home in the Salem area with William Bradford and finally by 1692 with the Thomas Putnam family.

Locker, George

A Salem yeoman married in 1692 to widow Lydia (Buffum) Hill, Locker was elected one of six Salem constables on March 9, 1691, and served for approximately one year in that capacity. His responsibilities included warnings for town meetings, collecting rates and serving warrants. Later in 1692 Locker signed a petition to assist accused witches John and Elizabeth Procter.

Noyes, Rev. Nicholas

Born in Newbury, Massachusetts, in 1647, Noyes graduated from Harvard College in 1667 and preached at Haddam, Connecticut, for thirteen years. During the King Philip's War he accompanied Connecticut troops and was present at the 1675 Great Swamp Fight. In 1682 Noyes was called to the Salem, Massachusetts church, being ordained as its teacher and assisting the elderly pastor, Rev. John Higginson. A bachelor and very corpulent, Noyes possessed a strong personality. He died in 1717.

Nurse, Francis

A traymaker living in Salem forty years prior to his moving in 1678 to a 300-acre village homestead, Nurse had begun renting the property with intent to purchase. Some people in Salem Village resented the Nurse family for what appeared to be a very shrewd land acquisition. In October 1691 Nurse was elected a member of the Village Committee. He died in 1695, and several years thereafter the homestead purchase was finally paid off by the surviving Nurse family.

Nurse, Rebecca

Born in 1622 in Yarmouth, England, to William and Joanna Towne, Rebecca Towne married Francis Nurse about 1644. A covenant member of the Salem church, Rebecca attended the closer village meeting house.

By early 1692 the nearly deaf and sickly matriarch of a large, grown family of eight was accused of practicing witchcraft. Though various friends, family, and neighbors petitioned and worked on her behalf, Nurse was tried in June. The jury at first brought in a "not guilty" verdict, but were instructed by the court to reconsider some points of evidence. Following her July 3 excommunication from the Salem church, she was hanged on July 19, 1692.

Nurse, Samuel

The second son of Francis and Rebecca, Samuel Nurse was born in 1678 and married Mary Smith in 1677. He was a yeoman and lived on the large family homestead. Following his father's death in 1695, Samuel inherited the homestead. He died about 1716.

Osburn, Sarah

Born about 1643 in Watertown, Massachusetts, to John and Margaret Warren, Sarah Warren married Robert Prince in 1662. Robert's sister had married Capt. John Putnam and Robert had been able to secure a large property in the village close to his Putnam in-laws. He was a supporter of village independence. When he died in 1674, Prince's estate was left in trust to his wife Sarah with his two small sons to come into their possession upon maturity. Sarah purchased the indenture of an Irishman, Alexander Osburn, to oversee the farm, and much gossip ensued over their living arrangements until about 1677, when the two married. Osburn and his wife attempted to obtain full legal control over the Prince land. After her arrest and examination, Sarah Osburn was committed to jail, where she died on May 10, 1692.

Parker, John

In 1673 Parker married Mary Cory, daughter of Giles and his first wife, Margaret Cory. During the examination of Parker's father-in-law's third wife, Martha Cory, one of the Needham family told the magistrates that Parker had "thought this woman [Martha] a witch."

Parris, Rev. Samuel

Born in 1653 to London merchant Thomas Parris, Samuel Parris was sent to Boston to attend Harvard College some time after Thomas moved to the Barbados. Upon the death of Thomas in 1673, Samuel left the school for the West Indies to take up a mercantile profession on inherited land. By 1680, after finding little economic advantage in the Barbados, Parris returned to Boston, and while continuing there as a merchant for several years, he decided to pursue the ministry at a time when Salem Village was looking for a new pastor. Tenaciously attempting to keep his position following the 1692 witchcraft era, Parris finally succumbed to the pressures of his enemies and quit the village pulpit in 1696. Pursuing occupations of minister, teacher, and retailer in several different communities, Parris died in Sudbury in 1720.

Parris, Elizabeth, Jr.

In 1692 Betty was the middle child of Samuel and Elizabeth Parris between Thomas (b. 1681) and Susannah (b. 1687). She was born in Boston on November 28, 1682. Grievously "afflicted" early on, Betty was sent by late March 1692 to live in Salem at the Stephen Sewall house. In 1710 in Sudbury she married Benjamin Barron.

Phillips, Mr.

Most probably Walter Phillips, Sr., he was granted an innholder's license in the village in 1689 when about 70 years of age. The tavern was located near the present Danvers-Peabody border on Sylvan Street. Phillips died in 1704.

Pope, Mrs.

Undoubtedly Bethshua Pope, she was the wife of Joseph Pope. Originally a Folger of Nantucket, Bethshua in 1692 was about 42 years of age. She, her husband and their children lived with Joseph's widowed mother Gertrude.

Porter, Elizabeth

Born in 1649 to Major William Hathorne and his wife Ann, one of the most prominent Salem families of the 17th century, Elizabeth married Israel Porter in 1672. Elizabeth's brother was Magistrate John Hathorne. Both Elizabeth and her husband signed the petition to assist Rebecca Nurse during her summer trial.

Porter, Israel

Baptized in Hingham, Massachusetts, in 1644, Porter was the son of John who soon after settled in the Salem Village area. Israel and two of his brothers prospered on their father's inheritance and their own ability. While residing in Salem Village, they had close economic and social ties with Salem Town. A gentleman farmer who retained his membership in the Salem church, Israel owned two mills and served six terms as a Salem Selectman, including in 1690-92. Opposed to Parris's ministry following the witchcraft era, Porter died in 1706.

Preston, Thomas
The son of Roger and Martha Preston, Thomas was born in Salem in 1643. A yeoman, he married Rebecca, daughter of Francis and Rebecca Nurse, in 1669. He died in 1697.

Procter, Elizabeth
Born about 1651 to William Bassett of Lynn, Massachusetts, Elizabeth Bassett became the third wife of John Procter in 1674. The couple had five children of their own besides the six from her husband's previous marriages. Elizabeth was arrested on April 11 prior to her husband for practicing witchcraft and condemned by the Court of Oyer and Terminer on August 5. As she was pregnant, she was given a temporary stay of execution until the birth of her child. The child, John, was born in January 1693, two days following the governor's reprieve of all the remaining condemned persons. Before the turn of the century, Elizabeth married Daniel Richards of Lynn.

Procter, John, Sr.
Born in England about 1632, John was an early inhabitant of Ipswich, Massachusetts, where he retained many ties and an extensive estate. Removing to the Salem area about 1666, he occupied a homestead on a major road leading to Boston and a short distance south of the Salem Village boundary. Pursuing farming here and on lands elsewhere, Procter prospered. He was also licensed to keep a tavern. In early April 1692, Procter was accused of witchcraft, and following a trial he was executed on August 19, 1692.

Putnam, Ann, Sr.
The youngest daughter of George and Elizabeth Carr of Salisbury, Massachusetts, Ann Carr was born in 1661 and married Thomas Putnam in 1678. Her sister, Mary Carr, was the wife of the first Salem Village minister, James Bayley. In 1692 Ann and Thomas had six living children, a seventh

having died in 1689. Pregnant during much of 1692, Ann gave birth to Abigail prior to October 30 of that year. Ann, Sr., died in 1699 just two weeks after her husband's death.

Putnam, Ann, Jr.
Born the eldest child to Ann and Thomas Putnam on October 18, 1679, Ann, Jr., following the witchcraft era, would always be referred to as a sickly person. She made a public confession concerning her role during the witchcraft episode when in 1706 she requested and was granted full membership into the Salem Village church. She died in 1716 never having married.

Putnam, Edward
The younger brother of Thomas, Jr., Putnam was born in 1654 to the village's richest couple, Lieutenant Thomas and Ann (Holyoke) Putnam. A yeoman, Putnam served as one of two deacons at the Salem Village church. He died in 1747.

Putnam, Jonathan
The eldest son of Captain John Putnam, Putnam was born in 1659. A cousin of Edward and Thomas, Jr., Jonathan was a yeoman who by 1692 was married to his second wife Lydia (Potter). Referred to as "Captain", Putnam also served as a constable in 1691. Until October of that year, he was also a member of the Village Committee when a new slate of members was voted into that position. Though he was one of the complainants of the 1692 warrant sworn out against Rebecca Nurse and Dorcas Good, Putnam later signed a statement with thirty-nine others indicating his never having cause to suspect Nurse of practicing witchcraft. He died in 1739.

Putnam, Captain John
Baptized at Aston Abbotts, England, in 1627, the son of John and Priscilla Putnam, Putnam moved to the village with his father in the 1640s. The large farming family prospered, John Putnam, Jr. becoming one of the wealthiest men in the village. Active in both town and church affairs, he supported the autonomy of Salem Village and its church. He was an original covenant member of the 1689 village church and a representative of Salem to the General Court for several terms. Capt. Putnam also served a number of terms on the Village Committee as well as Selectman in

Salem including in 1689, 1690 and 1692. A supporter of Parris, he died in 1710.

Putnam, Joseph

Following the death in 1665 of Lieutenant Thomas Putnam's first wife, Ann, Thomas married widow Mary Veren. In 1669 the marriage produced one child, Joseph, who was half-brother to Thomas Sr.'s other children, including Edward and Thomas, Jr. There was much animosity when, upon the father's death, it became evident that Joseph and the second Mrs. Putnam, not the elder brothers, had inherited the best part of this valuable Salem Village estate. Though the older brothers attempted to contest the will, Joseph, upon his eighteenth birthday, became one of the richest villagers. In 1690 Joseph married Elizabeth, daughter of Israel Porter, and in October 1691 he was elected to the Village Committee. Joseph Putnam's mother-in-law was the sister of Magistrate John Hathorne, and it might have been through that connection that he was asked to record the March 1 testimony. Thereafter, however, Joseph was a well-known opponent of the witchcraft proceedings and is traditionally supposed to have kept horses ready to flee if he himself were accused. Joseph was the father of the Revolutionary War folk hero Israel Putnam. Joseph died in 1725.

Putnam, Thomas

The eldest son of Lieutenant Thomas Putnam, Thomas, Jr., was born in 1652. He had fought in the King Philip's War. A yeoman and prominent village inhabitant, Putnam had served for many years as parish clerk. With his wife, he was one of the founding signers of the 1689 Salem Village church covenant. He died in 1699.

Rayment (Raymond), William, Jr.

Born ca. 1666, Rayment was most probably the son of William, a well-regarded inhabitant of Beverly who had close ties to the village. The son had served on a jury of inquest into the 1690 suicide of Christian Trask, the cause of which was described as "being violently asalted by the temptations of Satan . . . . "

Sewall, Stephen

Born in 1657, Sewall was the younger brother of prominent Boston merchant and later member of the special Court of Oyer and Ter-

miner, Samuel Sewall. Stephen took up residence in Salem, where he pursued a career as a merchant. He was also a military officer. In 1686 he was appointed Clerk of Inferior Court of Pleas and General Sessions of the Peace. In the summer of 1692 he was appointed first Registrar of Deeds for Essex County under the new charter, and he also served as clerk to the Court of Oyer and Terminer.

Sibley, Mary

Born in 1660 the daughter of Benjamin and Rebecca Woodrow, Mary married Samuel Sibley. She was admitted to the Salem Village church in 1690.

Sibley, Samuel

Born in 1657 the son of John Sibley, Sibley was a cooper by trade. Living near Thorndike Hill close to the village meeting house, Sibley was admitted as a covenant member of the village church in 1690, several months before his wife.

Tarbell, John

Born about 1653, Tarbell married Mary, daughter of Francis and Rebecca Nurse, in 1678. He was a yeoman and died in 1715.

Tituba

A slave, Tituba was one of three owned by Samuel Parris upon his coming to Salem Village in 1689. One slave referred to as "my Negro lad" is recorded to have died in 1689. Both Tituba and John are always referred to in the witchcraft court records as "the Indian" or "an Indian." Tradition holds that Tituba and John were acquired by Parris when in the Barbados, though no direct proof of this exists. In more recent times Tituba has been portrayed as a Black, though contemporaries did not so designate her. Her confession before the magistrates seemed so sincere and unwavering that many saw it as valid proof of the existence of a witchcraft conspiracy. It was later claimed by some that her master beat a confession out of her, and that following the witchcraft events Parris did not desire her and she was sold to somebody else upon payment of her jail fees. Out of her entire life's existence all we know of Tituba results from her activities in 1692.

Walcott, Mary

The daughter of Jonathan and Mary (Sibley), Walcott was born in 1675. In 1692 the

"the Devil hath been raised"

17-year-old Mary lived with her father and his second wife, Deliverance (Putnam), in a homestead a short distance northwesterly from the parsonage and near the village training field. Her father was a yeoman and captain of the village militia and her stepmother was an aunt of Ann Putnam, Jr. Nathaniel Ingersoll was Mary's great uncle.

Warren, Mary

Described as a servant in the home of John Procter and aged about 20, Mary Warren is not listed in March among the afflicted persons by Rev. Lawson in his narrative. According to her master she was among the group, however, and Procter believed a whipping would cure her. By April 18, Warren herself was accused of witchcraft. After confessing and remaining in jail until June, she was released and proceeded to accuse and give testimony against others. In an undated indictment of John Procter, Warren charged that on March 26 he had afflicted her. While in jail Warren had revealingly told her jailmates that when afflicted she thought she saw "the apparission of A hundred persons: for Shee said hir Head was Distempered . . . ."

Way, Aaron

Aaron Sr. and Jr. were living in Salem Village in 1692. The father was born about 1653 and the son in 1674. Both were yeomen. During later witch proceedings testimony was heard that accused witch John Willard had murdered "Aaron Way's child."

Williams, Abigail

A kinswoman described as a niece of Rev. Parris, Williams was a servant in the household and aged about 12 in 1692. Though some have speculated about a family connection with Rev. Roger Williams, her family background and post-1692 history are unknown.

Discovering Witches

During the 17th century English authors published a large body of work on the subject of witchcraft. While several refuted witchcraft, the majority wrote of its ever-present reality and meticulously described important contemporary cases. When the Salem outbreak occurred, magistrates and ministers alike looked to these volumes for guidance and as aids in the discovery of the truth. Mentioned throughout the writings and literature of the 1692 outbreak are the names of various of these English authors including Joseph Glanvill, William Perkins, John Gaule and Richard Baxter, as well as a 1682 volume credited to Sir Matthew Hale concerning a famous witch trial at Bury St. Edmonds. On the very day of the first Salem Village examination, Rev. Parris was presented with a William Perkins volume describing the proper method of detecting witchcraft. Given by a Boston First Church member, it was inscribed on the title page, "The gift of Deacon Robt. Sanderson to Samll. Parris March 1, 1691-2." It is also recorded that Boston minister Cotton Mather's 1689 work *Memorable Providences* was also utilized during the Salem outbreak.

Contemporary legal guides which included sections dealing with witchcraft were also consulted by Massachusetts authorities. Among the compilers of these English guides were Joseph Keble, Michael Dalton and Richard Bernard.

By late 1692, upon the urging of others, Cotton Mather himself hastily wrote a book defending the actions taken during the Massachusetts witch trials. Titled *Wonders of the Invisible World*, one of Mather's opening sections included excerpts from three noted English authors. Mather desired, " . . . to lay before my readers, a brief Synopsis of what has been written on the Subject, by a Triumvirate of as Eminent Persons as have ever handled it." He first quoted from the work of theologian William Perkins (1558-1602), whose book *A Discourse of the Damned Art of Witchcraft* was first published in 1608. Mather's second quote was derived from the body of work of John Gaule, a Puritan divine whose 1646 volume was titled *Select Cases of Conscience Touching Witches and Witchcrafts*. The last excerpt Mather used was from *A Guide to Grand Jury Men*, first published in 1627 and compiled by Richard Bernard (1568-1641).

These three examples give a defining view of what sort of evidence the authorities in early 1692 sought as proof of guilt. Many of these types of evidence were specifically relied upon as seen in questions of the Salem magistrates, and as mentioned by witnesses in a number of depositions. Unfortunately for the accused, a critical reading of these guidelines as to proofs of guilt, shows them to be markedly ambiguous.

An ABSTRACT of Mr. PERKIN'S Way for the Discovery of WITCHES.

I. THere are Presumptions, which do at least probably and conjecturally note one to be a Witch. These give occasion to Examine, yet they are no sufficient Causes of Conviction.

II. If any Man or Woman be notoriously defamed for a Witch, this yields a strong

"the Devil hath been raised"

Suspition. Yet the Judge ought carefully to look, that the Report be made by Men of Honesty and Credit.

III. If a Fellow-Witch, or Magician, give Testimony of any Person to be a Witch; this indeed is not sufficient for Condemnation; but it is a fit Presumption to cause a strait Examination.

IV. If after Cursing there follow Death, or at least some mischief: for Witches are wont to practise their mischievous Facts, by Cursing and Banning: This also is a sufficient matter of Examination, tho' not of Conviction.

V. If after Enmity, Quarrelling, or Threatening, a present mischief does follow; that also is a great Presumption.

VI. If the Party suspected be the Son or Daughter, the man-servant or maid-servant, the Familiar Friend, near Neighbor, or old Companion, of a known and convicted Witch; this may be likewise a Presumption; for Witchcraft is an Art that may be learned, and conveyed from man to man.

VII. Some add this for a Presumption: If the Party suspected be found to have the Devil's mark; for it is commonly thought, when the Devil makes his Covenant with them, he alwaies leaves his mark behind them, whereby he knows them for his own: —— a mark whereof no evident Reason in Nature can be given.

VIII. Lastly, If the party examined be Unconstant, or contrary to himself, in his deliberate Answers, it argueth a Guilty Conscience, which stops the freedom of Utterance. And yet there are causes of Astonishment, which may befal the Good, as well as the Bad.

IX. But then there is a Conviction, discovering the Witch, which must proceed from just and sufficient proofs, and not from bare presumptions.

X. Scratching of the suspected party, and Recovery thereupon, with several other such weak Proofs; as also, the fleeting of the suspected Party, thrown upon the Water; these Proofs are so far from being sufficient, that some of them are, after a sort, practices of Witchcraft.

XI. The Testimony of some Wizzard, tho' offering to shew the Witches Face in a Glass: This, I grant, may be a good Presumption, to cause a strait Examination; but a sufficient Proof of Conviction it cannot be. If the Devil tell the Grand Jury, that the person in question is a Witch, and offers withal to confirm the same by Oath, should the inquest receive his Oath or Accusation to condemn the man? Assuredly no. And yet, that is as much as the Testimony of another Wizzard, who only by the Devil's help reveals the Witch.

XII. If a man, being dangerously sick, and like to dye, upon Suspicion, will take it on his Death, that such a one hath bewitched him, it is an Allegation of the same nature, which may move the Judge to examine the Party, but it is of no moment for Conviction.

XIII. Among the sufficient means of Conviction, the first is, the free and volun-tary Confession of the Crime, made by the party suspected and acccused, after Examination. I say not, that a bare confession is sufficient, but a Confession after due Examination, taken upon pregnant presumptions. What needs now more witness or further Enquiry?

XIV. There is a second sufficient Conviction, by the Testimony of two Witnesses, of good and honest Report, avouching before the Magistrate, upon their own Knowledge, these two things: either that the party accused hath made a League with the Devil, or hath done some known practice of witchcraft. And, all Arguments that do necessarily prove either of these, being brought by two sufficient Witnesses, are of force fully to convince the party suspected.

XV. If it can be proved, that the party suspected hath called upon the Devil, or desired his Help, this is a pregnant proof of a League formerly made between them.

XVI. If it can be proved, that the party hath entertained a Familiar Spirit, and had Conference with it, in the likeness of some visible Creatures; here is Evidence of witchcraft.

XVII. If the witnesses affirm upon Oath, that the suspected person hath done any action or work which necessarily infers a Covenant made, as, that he hath used Enchantments, divined things before they come to pass, and that peremptorily, raised Tempests, caused the Form of a dead man to appear; it proveth sufficiently, that he or she is a Witch. This is the Substance of Mr. Perkins.

Take next the Sum of Mr. Gaules Judgment about the Detection of Witches. '1. Some Tokens for the Trial of Witches, are altogether unwarrantable. Such are the old Paganish Sign, the Witches Long Eyes; the Tradition of Witches not weeping; the casting of the Witch into the Water, with Thumbs and Toes ty'd a-cross. And many more such marks, which if they are to know a Witch by, certainly 'tis no other Witch, but the User of them. 2. There are some Tokens for the Trial of Witches, more probable, and yet not so certain as to afford Conviction. Such are strong and long Suspicion: Suspected Ancestors, some appearance of Fact, the Corps bleeding upon the Witches touch, the Testimony of the Party bewitched, the supposed Witches unusual Bodily marks, the Witches usual Cursing and Banning, the Witches lewd and naughty kind of Life. 3. Some Signs there are of a Witch, more certain and infallible. As, firstly, Declining of Judicature, or faultering, faulty, unconstant, and contrary Answers, upon judicial and deliberate examination. Secondly, When upon due Enquiry into a person's Faith and Manners, there are found all or most of the Causes which produce Witchcraft, namely, God forsaking, Satan invading, particular Sins disposing; and lastly, a compact completing all. Thirdly, The Witches free Confession, together with full Evidence of the Fact. Confession without Fact may be a meer Delusion, and Fact without Confession may be a meer Accident. 4thly, The semblable Gestures and Actions of suspected Witches, with the comparable Expressions of Affections, which in all Witches have been observ'd and found very much alike. Fifthly, The Testimony of the Party bewitched, whether pining or dying, together with the joynt Oaths of sufficient persons, that have seen certain prodigious Pranks or Feats, wrought by the Party accused. 4. Among the most unhappy circumstances to convict a Witch, one is, a maligning and oppugning the Word, Work, and Worship of God, and by any extraordinary sign seeking to seduce any from it. See Deut. 13. 1, 2. Mat. 24.24. Act.13. 8, 10. 2, Tim. 3. 8 Do but mark well the places, and for this very Property (of thus opposing and perverting) they are all there concluded arrant and absolute Witches. 5. It is not requisite, that so palpable Evidence of Conviction should here come in, as in other more sensible matters; 'tis enough, if there be but so much circumstantial Proof or Evidence, as the Substance, Matter, and Nature of such an abstruse Mystery of Iniquity will well admit. [I suppose he means, that whereas in other Crimes we look for more direct proofs, in this there is a greater use of consequential ones.] "But I could heartily wish, that the Juries were empanell'd of the most eminent Physicians, Lawyers, and

Divines that a Country could afford. In the mean time 'tis not to be called a Toleration, if Witches escape, where Conviction is wanting.' To this purpose our Gaule.

I will transcribe a little from one Author more, 'tis the Judicious Bernard of Batcomb, who in his *Guide to grand Jurymen*, after he has mention'd several things that are shrewd Presumptions of a Witch, proceeds to such things as are the Convictions of such an one. And he says, 'A witch in league with the Devil is convicted by these Evidences; I. By a witches Mark; which is upon the Baser sort of Witches; and this, by the Devils either Sucking or Touching of them. Tertullian says, It is the Devils custome to mark his. And note, That this mark is Insensible, and being prick'd it will not Bleed. Some times, its like a Teate; sometimes but a Blewish Spot; sometimes a Red one; and sometimes the flesh Sunk: but the Witches do sometimes cover them. II. By the Witches Words. As when they have been heard calling on, speaking to, or Talking of their Familiars; or, when they have been heard Telling of Hurt they have done to man or beast: Or when they have been heard Threatning of such Hurt; Or if they have been heard Relating their Transportations. III. By the Witches Deeds. As when they have been seen with their Spirits, or seen secretly Feeding any of their Imps. Or, when there can be found their Pictures, Poppets, and other Hellish Compositions. IV. By the Witches Extasies: With the Delight whereof, Witches are so taken, that they will hardly conceal the same: Or, however at some time or other, they may be found in them. V. By one or more Fellow-Witches, Confessing their own Witchcraft, and bearing Witness against others; if they can make good the Truth of their Witness, and give sufficient proof of it. As, that they have seen them with their Spirits, or, that they have Received Spirits from them; or that they can tell, when they used Witchery-Tricks to Do Harm; or, that they told them what Harm they had done; or that they can show the mark upon them; or, that they have been together in their Meetings; and such like. VI. By some Witness of God Himself, happening upon the Execrable Curses of Witches upon themselves, Praying of God to show some Token, if they be Guilty. VII. By the Witches own Confession, of Giving their Souls to the Devil. It is no Rare thing, for Witches to Confess.'

135

(Cotton Mather, The Wonders of the Invisible World, *"Enchantments Encounter'd"* [London, 1693] p. 14-[17])

Appendices

Post-March Narratives

Following the witchcraft trials of 1692-93, a small but significant flurry of writings was produced as various authors attempted to espouse a particular point of view or explain the meaning of the occurrences. The following excerpts taken from these earliest of the Salem witchcraft histories are included here since they exhibit further information not found in the surviving case documents themselves or are information looked at in a different manner, all of which relate to the first month of the outbreak. These accounts are recorded by people who were involved in the witch proceedings with the exception of Robert Calef, who nonetheless had access to witnesses and information not preserved elsewhere.

Conclusion of Rev. Lawson's Narrative

The small pamphlet authored by Rev. Lawson included only one post-March description, this a fanciful notation of what Mercy Lewis said she saw during one of her fits. Lawson followed this April 1, 1692, account with some general observations concerning the deportment of both the afflicted and the accused. As this pamphlet was probably published shortly after early April, Lawson's remarks about the accused and the afflicted are narrowly confined to this genesis period of the witchcraft outbreak.

The first of April, Marcy Lewis, Thomas Putnam's Maid, in her fitt, said, they did eat Red Bread like Mans Flesh, and would have had her eat some: but she would not; but turned away her head, and Spit at them, and said, "I will not Eat, I will not Drink, it is Blood" etc. She said, "That is not the Bread of Life, that is not the Water of Life; Christ gives the Bread of Life, I will have none of it!" This first of April also Marcy Lewis aforesaid saw in her fitt a White man and was with him in a Glorious Place, which had no Candles nor Sun, yet was full of Light and Brightness; where was a great Multitude in White glittering Robes, and they Sung the Song in the fifth of Revelation the Ninth verse, and the 110 Psalm, and the 149 Psalm; and said with her self, "How long shall I stay here? let me be along with you": She was loth to leave this place, and grieved that she could tarry no longer. This White-man hath appeared several times to some of them, and given them notice how long it should be before they had another Fit, which was sometimes a day, or day and half, or more or less: it hath fallen out accordingly.

Remarks of things more than ordinary about the Afflicted Persons.

1. They are in their Fits tempted to be Witches, are shewed the List of the Names of others, and are tortured, because they will not yield to Subscribe, or meddle with, or touch the Book, and are promised to have present Relief if they would do it.
2. They did in the Assembly mutually Cure each other, even with a Touch of their Hand, when Strangled, and otherwise Tortured; & would endeavour to get to their Afflicted, to Relieve them.
3. They did also foretel when anothers Fit was a-coming, and would say, "Look

"the Devil hath been raised"

to her! she will have a Fit presently," which fell out accordingly, as many can bear witness, that heard and saw it.

4. That at the same time, when the Accused Person was present, the Afflicted Persons saw her Likeness in other places of the Meeting-House, suckling her Familiar, sometimes in one place and posture, and sometimes in another.

5. That their Motions in their Fits are Preternatural, both as to the manner, which is so strange as a well person could not Screw their Body into; & as to the violence also it is preternatural, being much beyond the Ordinary force of the same person when they are in their right mind.

6. The eyes of some of them in their fits are exceeding fast closed, and if you ask a question they can give no answer, and I do believe they cannot hear at that time, yet do they plainly converse with the Appearances, as if they did discourse with real persons.

7. They are utterly pressed against any persons Praying with them, and told by the appearances, they shall not go to Prayer, so Tho. Putmans wife was told, I should not Pray; but she said, I should: and after I had done, reasoned with the Appearance, "Did not I say he should go to Prayer!"

8. The forementioned Mary W. being a little better at ease, the Afflicted persons said, she had signed the book; and that was the reason she was better. Told me by Edward Putman.

Remarks concerning the Accused

1. For introduction to the discovery of those that afflicted them, It is reported Mr. Parris's Indian Man and Woman made a Cake of Rye Meal, and the Childrens water, baked it in the Ashes, and gave it to a Dogge, since which they have discovered, and seen particular persons hurting of them.

2. In Time of Examination, they seemed little affected, though all of the Spectators were much grieved to see it.

3. Natural Actions in them produced Preternatural actions in the Afflicted, so that they are their own Image with out any Poppits of Wax or otherwise.

4. That they are accused to have a Company about 23 or 24 and they did Muster in Armes, as it seemed to the Afflicted Persons.

5. Since they were confined, the Persons have not been so much Afflicted with their appearing to them, Biteing or Pinching of them, etc.

6. They are reported by the Afflicted Persons to keep dayes of Fast and dayes of Thanksgiving, and Sacraments; Satan endeavours to Transforme himself to an Angel of Light, and to make his Kingdom and Adminsitrations to resemble those of our Lord Jesus Christ.

7. Satan Rages Principally amongst the Visible Subjects of Christ's Kingdom and makes use (at least in appearance) of some of them to Afflict others; that Christ's Kingdom may be divided against it self, and so be weakened.

8. Several things used in England at Tryal of Witches, to the Number of 14 or 15, which are wont to pass instead of, or in Concurrence with Witnesses, at least 6 or 7 of them are found in these accused: see Keebles Statutes.

9. Some of the most solid Afflicted Persons do affirme the same things concerning seeing the accused out of their Fitts as well as in them.

10. The Witches had a Fast, and told one of the Afflicted Girles, she must not

Eat, because it was Fast Day, she said, she would: they told her they would Choake her then; which when she did eat, was endeavoured.

Finis.

138

(Deodat Lawson, A Brief and True Narrative [Boston, 1692] p. 8-10)

Calef's More Wonders

Published in London in 1700, Robert Calef's More Wonders of the Invisible World *found little support or enthusiasm in Massachusetts among those magistrates and ministers involved with the 1692 witchcraft cases. Calef, a Boston merchant, used the volume to espouse what he believed to be the blatant abuses done during the witchcraft proceedings. Rev. Cotton Mather was a particular target viciously attacked by Calef, the minister commenting in his private diary in November 1700, ". . . I am the cheef Butt of his Malice."*

In part five of the work, Calef describes the beginnings of the 1692 witchcraft utilizing other sources as well as relying very heavily upon Deodat Lawson's A Brief and True Narrative. *Calef, however, sometimes gives his accounting of events a different twist. As an example, Calef takes the mistaken date used by Lawson of April 3 for the March 27 Sacrament Day, and explains that as she left the meeting house, Sarah Cloyce did not slam the door (a sign of unique disrespect) but that the wind shut the door forcibly.*

PART V.

An Impartial Account of the most Memorable Matters of Fact, touching the supposed Witchcraft in New England,

Mr. Parris had been some years a Minister in Salem-Village, when this sad Calamity (as a deluge) overflowed them, spreading it self far and near: He was a Gentleman of Liberal Education, and not meeting with any great Encouragement, or Advantage in Merchandizing, to which for some time he apply'd himself, betook himself to the work of the Ministry; this Village being then vacant, he met with so much Encouragement, as to settle in that Capacity among them.

After he had been there about two years, he obtained a Grant from a part of the Town, that the House and Land he Occupied, and which had been Alotted by the whole People to the Ministry, should be and remain to him, etc. as his own Estate in Fee Simple. This occasioned great Divisions both between the Inhabitants themselves, and between a considerable part of them and their said Minister, which Divisions were but as a beginning or Præludium to what immediately followed.

It was the latter end of February 1691. when divers young Persons belonging to Mr. Parris's Family, and one or more of the Neighbourhood, began to Act, after a strange and unusual manner, *viz.* as by getting into Holes, and creeping under Chairs and Stools, and to use sundry odd Postures and Antick Gestures, uttering foolish, ridiculous Speeches, which neither they themselves nor any others could make sense of; the Physicians that were called could assign no reason for this ; but it seems one of them, having recourse to the old shift, told them, he was afraid they were Bewitched; upon such suggestions, they that were concerned, applied themselves to Fasting and Prayer, which was attended not only in their own private Families, but with calling in the help of others.

"the Devil hath been raised"

March the 11th. Mr. Parris invited several Neighbouring Ministers to join with him in keeping a Solemn day of Prayer at his own House; the time of the exercise those Persons were for the most part silent, but after any one Prayer was ended, they would Act and Speak strangely and Ridiculously, yet were such as had been well Educated and of good Behaviour, the one, a Girl of 11 or 12 years old, would sometimes seem to be in a Convulsion Fit, her Limbs being twisted several ways, and very stiff, but presently her Fit would be over.

A few days before this Solemn day of Prayer, Mr. Parris's Indian Man and Woman made a Cake of Rye Meal, with the Childrens Water, and Baked it in the Ashes, and as is said, gave it to the Dog; this was done as a means to Discover Witchcraft; soon after which those ill affected or afflicted Persons named several that they said they saw, when in their Fits, afflicting of them.

The first complain'd of, was the said Indian Woman, named Tituba, she confessed that the Devil urged her to sign a Book, which he presented to her, and also to work Mischief to the Children, etc. She was afterwards Committed to Prison, and lay there till Sold for her Fees. The account she since gives of it is, that her Master did beat her and otherways abuse her, to make her confess and accuse (such as he call'd) her Sister-Witches, and that whatsoever she said by way of confessing or accusing others, was the effect of such usage; her Master refused to pay her Fees, unless she would stand to what she had said.

The Children complained likewise of two other Women, to be the Authors of their Hurt, *Viz.* Sarah Good, who had long been counted a Melancholy or Distracted Woman, and one Osburn, an Old Bed-rid Woman; which two were Persons so ill thought of, that the accusation was the more readily believed; and after Examination before two Salem Magistrates, were committed: *March the 19th,* Mr. Lawson (who had been formerly a Preacher at the said Village) came thither, and hath since set fourth in Print an account of what then passed, about which time, as he saith, they complained of Goodwife Cory, and Goodwife Nurse, Members of the Churches at the Village and at Salem, many others being by that time Accused.

March the 21st, Goodwife Cory was examined before the Magistrates of Salem, at the Meeting House in the Village, a throng of Spectators being present to see the Novelty. Mr. Noyes, one of the Ministers of Salem, began with Prayer, after which the Prisoner being call'd, in order to answer to what should be Alledged against her, she desired that she might go to Prayer, and was answered by the Magistrates, that they did not come to hear her pray, but to examine her.

The number of the Afflicted were at that time about Ten, *Viz.* Mrs. Pope, Mrs. Putman, Goodwife Bibber, and Goodwife Goodall, Mary Wolcott, Mercy Lewes (at Thomas Putmans) and Dr. Griggs Maid, and three Girls, *Viz.* Elizabeth Parris, Daughter to the Minister, Abigail Williams his Neice, and Ann Putman, which last three, were not only the beginners, but were also the chief in these Accusations. These Ten were most of them present at the Examination, and did vehemently accuse her of Afflicting them, by Biting, Pinching, Strangling, etc. And they said, they did in their Fits see her likeness coming to them, and bringing a Book for them to Sign; Mr. Hathorn, a Magistrate of Salem, asked her, why she Afflicted those Children? she said, she did not Afflict them, he asked her, who did then? she said, "I do not know, how should I know?" she said, they were Poor Distracted Creatures, and no heed to be given to what they said; Mr. Hathorn and Mr. Noyes replied that it was the Judgment of all that were there present, that they were bewitched, and

Appendices

only she (the Accused) said they were Distracted: She was Accused by them, that the Black Man Whispered to her in her Ear now (while she was upon Examination) and that she had a Yellow Bird, that did use to Suck between her Fingers, and that the said Bird did Suck now in the Assembly; order being given to look in that place to see if there were any sign, the Girl that pretended to see it said, that it was too late now, for she had removed a Pin, and put it on her Head, it was upon search found, that a Pin was there sticking upright. When the Accused had any motion of their Body, Hands or Mouth, the Accusers would cry out, as when she bit her Lip, they would cry out of being bitten, if she grasped one hand with the other, they would cry out of being Pinched by her, and would produce marks, so of the other motions of her Body, as complaining of being Prest, when she lean'd to the seat next her, if she stirred her Feet, they would stamp and cry out of Pain there. After the hearing the said Cory was committed to Salem Prison, and then their crying out of her abated.

March the 24th, Goodwife Nurse was brought before Mr. Hathorn and Mr. Curwin (Magistrates) in the Meeting House. Mr. Hale, Minister of Beverly, began with Prayer, after which she being Accus'd of much the same Crimes made the like answers, asserting her own Innocence and earnestness. The Accusers were mostly the same, Tho. Putmans Wife, etc. complaining much. The dreadful Shreiking from her and others, was very amazing, which was heard at a great distance; she was also Committed to Prison.

A Child of Sarah Goods, was likewise apprehended, being between 4 and 5 years Old. The Accusers said this Child bit them, and would shew such like marks, as those of a small Sett of Teeth upon their Arms; as many of the Afflicted as the Child cast its Eye upon, would complain they were in Torment: which Child they also Committed.

Concerning these that had been hitherto Examined and Committed, it is among other things observed by Mr. Lawson (in Print) that they were by the Accusers charged, to belong to a Company that did muster in Arms, and were reported by them to keep Days of Fast, Thanksgiving and Sacraments; and that those Afflicted (or Accusers) did in the Assembly, Cure each others, even with a touch of their Hand, when strangled and otherways tortured, and would endeavour to get to the Afflicted to relieve them thereby (for hitherto they had not used the Experiment of bringing the Accused to touch the Afflicted, in order to their Cure) and could foretel one anothers Fits to be coming, and would say, look to such a one, she will have a Fit presently and so it happened, and that at the same time when the Accused person was present, the Afflicted said they saw her Spectre or likeness in other places of the Meeting House Suckling of their Familiars.

The said Mr. Lawson being to Preach at the Village, after the Psalm was Sung, Abigail Williams said, "Now stand up and name your Text", after it was read, she said, "It is a long Text." Mrs. Pope in the beginning of Sermon said to him, "Now there is enough of that." In Sermon, he referring to his Doctrine, Abigail Williams said to him, "I know no Doctrine you had, if you did name one I have forgot it." Ann Putman, an afflicted Girl, said, There was a Yellow Bird sate on his Hat as it hung on the Pin in the Pulpit.

March 31, 1692. Was set apart as a day of Solemn Humiliation at Salem, upon the Account of this Business, on which day Abigail Williams said, That she saw a great number of Persons in the Village at the Administration of a Mock Sacrament, where they had Bread as read as raw Flesh, and red Drink.

April 1. Mercy Lewis affirmed, That she saw a man in white, with whom she went into a Glorious Place, *viz.* In her fits, where was no Light of the Sun, much less of Candles, yet was full of Light and Brightness, with a great Multitude in White Glittering Robes, who Sang the Song in 5. Rev. 9. and the 110 and 149 Psalms; And was grieved that she might tarry no longer in this place. This White Man is said to have appeared several times to others of them, and to have given them notice how long it should be before they should have another Fit.

April the 3d. Being Sacrament Day at the Village, Sarah Cloys, Sister to Goodwife Nurse, a Member to one of the Churches, was (tho' it seems with difficulty prevail'd with to be) present; but being entred the place, and Mr. Parris naming his Text, 6 John, 70. *Have not I chosen you Twelve, and one of you is a Devil* (for what cause may rest as a doubt whether upon the account of her Sisters being Committed, or because of the choice of that Text) she rose up and went out, the wind shutting the Door forcibly, gave occasion to some to suppose she went out in Anger, and might occasion a suspicion of her; however she was soon after complain'd of, examin'd and Committed.

(Robert Calef, More Wonders of the Invisible World *[London, 1700]*
p. 90-93.)

Rev. Hale's Enquiry

Rev. John Hale, minister at Beverly, which adjoined both Salem and Salem Village, was intimately involved in the witchcraft events. Following 1692 Hale began reflecting on what happened during that turbulent year. Like others, he concluded that mistakes had been made in the prosecution of some of the accused, and that though the Devil was still a real presence and threat in the world, and though witchcraft incidents had indeed taken place, innocent people had been executed. In 1697 Hale wrote a manuscript outlining this thesis that mistakes made during the trial were the results of using incorrect principles and unfounded traditions in pursuing witches, rather than using the scriptures as a guide. Thus through the mistaken use of these unreliable methods to discover witches, Satan was able to use his own devious powers and men's reliance upon ill-found proofs both of which resulted in innocent persons being accused and executed. Having been present during many of the witch examinations and knowing many of the people involved, Hale believed his experience and knowledge of the scriptures could be used as a guide for others, "... to shun the Rocks by which we were bruised, and narrowly escaped Shipwrack upon."

Cotton Mather in his highly acclaimed book Magnalia Christi Americana *first published the section of the Hale manuscript dealing with the origins of the Salem Witchcraft events themselves. He credited Hale as its author, saying of Hale's writing, "And I will assure the Reader that he hath now to do with a Writer, who would not for a World be guilty of over-doing the Truth in an History of this importance."*

The full Hale volume itself, titled A Modest Enquiry Into the Nature of Witchcraft, *was not published until 1702, after Hale's death. A major portion of chapter two of this volume, the section printed by Mather, told of the early witchcraft outbreak, and further expands our knowledge of these February and March 1692, occurrences as recorded by a contemporary of the events.*

Appendices

Chapter II.

I. In the latter end of the year 1691, Mr. Samuel Paris, Pastor of the Church in Salem-Village, had a Daughter of Nine, and a Neice of about Eleven years of Age, sadly Afflicted of they knew not what Distempers; and he made his application to Physitians, yet still they grew worse: And at length one Physitian gave his opinion, that they were under an Evil Hand. This the Neighbours quickly took up, and concluded they were bewitched. He had also an Indian Man servant, and his Wife who afterwards confessed, that without the knowledge of their Master or Mistress, they had taken some of the Afflicted persons Urine, and mixing it with meal had made a Cake, & baked it, to find out the Witch, as they said. After this, the Afflicted persons cryed out of the Indian Woman, named Tituba, that she did pinch, prick, and grievously torment them, and that they saw her here and there, where no body else could. Yea they could tell where she was, and what she did, when out of their humane sight. These Children were bitten and pinched by invisible agents; their arms, necks, and backs turned this way and that way, and returned back again, so as it was impossible for them to do of themselves, and beyond the power of any Epileptick Fits, or natural Disease to effect. Sometimes they were taken dumb, their mouths stopped, their throats choaked, their limbs wracked and tormented so as might move an heart of stone, to sympathize with them, with bowels of compassion for them. I will not enlarge in the description of their cruel Sufferings, because they were in all things afflicted as bad as John Goodwins Children at Boston, in the year 1689. So that he that will read Mr. Mathers Book of *Memorable Providences*, page 3, etc., may Read part of what these Children, and afterwards sundry grown persons suffered by the hand of Satan, at Salem Village, and parts adjacent, *Anno* 1691, 2. Yet there was more in these Sufferings, than in those at Boston, by pins invisibly stuck into their flesh, pricking with Irons, (As in part published in a Book Printed 1693, *viz. The Wonders of the Invisible World*). Mr. Paris seeing the distressed condition of his Family, desired the presence of some Worthy Gentlemen of Salem, and some Neighbour Ministers to consult together at his House; who when they came, and had enquired diligently into the Sufferings of the Afflicted, concluded they were preternatural, and feared the hand of Satan was in them.

II. The advice given to Mr. Paris by them was, that he should sit still and wait upon the Providence of God to see what time might discover; and to be much in prayer for the discovery of what was yet secret. They also Examined Tituba, who confessed the making a Cake, as is above mentioned, and said her Mistress in her own Country was a Witch, and had taught her some means to be used for the discovery of a Witch and for the prevention of being bewitched, etc. But said that she her self was not a Witch.

III. Soon after this, there were two or three private Fasts at the Ministers House, one of which was kept by sundry Neighbour Ministers, and after this, another in Publick at the Village, and several days afterwards of publick Humiliation, during these molestations, not only there, but in other Congregations for them. And one General Fast by Order of the General Court, observed throughout the Colony to seek the Lord that he would rebuke Satan, and be a light unto his people in this day of darkness.

But I return to the History of these troubles. In a short time after other persons who were of age to be witnesses, were molested by Satan, and in their fits cryed

"the Devil hath been raised"

out upon Tituba and Goody O. and S. G. that they or Specters in their Shapes did grievously torment them; hereupon some of their Village Neighbours complained to the Magistrates at Salem, desiring they would come and examine the afflicted & accused together; the which they did: the effect of which examination was, that Tituba confessed she was a Witch, and that she with the two others accused did torment & bewitch the complainers, and that these with two others whose names she knew not, had their Witch-meeting together; relating the times when and places where they met, with many other circumstances to be seen at large. Upon this the said Tituba and O. & S. G. were committed to Prison upon suspicion of acting Witchcraft. After this the said Tituba was again examined in Prison, and owned her first confession in all points, and then was her self afflicted and complained of her fellow Witches tormenting of her, for her confession, and accusing them, and being searched by a Woman, she was found to have upon her body the marks of the Devils wounding of her.

IV. Here were these things rendred her confession credible. (1.) That at this examination she answered every question just as she did at the first. And it was thought that if she had feigned her confession, she could not have remembered her answers so exactly. A lyar we say, had need of a good memory, but truth being always consistent with it self is the same to day as it was yesterday. (2.) She seemed very penitent for her Sin in covenanting with the Devil. (3.) She became a sufferer her self & as she said for her confession. (4.) Her confession agreed exactly (which was afterwards verified in the other confessors) with the accusations of the afflicted. Soon after these afflicted persons complained of other persons afflicting of them in their fits, and the number of the afflicted and accused began to increase. And the success of Tituba's confession encouraged those in Authority to examine others that were suspected, and the event was, that more confessed themselves guilty of the Crimes they were suspected for. And thus was this matter driven on.

V. I observed in the prosecution of these affairs, that there was in the Justices, Judges and others concerned, a conscientious endeavour to do the thing that was right. And to that end they consulted the Presidents of former times and precepts laid down by Learned Writers about Witchcraft. As Keeble on the *Common Law*, Chapt. Conjuration, (an Author approved by the Twelve Judges of our Nation.) Also Sir Mathew Hales *Tryal of Witches*, Printed *Anno* 1682. Glanvils *Collection of sundry tryals in England and Ireland*, in the years 1658, 61, 63, 64, and 81. Bernards *Guide to Jurymen*, Baxter and R. Burton, their Histories about Witches and their discoveries. Cotton Mather's *Memorable Providences relating to Witchcrafts*, Printed *Anno* 1689.

(*John Hale*, A Modest Enquiry Into the Nature of Witchcraft
[Boston, 1702] p. 23-28)

Rev. Lawson's 1704 Edition

Rev. Lawson was living in England by 1704, and in that year he cooperated in the reprinting of his March 24, 1692, Salem Village sermon. As an appendix to this sermon, the minister addressed to his readers the story of how he came to return to Salem Village in early 1692, some previously unpublished details of what he had observed while there, and some personal reflections on these events of twelve years earlier.

Appendices

As this Lawson publication expanded upon his original 1692 observations of the actions of the accused and accusers, that information is reprinted below. It should be noted, however, that in 1704 Lawson was commenting upon the entire breadth of events and trends taking place during the full eight months of the witchcraft. Certain passages, including number five under matters "Relating to the afflicted" and number thirteen under matters "Relating to the accused," which refers to the case of Rev. George Burroughs, and number seventeen concerning the executions, are obviously post-March occurrences. Not included here is the section dealing with the confessing witches, as except for Tituba, this phenomenon did not take place until after March 1692.

At the request of several worthy ministers and Christian friends, I do here annex, by way of appendix to the preceding sermon, some brief account of those amazing things which occasioned that discourse to be delivered. Let the reader please therefore to take it in the brief remarks following, and judge as God shall incline him.

It pleased God, in the year of our Lord 1692, to visit the people at a place called Salem Village, in New England, with a very sore and grievous affliction, in which they had reason to believe that the sovereign and holy God was pleased to permit Satan and his instruments to affright and afflict those poor mortals in such an astonishing and unusual manner.

Now, I having for some time before attended the work of the ministry in that village, the report of those great afflictions came quickly to my notice, and the more readily because the first person afflicted was in the minister's family who succeeded me after I was removed from them. In pity, therefore, to my Christian friends and former acquaintance there, I was much concerned about them, frequently consulted with them, and fervently, by divine assistance, prayed for them; but especially my concern was augmented when it was reported, at an examination of a person suspected for witchcraft, that my wife and daughter, who died three years before, were sent out of the world under the malicious operations of the infernal powers, as is more fully represented in the following remarks. I did then desire, and was also desired by some concerned in the Court, to be there present, that I might hear what was alleged in that respect; observing, therefore, when I was amongst them, that the case of the afflicted was very amazing and deplorable, and the charges brought against the accused such as were ground of suspicions, yet very intricate, and difficult to draw up right conclusions about them; I thought good, for the satisfaction of myself and such of my friends as might be curious to inquire into those mysteries of God's providence and Satan's malice, to draw up and keep by me a brief account of the most remarkable things that came to my knowledge in those affairs, which remarks were afterwards (at my request) revised and corrected by some who sat judges on the bench in those matters, and were now transcribed from the same paper on which they were then written. After this, I being by the providence of God called over into England in the year 1696, I then brought that paper of remarks on the witchcraft with me; upon the sight thereof some worthy ministers and Christian friends here desired me to reprint the sermon, and subjoin the remarks thereunto in way of appendix; but for some particular reasons I did then decline it. But now, forasmuch as I myself had been an eye and ear witness of most of those amazing things, so far as they came within the notice of human senses, and the requests of my friends were renewed since I came to dwell in London, I have given way to the publishing of them, that I may satisfy such as are not resolved to the contrary, that

"the Devil hath been raised"

there may be (and are) such operations of the powers of darkness on the bodies and minds of mankind by divine permission. and that those who sat judges on those cases may, by the serious consideration of the formidable aspect and perplexed circumstances of that afflictive providence, be in some measure excused, or at least be less censured, for passing sentence on several persons as being the instruments of Satan in those diabolical operations, when they were involved in such a dark and dismal scene of providence, in which Satan did seem to spin a finer thread of spiritual wickedness than in the ordinary methods of witchcraft: hence the judges, desiring to bear due testimony against such diabolical practices, were inclined to admit the validity of such a sort of evidence as was not so clearly and directly demonstrable to human senses as in other cases is required, or else they could not discover the mysteries of witchcraft. I presume not to impose upon my Christian or learned reader any opinion of mine how far Satan was an instrument in God's hand in these amazing afflictions which were on many persons there about that time; but I am certainly convinced, that the great God was pleased to lengthen his chain to a very great degree for the hurting of some and reproaching of others, as far as he was permitted so to do. Now, that I may not grieve any whose relations were either accused or afflicted in those times of trouble and distress, I choose to lay down every particular at large, without mentioning any names or persons concerned (they being wholly unknown here); resolving to confine myself to such a proportion of paper as is assigned to these remarks in this impression of the book, yet, that I may be distinct, shall speak briefly to the matter under three heads; viz.: —

1. Relating to the afflicted.

2. Relating to the accused. And,

3. Relating to the confessing witches.

To begin with the afflicted. —

1. One or two of the first that were afflicted complaining of unusual illness, their relations used physic for their cure; but it was altogether in vain.

2. They were oftentimes very stupid in their fits, and could neither hear nor understand, in the apprehension of the standers-by; so that, when prayer hath been made with some of them in such a manner as might be audible in a great congregation, yet, when their fit was off, they declared they did not hear so much as one word thereof.

3. It was several times observed, that, when they were discoursed with about God or Christ, or the things of salvation, they were presently afflicted at a dreadful rate; and hence were oftentimes outrageous, if they were permitted to be in the congregation in the time of the public worship.

4. They sometimes told at a considerable distance, yea, several miles off, that such and such persons were afflicted, which hath been found to be done according to the time and manner they related it; and they said the spectres of the suspected persons told them of it.

5. They affirmed that they saw the ghosts of several departed persons, who, at their appearing, did instigate them to discover such as (they said) were instruments to hasten their deaths, threatening sorely to afflict them if they did not make it known to the magistrates. They did affirm at the examination, and again at the trial of an accused person, that they saw the ghosts of his two wives (to whom he had carried very ill in their lives, as was proved by several testimonies), and also that they saw the ghosts of my wife and daughter (who died above three years before); and they

Appendices

did affirm, that, when the very ghosts looked on the prisoner at the bar, they looked red, as if the blood would fly out of their faces with indignation at him. The manner of it was thus: several afflicted being before the prisoner at the bar, on a sudden they fixed all their eyes together on a certain place of the floor before the prisoner, neither moving their eyes nor bodies for some few minutes, nor answering to any question which was asked them: so soon as that trance was over, some being removed out of sight and hearing, they were all, one after another, asked what they saw; and they did all agree that they saw those ghosts above mentioned. I was present, and heard and saw the whole of what passed upon that account, during the trial of that person who was accused to be the instrument of Satan's malice therein.

6. In this (worse than Gallick) persecution by the dragoons of hell, the persons afflicted were harassed at such a dreadful rate to write their names in a Devil-book presented by a spectre unto them: and one, in my hearing, said, "I will not, I will not write! It is none of God's book, it is none of God's book: it is the Devil's book, for aught I know;" and, when they steadfastly refused to sign, they were told, if they would but touch, or take hold of, the book, it should do; and, lastly, the diabolical propositions were so low and easy, that, if they would but let their clothes, or any thing about them, touch the book, they should be at ease from their torments, it being their consent that is aimed at by the Devil in those representations and operations.

7. One who had been long afflicted at a stupendous rate by two or three spectres, when they were (to speak after the manner of men) tired out with tormenting of her to force or fright her to sign a covenant with the Prince of Darkness, they said to her, as in a diabolical and accursed passion, "Go your ways, and the Devil go with you; for we will be no more pestered and plagued about you." And, ever after that, she was well, and no more afflicted, that ever I heard of.

8. Sundry pins have been taken out of the wrists and arms of the afflicted; and one, in time of examination of a suspected person, had a pin run through both her upper and lower lip when she was called to speak, yet no apparent festering followed thereupon, after it was taken out.

9. Some of the afflicted, as they were striving in their fits in open court, have (by invisible means) had their wrists bound fast together with a real cord, so as it could hardly be taken off without cutting. Some afflicted have been found with their arms tied, and hanged upon an hook, from whence others have been forced to take them down, that they might not expire in that posture.

10. Some afflicted have been drawn under tables and beds by undiscerned force, so as they could hardly be pulled out; and one was drawn half-way over the side of a well, and was, with much difficulty, recovered back again.

11. When they were most grievously afflicted, if they were brought to the accused, and the suspected person's hand but laid upon them, they were immediately relieved out of their tortures; but, if the accused did but look on them, they were instantly struck down again. Wherefore they used to cover the face of the accused, while they laid their hands on the afflicted, and then it obtained the desired issue: for it hath been experienced (both in examinations and trials), that, so soon as the afflicted came in sight of the accused, they were immediately cast into their fits; yea, though he accused were among the crowd of people unknown to the sufferers, yet, on the first view, were they struck down, which was observed in a child of four or five years of age, when it was apprehended, that so many as she could look upon,

"the Devil hath been raised"

either directly or by turning her head, were immediately struck into their fits.

12. An iron spindle of a woollen wheel, being taken very strangely out of an house at Salem Village, was used by a spectre as an instrument of torture to a sufferer, not being discernible to the standers-by, until it was, by the said sufferer, snatched out of the spectre's hand, and then it did immediately appear to the persons present to be really the same iron spindle.

13. Sometimes, in their fits, they have had their tongues drawn out of their mouths to a fearful length, their heads turned very much over their shoulders; and while they have been so strained in their fits, and had their arms and legs, &c., wrested as if they were quite dislocated, the blood hath gushed plentifully out of their mouths for a considerable time together, which some, that they might be satisfied that it was real blood, took upon their finger, and rubbed on their other hand. I saw several together thus violently strained and bleeding in their fits, to my very great astonishment that my fellow-mortals should be so grievously distressed by the invisible powers of darkness. For certainly all considerate persons who beheld these things must needs be convinced, that their motions in their fits were preternatural and involuntary, both as to the manner, which was so strange as a well person could not (at least without great pain) screw their bodies into, and as to the violence also, they were preternatural motions, being much beyond the ordinary force of the same persons when they were in their right minds; so that, being such grievous sufferers, it would seem very hard and unjust to censure them of consenting to, or holding any voluntary converse or familiarity with, the Devil.

14. Their eyes were, for the most part, fast closed in their trance-fits, and when they were asked a question they could give no answer; and I do verily believe, they did not hear at that time; yet did they discourse with the spectres as with real persons, asserting things and receiving answers affirmative or negative, as the matter was. For instance, one, in my hearing, thus argued *with*, and railed *at*, a spectre: "Goodw—, begone, begone, begone! Are you not ashamed, a woman of your profession, to afflict a poor creature so? What hurt did I ever do you in my life? You have but two years to live, and then the Devil will torment your soul for this. Your name is blotted out of God's book, and it shall never be put into God's book again. Begone! For shame! Are you not afraid of what is coming upon you? I know, I know what will make you afraid, — the wrath of an angry God: I am sure that will make you afraid. Begone! Do not torment me. I know what you would have" (we judged she meant her soul): "but it is out of your reach; it is clothed with the white robes of Christ's righteousness." This sufferer I was well acquainted with, and knew her to be a very sober and pious woman, so far as I could judge; and it appears that she had not, in that fit, voluntary converse with the Devil, for then she might have been helped to a better guess about that woman abovesaid, as to her living but two years, for she lived not many months after that time. Further, this woman, in the same fit, seemed to dispute with a spectre about a text of Scripture: the apparition seemed to deny it; she said she was sure there was such a text, and she would tell it; and then said she to the apparition, "I am sure you will be gone, for you cannot stand before that text." Then was she sorely afflicted, — her mouth drawn on one side, and her body strained violently for about a minute; and then said, "It is, it is, it is," three or four times, and then was afflicted to hinder her from telling; at last, she broke forth, and said, "It is the third chapter of the Revelations." I did manifest some scruple about reading it, lest Satan should draw any thereby superstitiously to improve the

Appendices

word of the eternal God; yet judging I might do it once, for an experiement, I began to read; and, before I had read through the first verse, she opened her eyes, and was well. Her husband and the spectators told me she had often been relieved by reading texts pertinent to her case, — as Isa. 40, 1, ch. 49, 1, ch. 50, 1, and several others. These things I saw and heard from her.

15. They were vehemently afflicted, to hinder any persons praying with them, or holding them in any religious discourse. The woman mentioned in the former section was told by the spectre I should not go to prayer; but she said I should, and, after I had done, reasoned with the apparition, "Did not I say he should go to prayer?" I went also to visit a person afflicted in Boston; and, after I was gone into the house to which she belonged, she being abroad, and pretty well, when she was told I was there, she said, "I am loath to go in; for I know he will fall into some good discourse, and then I am sure I shall go into a fit." Accordingly, when she came in, I advised her to improve all the respite she had to make her peace with God, and sue out her pardon through Jesus Christ, and beg supplies of faith and every grace to deliver her from the powers of darkness; and, before I had uttered all this, she fell into a fearful fit of diabolical torture.

16. Some of them were asked how it came to pass that they were not affrighted when they saw the *black-man:* they said they were at first, but not so much afterwards.

17. Some of them affirmed they saw the *black-man* sit on the gallows, and that he whispered in the ears of some of the condemned persons when they were just ready to be turned off, even while they were making their last speech.

18. They declared several things to be done by witchcraft, which happened before some of them were born, — as strange deaths of persons, casting away of ships, &c.; and they said the spectres told them of it.

19. Some of them have sundry times seen a *white-man* appearing amongst the spectres, and, as soon as he appeared, the *black-witches* vanished: they said this white-man had often foretold them what respite they should have from their fits, as sometimes a day or two or more, which fell out accordingly. One of the afflicted said she saw him, in her fit, and was with him in a glorious place which had no candle nor sun, yet was full of light and brightness, where there was a multitude in white, glittering robes, and they sang the song in Rev. 5, 9; Psal. 110, 149. She was loath to leave that place, and said, *"How long shall I stay here? Let me be along with you."* She was grieved she could stay no longer in that place and company.

20. A young woman that was afflicted at a fearful rate had a spectre appeared to her with a white sheet wrapped about it, not visible to the standers-by until this sufferer (violently striving in her fit) snatched at, took hold, and tore off a corner of that sheet. Her father, being by her, endeavored to lay hold upon it with her, that she might retain what she had gotten; but, at the passing-away of the spectre, he had such a violent twitch of his hand as if it would have been torn off: immediately thereupon appeared in the sufferer's hand the corner of a sheet, — a real cloth, *visible* to the spectators, which (as it is said) remains still to be seen.

Remarkable Things Relating To The Accused.

1. A woman, being brought upon public examination, desired to go to prayer. The magistrates told her they came not there to hear her pray, but to examine her in what was alleged against her relating to suspicions of witchcraft.

"the Devil hath been raised"

2. It was observed, both in times of examination and trial, that the accused seemed little affected with what the sufferers underwent, or what was charged against them as being the instruments of Satan therein, so that the spectators were grieved at their unconcernedness.

3. They were sometimes their *own image*, and not always practising upon poppets made of clouts, wax, or other materials, (according to the old methods of witch-craft); for *natural* actions in them seemed to produce preternatural impressions on the afflicted, as biting their lips in time of examination and trial caused the sufferers to be bitten so as they produced the marks before the magistrates and spectators: the accused pinching their hands together seemed to cause the sufferers to be *pinched*; those again *stamping* with their feet, *these* were tormented in their legs and feet, so as they *stamped fearfully*. After all this, if the accused did but lean against the bar at which they stood, some very sober women of the afflicted complained of their breasts, as if their bowels were torn out; thus, some have since confessed, they were wont to afflict such as were the objects of their malice.

4. Several were accused of having familiarity with the *black-man* in time of exami-nation and trial; and that he whispered in their ears, and therefore they could not hear the magistrates; and that one woman accused rid (in her shape and spectre) by the place of judicature, behind the black man, in the very time when she was upon examination.

5. When the suspected were standing at the bar, the afflicted have affirmed that they saw their shapes in other places suckling a yellow bird; sometimes in one place and posture, and sometimes in another. They also foretold that the spectre of the prisoner was going to afflict such or such a sufferer, which presently fell out accordingly.

6. They were accused by the sufferers to keep days of hellish fasts and thanks-givings; and, upon one of their fast-days, they told a sufferer she must not eat, it was fast-day. She said she would: they told her they would choke her then, which, when she did eat, was endeavored.

7. They were also accused to hold and administer diabolical sacraments; viz., a mock-baptism and a Devil-supper, at which cursed imitations of the sacred insti-tutions of our blessed Lord they used forms of words to be trembled at in the very rehearsing: concerning baptism I shall speak elsewhere. At their cursed supper, they were said to have red bread and red drink; and, when they pressed an afflicted per-son to eat and drink thereof, she turned away her head, and spit at it, and said, "I will not eat, I will not drink: it is blood. That is not the bread of life, that is not the water of life; and I will have none of yours." Thus horribly doth Satan endeavor to have his kingdom and administrations to resemble those of our Lord Jesus Christ.

8. Some of the most *sober* afflicted persons, when they were well, did affirm the spectres of such and such as they did complain of in their fits did appear to them, and could relate what passed betwixt them and the apparitions, after their fits were over, and give account after what manner they were hurt by them.

9. Several of the accused would neither in time of examination nor trial confess any thing of what was laid to their charge: some would not admit of any minister to pray with them, others refused to pray for themselves. It was said by some of the confessing witches, that such as have received the Devil-sacrament can never confess: only one woman condemned, after the death-warrant was signed, freely confessed, which occasioned her reprieval for some time; and it was observable this

149

woman had one lock of hair of a very great length, viz., four foot and seven inches long by measure. This lock was of a different color from all the rest, which was short and gray. It grew on the hinder part of her head, and was matted together like an elf-lock. The Court ordered it to be cut off, to which she was very unwilling, and said she was told if it were cut off she should die or be sick; yet the Court ordered it so to be.

10. A person who had been frequently transported to and fro by the devils for the space of near two years, was struck dumb for about nine months of that time; yet he, after that, had his speech restored to him, and did depose upon oath, that, in the time while he was dumb, he was many times bodily transported to places where the witches were gathered together, and that he there saw feasting and dancing; and, being struck on the back or shoulder, was thereby made fast to the place, and could only see and hear at a distance. He did take his oath that he did, with his bodily eyes, see some of the accused at those witch-meetings several times. I was present in court when he gave his testimony. He also proved by sundry persons, that, at those times of transport, he was bodily absent from his abode, and could nowhere be found, but being met with by some on the road, at a distance from his home, was suddenly conveyed away from them.

11. The afflicted persons related that the spectres of several eminent persons had been brought in amongst the rest; but, as the sufferers said the Devil could not hurt them in their shapes, but two witches seemed to take them by each hand, and lead them or force them to come in.

12. Whiles a godly man was at prayer with a woman afflicted, the daughter of that woman (being a sufferer in the like kind) affirmed that she saw two of the persons accused at prayer to the Devil.

13. It was proved by substantial evidences against one person accused, that he had such an unusual strength (though a very little man), that he could hold out a gun with one hand behind the lock, which was near seven foot in the barrel, being as much as a lusty man could command with both hands after the usual manner of shooting. It was also proved, that he lifted barrels of meat and barrels of molasses out of a canoe alone, and that putting his fingers into a barrel of molasses (full within a finger's length according to custom) he carried it several paces; and that he put his finger into the muzzle of a gun which was more than five foot in the barrel, and lifted up the butt-end thereof, lock, stock, and all, without any visible help to raise it. It was also testified, that, being abroad with his wife and his wife's brother, he occasionally staid behind, letting his wife and her brother walk forward; but, suddenly coming up with them, he was angry with his wife for what discourse had passed betwixt her and her brother: they wondering how he should know it, he said, "I know your thoughts;" at which expression, they, being amazed, asked him how he could do that; he said, "My God, whom I serve, makes known your thoughts to me."

I was present when these things were testified against him, and observed that he could not make any plea for himself (in these things) that had any weight: he had the liberty of challenging his jurors before empanelling, according to the statute in that case, and used his liberty in challenging many; yet the jury that were sworn brought him in guilty.

14. The magistrates privately examined a child of four or five years of age, mentioned in the remarks of the afflicted, sect. 11: and the child told them it had a little

"the Devil hath been raised"

snake which used to suck on the lowest joint of its forefinger; and, when they (inquiring where) pointed to other places, it told them not *there* but *here*, pointing on the lowest joint of the forefinger, where they observed a deep red spot about the bigness of a flea-bite. They asked it who gave it that snake, whether the black man gave it : the child said no, its mother gave it. I heard this child examined by the magistrates.

15. It was proved by sundry testimonies against some of the accused, that. upon their malicious imprecations, wishes, or threatenings, many observable deaths and diseases, with many other odd inconveniences, have happened to cattle and other estate of such as were so threatened by them, and some to the persons of men and women.

(As reprinted in Charles W. Upham, Salem Witchcraft *[Boston, 1867] V.2, p. 527-535.)*

Appendices

Index

153

Index

"the Devil hath been raised"

155

Index

"The Devil hath been raised"

has been published in a first edition
of two thousand sewn, softcover copies.
Designed by A. L. Morris,
the text was composed in Bem
and printed by Knowlton & McLeary
in Farmington, Maine, on Mohawk Vellum.
The binding was executed by New Hampshire Bindery
in Concord, New Hampshire.

———